Katie & the Carpenter

Katie & the Carpenter

Rob W. Proctor

ISBN: 1535453079
ISBN 13: 9781535453073

To Denni, Katie, & Brian.

Katie & the Carpenter

Chapter List

PART I
The Best Laid Plans

PROLOGUE

Cincinnati, Ohio 1993

RICHARD SORENSEN COULDN'T HAVE HAD any idea that this day would be his daughter's last. After all, the collision wasn't that severe, and Amber was taken to the hospital mostly as a matter of precaution. A few hours later, though, his little girl was dead. How could everything have spiraled out of control so quickly?

As a manager for State Farm Insurance in Cincinnati, I worked with the unit that received the claim involving Richard Sorensen and his daughter Amber (not their real names). The other vehicle had turned suddenly in front of Sorensen's car, causing the accident. Three-and-a-half-year-old Amber had been properly restrained in the back seat. She complained that her head hurt, so Amber was taken to Cincinnati Children's Hospital for examination. Unfortunately, it was the beginning of a horrible nightmare.

Shortly after arriving at the hospital, Amber complained of a more severe headache, began vomiting, and showed signs of a seizure. Her condition worsened, and a Magnetic Resonance Image (MRI) was requested. The scan revealed a brain tumor, previously unknown to anyone. The force of the accident had caused the tumor to rupture, and it was now causing numerous complications. Pediatric neurosurgeon Dr. Kerry Crone was brought in for emergency surgery, but a few hours later Amber Sorensen tragically died.

For me, one of the most difficult aspects of handling bodily injury insurance claims was placing a dollar value on someone else's suffering. But money is the only remedy an insurance policy provides, so my team began the emotional task of determining the economic value of Amber Sorensen's claim. Evaluating any claim involving death is difficult, and when a child is involved it becomes even more challenging.

This case had an unusual twist. The medical records indicated the brain tumor Amber had was an astrocytoma, which would have become evident within a few months. Amber would have begun to have headaches and potentially other symptoms, including vomiting and double vision. Furthermore, a brain tumor like the one Amber had could possibly have resulted in her death within the next two to five years.

Normally the investigation components of the claim were handled by claims adjusters like the ones who worked for me. Due to the unusual nature of the claim, and for reasons I couldn't fully articulate, I felt the need to assume some of the investigative responsibilities. I contacted Dr. Jeff Acker, a high school friend and oncologist who attended medical school at Duke University, one of the leading cancer research facilities in the nation. Dr. Acker provided me with some information on brain tumors as well as a list of commonly used medical textbooks on the subject. I went so far as to obtain a temporary University of Cincinnati student library card, and made several trips to the UC Medical School library, where I took on a self-guided study of pediatric brain tumors.

The claim of Amber Sorensen eventually settled. The amount of the settlement isn't what I remember. I'll never forget the tears that flowed as we discussed in detail the heartbreaking death of this child when I presented the claim to the other managers for evaluation. For some reason this claim always stuck out in my mind. In fact, for several years I kept a portion of the file in a drawer in my desk, the only time I did such a thing.

I had been involved in overseeing hundreds of claims involving serious injury and tragic deaths, as well as unusual medical issues. Never before had I taken such significant steps to become personally knowledgeable about an obscure medical condition. But why? The answer to that question would become evident some seven years later.

CHAPTER 1

"Are You Sitting Down?" January 18, 2000

DENNI HAD BARELY STEPPED IN the door when the reproduction antique phone on the wall clanged with its old phone sound. She threw her purse on the island in the kitchen and said, "I'm coming," as if the person calling could hear her.

"Hello, Denni Proctor? It's Cecilia Profit."

Dr. Profit was the ear, nose, and throat specialist who'd been seeing our four-year-old daughter Katie, and my wife Denni was surprised by the call. Denni and Katie had just returned from Bronson Hospital in Kalamazoo, Michigan, where less than two hours earlier Katie had a CAT scan. At my wife's insistence, Katie had a hearing test that revealed she was completely deaf in her right ear. The doctors suspected Katie had a problem with the nerve in her ear, and simply wanted to verify it so they could move ahead with a procedure to repair the nerve. They told us the CAT scan was routine, a precautionary measure to rule out anything else.

"Are you sitting down?" Dr. Profit asked.

Denni could feel the oxygen leaving her body, as she knew nothing good could ever follow a statement like that.

"Yes," she lied.

"Denni, the CAT scans showed a mass on Katie's brain. I'm very sorry. We've made an appointment for you with a neurosurgeon here in Kalamazoo first thing tomorrow morning."

"What? A mass? What do you mean?" was all Denni could muster.

"I'm sorry, Denni. Katie has a brain tumor."

I was at my office in Kalamazoo beginning a presentation to a group of incoming State Farm agents. Just as I started my introductory remarks to the group, my secretary, Diana, peeked in the door and motioned to me. I was prepared to tell her whatever it was could wait, but Diana looked determined.

"Rob, your wife needs to talk to you. I told her you were in a meeting, but she said it's really urgent, and she's holding right now," Diana said.

As I walked to my office, I was thinking whatever issue was going on as likely as not related to our house. After all, living in a house that was over one hundred and thirty years old, rarely a week went by without some form of house repair or maintenance issue.

"Hey, it's me," I said as I picked up the phone. "What's up?"

"There's a mass," Denni said.

I had the same reaction as Denni.

"What? What did you say?"

"There's a mass on Katie's brain. She has a brain tumor."

"Oh my God!" I said, as struggled to breathe and maintain my composure.

"We have an appointment with Dr. Hopkins tomorrow morning. He's a neurosurgeon in Kalamazoo. You've got to come home now," Denni said, as her voice started to crack.

"I'm on my way," I said and quickly hung up the phone.

Through my mental fog I made the thirty-five-mile trip from Kalamazoo to our home in Allegan. As I drove, my mind was overwhelmed. I thought about my daughter Katie, my wife Denni, and the past few years of our lives in Allegan. Our path had seemed so clear up until a few moments ago.

CHAPTER 2

The Best Laid Plans 1994-1995

ALLEGAN WAS A CHARMING TOWN of five thousand people on the banks of the Kalamazoo River in southwest Michigan. Denni and I had relocated to Allegan almost six years earlier. We had taken a sudden change in course from our career-oriented path in Cincinnati, Ohio, to Michigan - for a house. Not just any house - the Pritchard House.

The house was built in 1865 by my great-great grandfather, Benjamin D. Pritchard. As commander of the Fourth Michigan Cavalry in the Civil War, he was credited with capturing Confederate President Jefferson Davis, essentially ending the Confederacy. In May of 1865, the Fourth Michigan regiment tracked Davis and his party through the backwoods of Georgia as the Confederate group tried to escape to Florida, and potentially the Caribbean. In a world before smartphones and CNN, Pritchard and his men knew nothing of President Lincoln's assassination a month earlier. After the capture, and eventually hearing the news, he said it was a good thing they didn't know of Lincoln's death or his men likely would have made the same fate for Jefferson Davis.

At the age of thirty-two, Benjamin Pritchard returned to Allegan a Brigadier General and nationally acclaimed war hero. He went back to his law practice, founded the first national bank in the entire state of Michigan, and served as State Treasurer. A skilled artist and carpenter, he built a magnificent Gothic-style home on the hill overlooking the city with an expansive view of the Kalamazoo River. After his death in 1907, several generations of the Pritchard family lived in the house. Since the late 1950s, my grandfather Dudley, and his wife, Ada, whom we called Mimi, had been the caretakers.

Growing up, I visited Allegan frequently and our family spent several weeks in the Pritchard House every summer, as well as the occasional fall and winter trips. When I was a young boy, I told my mother and Mimi that one day I'd live in the Pritchard House. I'm sure both of them passed it off as another boyhood dream.

In the spring of 1994, Mimi had fallen in the house and broken her hip. Although ninety-seven years old at the time, she recovered in remarkable fashion. Even so, it became clear to the rest of the family that it was no longer safe for Mimi & Grandpa to live unassisted. Something would have to be done about their living arrangements, including determining the fate of the house. In one of the most difficult moments of my life to that point, I had to tell my grandparents they needed to move out of the Pritchard House and into a nursing home. After Mimi was discharged from the hospital, my grandparents relocated to the Veterans Home in Grand Rapids. Later, while going through some boxes in the house, I found an invitation to the groundbreaking ceremony of the Veterans Home in 1889. General Pritchard had been a guest of honor on the podium at that ceremony, over one hundred earlier. I thought it was quite fitting that my grandparents became residents there.

The situation weighed on my mind, and I couldn't bear the thought of the Pritchard House leaving our family. It was a beautiful house: fifteen rooms filled with Victorian features, including pocket doors made from mahogany and a hand-carved hanging circular staircase crafted by "The General." The staircase was so unusual the Engineering department from the University of Michigan came to study it. Practically every room in the house was fully furnished with heirlooms from the 1820s to the early 1900s. The property had been included in the National Historic Register for years.

The house had leaded glass windows, a full butler's pantry, servants' quarters, and a real woodshed. Over two acres of grounds included towering oak, walnut, hickory, and maple trees, plus a formal garden. Several other houses dating from the Civil War were situated alongside the Pritchard House on Davis Street, which had come to be known as "General's Row."

The list of family members who might be interested in taking over the house was short. My grandparents had one child, my mother Alice. She'd been living in Ohio since the early 1960s, and had no interest in taking over the house. Nor did my brother, Rick, a professor at Siena College near Albany, New York. If anyone in the family was going to live in the Pritchard House, it was going to be up to Denni and me.

I was an aspiring first-line manager at State Farm in Cincinnati, and was determined to have a successful career with the company. Denni had a job as a school teacher in a district twenty miles northeast of Cincinnati. Denni and I met at Eastern Kentucky University and married in 1987 when we were both twenty-four years old. In the seven years since we were married, we moved from Cincinnati to Toledo and back again for positions at State Farm. The two of us were considering putting down some roots in Cincinnati when the Pritchard House opportunity arose.

"Are you sure you want to transfer to Allegan?" Denni asked me, when I approached her about moving to Michigan. "You know I'll go where you want. For Pete's sake, I moved to Toledo with you, but I want you to be sure this is really what *you* want to do. It sounds like this is really going to limit your career options, at least for a while if not forever. We've been talking about you becoming a State Farm agent here, and I love teaching where I do. Your mom is only two hours away and most of my family is close. It's a big step for both of us. I'm going to have to give up my teaching position, and I have no idea what the employment situation is in Michigan."

"I know it's a big step," I said. "But I want to do this. I know it's just a house, but it feels like so much more than that. There's something about it that seems bigger than us. I've been going there since I was a kid and took my first steps on the porch there. You love the house, too. You've said a number of times there's something about the way it makes you feel. It's hard to describe, but it's real. I really want to do this. I feel like we *have* to do this."

"OK, then I'm in," Denni said. "Under one condition; you can never leave me!"

My co-workers had a more puzzled response than my wife. Lots of employees at State Farm moved around with the company, but very few people transferred to Michigan and even fewer transferred back out. For me it wasn't the job that was the driving force. It was something much bigger.

"You're moving to where?" my colleagues asked.

My answer, "Allegan, it's halfway between Grand Rapids and Kalamazoo," didn't help much.

I had learned the proper Michigan technique to showing locations around the state. When asked where one lived, true Michiganders hold up their right hand, which makes a perfect template of the state of Michigan, and one uses the other index finger to point out the exact location on the hand-map. Allegan is in the meaty part of the palm, straight down from the inside of the pinky finger, two-thirds of the way towards the bottom of the hand. Detroit is in the crook of the thumb and index finger, three hours to the other side of the hand. (When you're done looking at your hand, you can start reading again.)

In the summer of 1994, Denni and I moved into the Pritchard House to become the fifth generation of the Pritchard family to occupy the house. That month we also celebrated Mimi & Grandpa's 70th wedding anniversary. Seventy years is a long time for any couple, but for this pair it was all the more special. By the time they married in 1924, Mimi was a twenty-seven-year-old schoolteacher. She would have been an old-maid school teacher by definition. Then, in the fall, two days before his 97th birthday, my grandfather Dudley died. Since Dudley was a World War I vet and grandson of the town's greatest war hero, the city of Allegan flew the flag at half-mast, and he was given military honors including a gun salute from the Pritchard Brigade, the Civil War reenactment group bearing the name of his grandfather.

At the funeral, I remembered some of the stories my grandpa had told me. Stories of when he was a little boy at the turn of the 1900s. For years, the General hosted reunions of the 4th Michigan Cavalry on the grounds of the Pritchard House. My grandpa talked of men who rode to Allegan on horseback, just as they did in the Civil War, and not in one of those newfangled "horseless-carriage" automobiles. The soldiers made campfires in the yard and told stories about the war that were apparently too much for a little boy's ears, so my grandpa would be sent to bed.

I thought how hard it must have been as the grandson of such a legend, always living in the General's shadow. Dudley was laid to rest in the family plot in Allegan, alongside his grandfather, the war hero, lawyer, banker, artist, State Treasurer, and all around overachiever, General Benjamin Dudley Pritchard.

My grandpa's death was a big loss for me, as he was one of the greatest people I've ever known. My mom has told me I've always been a lot like him, which I take as a huge compliment. I have a very sarcastic sense of humor, and I know exactly where I got it from. Grandpa was my humor role model, and though it's earned me some face time with school principals and less than amused bosses, I've always found humor wherever I could. I thank my grandfather for that.

In the move from Ohio I transferred to the State Farm office in Grand Rapids, forty-five miles to the north of Allegan. Denni got a job as a computer training analyst at Perrigo Company, the country's leading manufacturer of store brand pharmaceuticals, based in Allegan. Perrigo had been a locally-grown company, founded by Allegan chemist Luther Perrigo in 1886. The Perrigo's had been next-door neighbors of the Pritchard family since the 1940s. Not much changes on General's Row.

Shortly after moving in, Denni and I came up with a "Five-Year Plan." While we weren't entirely sure of the longer-term horizon, we figured we'd spend five years restoring the house. We both knew the house needed some restoration work, but neither of us had any idea what we were getting into. We immediately dove into the restoration project, and I reached out to the Public Broadcasting Service television series *This Old House.* State Farm was a sponsor and the house had some historical appeal, so I thought it might be a good candidate for the show. An initial inquiry revealed we needed in the neighborhood of $250,000 in cash or liquid assets to undertake a project worthy of the show. According to my math, we were several hundred thousand dollars short in the liquid assets area, so I found a great local contractor and started our own version of *This Old Pritchard House.*

Up to this point in my life, in addition to being hell-bent towards a successful career, I was staunchly opposed to the idea of having children. When we were engaged, Denni and I had talked briefly about having children, and my response was simple - "Never." Not just never, but "never, ever, ever." If anyone asked, that was my immediate, unwavering response. Denni, herself adopted, would admit later that the thought of being childless made her sad, and she was hopeful I would change my mind someday. She told me she had no intentions of raising children without my help. For the first years of our marriage having children was not on my radar. It wasn't that I disliked them, I just didn't think I wanted them.

After turning thirty and making the transition from Ohio to Michigan, I began to have second thoughts about my philosophy regarding children. Something about living in my family home made me rethink that position, and it didn't take any convincing for Denni to want to start a family.

In September 1995, we were blessed with the birth of a baby girl. We'd originally planned on naming her Victoria – as in the Victorian era of the Pritchard House. But when we saw her lying swaddled in the newborn crib at Allegan General Hospital, Denni and I looked at her, then each other, and we both said at the same time, "Katie." Katie had been on our short list of possible names since Denni's Maid of Honor, best friend, and college roommate was named Katie. Kathleen Elizabeth Proctor – "Katie" - it was. I couldn't help but feel The General would be proud to know his great-great-great granddaughter would be living in his house.

In a very short period of time, Denni and I had come to love to our Mayberry-like life. We were both infatuated with Allegan, and the birth of our daughter was more incredible than either one of us imagined. I've been wrong about a lot of things in my life, but my earlier philosophy against having children was as far off the mark as possible. Apparently, there is something to be said for the phrase "never say never."

Just a few years before, my life was on a career-oriented, childless path in Cincinnati. Now, here I was in Allegan, clearly side-tracking and potentially permanently limiting my career, uprooting Denni from her teaching position, and moving her further away from her own family. We were undertaking a huge restoration project, the scope of which neither of us could fathom. And now, most recently, holding my beautiful baby girl in my arms. Everything had changed.

So much for those best laid plans. Life's funny like that.

General B.D. Pritchard House, built in 1865 – Allegan, MI

CHAPTER 3

Didn't See That Coming 1995-2000

§

The addition of a child did not initially sidetrack Denni and me from our Five-Year Plan for restoring the Pritchard House. Since moving in, we'd tackled one project after another, and made slow but steady, and expensive, progress. We started at the top by replacing the roof, and then did a complete remodel of the kitchen. Anyone who lives in a true Victorian house knows that there is no such thing as a dream Victorian kitchen. In that era, kitchens were servant's quarters, designed for function rather than aesthetics. During the summer before Katie was born, we found ourselves in need of a nursery, and renovated a bedroom in the house. It turned out to be one of the first surprises we came upon in our remodeling endeavors.

The bedroom in question was the Pink Room, named for the pink walls and the pink curtains that hung from the windows. One might conclude with a pink theme, we could have taken our chances on the baby being a girl and left it that way. However, leaving the room intact was not a realistic option. The plaster had numerous cracks in need of repair, and the paint was cracked and peeling. Worse yet, the walls had paint over wallpaper - something we found throughout the house. When we removed the paint to uncover the wallpaper, it became apparent from the design that this room at one time, had been a nursery. As we progressed, we discovered that three of the walls had the nursery wallpaper design but the fourth wall did not. A little research led us to an eerie conclusion.

After the General's death in 1907, his daughter Bertha lived in the house with her husband Charles Wilkes. In 1919, they had a baby girl named Francis, who survived only nineteen days. Just down from the Pritchard family plot at the cemetery is the Wilkes plot. Buried next to her mother Bertha is "Baby Francis Wilkes." We concluded that Bertha and Charles had not yet finished the nursery when the unthinkable occurred, and rather than complete the room, they painted over it. On the night Katie turned nineteen days old, Denni wouldn't let our daughter sleep in her crib in the nursery. Instead, Katie slept soundly in a makeshift crib in our room.

Another massive undertaking for the house included a new paint job. The house had been touched up for my mother's wedding in 1957, but in the forty years since then, the onslaught of Michigan weather had taken its toll, and the exterior was clearly in a need of a total makeover. In a project that lasted over four months, the entire house was sandblasted, rotting boards were replaced, and every seam between every board was caulked.

Considering the cost was as much as a luxury car at the time, we couldn't have been more thrilled with the outcome. The house gleamed a shining white, with burgundy and hunter green accents that showcased the Gothic and Victorian features.

Just as we were prepared to enjoy our newly beautified house, we encountered something we didn't anticipate, another unexpected development that would fit into the "Didn't see that coming" category. Over the years we lived in the Pritchard House, Denni and I would say that phrase dozens of times.

When Katie went for her checkup several weeks after the house painting was completed, she had significantly elevated levels of lead in her blood. The house's mixture of milk, lead, and latex paint caused the dust from the sandblasting to increase Katie's lead levels. The counts were just below the pediatrician having to notify the authorities, so we embarked on a campaign to return them to normal. The program consisted of washing all of Katie's toys daily. Denni separated her toys into several batches so she'd have a set to play with while the other ones went through the dishwasher. Not only did her toys need washing, but also the floors needed to be mopped, the house wet-dusted, and the carpets vacuumed. The house was over five thousand square feet of wooden floors and antique oriental rugs, which made this a monumental task. After several months of the daily cleaning and much griping from me, Katie's lead levels returned to normal, and we figured that was the end of any health issues.

For the next year and a half, aside from a rather strange incident when Katie vomited to the point she got dehydrated and was hospitalized, she seemed very healthy and enjoyed a typical toddlerhood. Katie and Denni continued their rituals around town. She played with her friends from daycare, and she was as smitten with our dog, Rocky, as he was with her. Rocky was our ninety-pound boxer, who looked intimidating, but Katie had him wrapped tightly around her little finger. When Katie was an infant, she sat in a swing that gently rocked her for hours on end. Rocky would lie in front of the swing and protect her from any potential dangers lurking around.

Life in our house seemed almost normal as we went through one renovation project after another. We had become accustomed to the chaos, and had settled into a routine. In the fall of 1998 I moved offices to work in Kalamazoo some thirty-five miles to the south of Allegan. Both Denni and I thought it would be an opportune time for Katie to go to preschool in Kalamazoo. Denni gave me an ample supply of kiddie music to play during the commute. After a short time, I realized that I couldn't endure another chorus of "Baby Beluga & the Deep Blue Sea," so I called an audible, and Katie and I listened to a wide variety of music and programs during our daily drive, from classic rock to *The Bob & Tom Show*, an adult comedy program, whose humor I figured was so far over Katie's head that it would be harmless.

It worked pretty well, until one evening at dinner when Katie belted out a rousing version of John Mellencamp's "I Need a Lover." After giving me a stern look, Denni asked Katie what else she listened to during her ride with Daddy. Katie raised her fist and shouted, "Bob & Tom Rock!" I could hear DJ Denni loud and clear, "We now return you to your regular children's music programming." Welcome back, Baby Beluga.

Summertime came and went in Michigan in 1999, and on a number of mornings Katie was sick to her stomach shortly after waking. Sometimes she just couldn't stop it, and in October, Katie was hospitalized for dehydration. It created quite a stir for Denni, because, of all the wonderful traits my wife possesses, her ability to deal with the act of vomiting is pretty limited. OK, it's almost non-existent. The mere sound of someone getting sick causes Denni herself to gag, and sometimes triggers her to join the vomiting festivities.

Denni informed the pediatrician that her gut told her something wasn't right. The pediatrician said Katie probably just had a sensitive stomach and not to worry. She did refer Katie to an allergist, I suspected if nothing else to get Denni to stop bringing it up. After all, moms are the ultimate worrywarts.

The allergist assured us there was nothing to be alarmed about, but said allergies or possibly migraines were likely the source of her issues. The morning sickness continued sporadically, and then Denni noticed something else she thought was strange. Whenever Katie talked to her grandparents on the phone, she held the phone up to her left ear. Denni started putting the phone up to Katie's right ear, and Katie would instinctively move it to her left ear. The pediatrician continued to tell Denni not to worry, and said that it was probably just a habit. Denni wondered if the nausea and hearing issues might be connected. She pushed the doctor to order a hearing test, convinced that something just wasn't right, and the doctor relented.

In addition to Katie's medical issues, October turned into an emotional month for our family. We celebrated Mimi Pritchard's 102nd birthday. Born in 1897, Mimi said that one of her goals was to live in three different centuries. She came within nine weeks of that goal, and died a week later on October 24, 1999.

As had happened several times at work over the preceding few months, at the funeral I felt an unusually strong sense of stress in addition to sadness. I assumed it was some form of anxiety attack. While it was sad to say goodbye to my grandmother, she lived a long and healthy life, so I didn't have the grief associated with a tragic or unexpected loss. As the pastor spoke, I almost couldn't contain my thoughts, and for a moment I was concerned I was having a panic attack. I sensed that it wasn't only my grandmother's death on my mind. I feared it was something else, I just couldn't put my finger on what it was.

One night as we lay in bed, I mentioned my anxiety issues to Denni. "This is so strange," Denni said. "I've been having a recurring nightmare. I'm driving in our car with Katie in the back seat, and we go off a bridge into water, and I can't save her. I'm so worried."

"Everything will be fine," I replied, although I wasn't sure I sounded convincing to either myself or Denni. "Just don't go over any bridges."

The hearing test finally took place in mid-December 1999. The first test validated Denni's suspicion that Katie had some hearing loss in her right ear. Due to the findings of the initial test, Katie had a more thorough hearing test that revealed Katie was completely deaf in her right ear. The ENT doctor said Katie's hearing issues could be the result of two potential sources.

The first and most likely cause related to nerve damage in her ear, and could be repaired by a relatively simple procedure. The less likely cause was a mass, and even though nerve damage was the suspected cause of the deafness, the doctor ordered a CAT scan "just to make sure" there was nothing else going on.

The second hearing test was completed the week of Christmas. The doctor told Denni it would be fine to schedule the follow-up appointment for the CAT scan after the hustle and bustle of the holiday season. As if we needed anything else on our plate, two days before the hearing test, it was confirmed that Denni was pregnant with an August due date. Denni had suffered a miscarriage the previous year, and had decided not to make any widespread announcement until she was further along in her pregnancy. Instead, she told a few doctors, and kept it on a need-to-know basis.

Over the holidays Katie seemed to be in good health, and our family enjoyed a beautiful Michigan Christmas, along with the ringing in of the new millennium. Denni and I began to regret the delay when Katie had another bout of vomiting after the New Year. When the appointment finally arrived, it was none too soon for us.

At Bronson Hospital in Kalamazoo earlier that day, the CAT scan had a routine feel about it. The technician joked throughout the procedure, and as we left he said matter-of-factly, "I didn't see anything." I never stopped to think that the technician had no medical training, as he was really more of a patient transfer agent, like the workers who move the elderly through airports. He certainly wasn't in a position to offer a medical opinion of any kind. Yet his comments somehow comforted me as I left the hospital and returned to my office in Kalamazoo, while Denni and Katie headed home to Allegan, thirty-five miles away.

The trip home from my office in Kalamazoo had seemed like an eternity. Considering the time frame I'd traveled through in my mind, it had been quite a journey. As I steered the car down the long, circular driveway of the Pritchard House, my head was spinning from the unbelievable turn of events. Katie has a brain tumor. How could this be? We certainly didn't see it coming. And the cause of my anxiety and Denni's nightmares for the past few months? At least now we had found the source.

PART II

"I've Got This"

CHAPTER 4

Chance of Survival January 21, 2000

AFTER UNDERGOING A SERIES OF neurological tests, Katie sat on the floor in Dr. Hopkins's office and played quietly with her doll while Denni and I talked with the neurosurgeon. With a name like John Hopkins, I figured he didn't have much of a choice besides a medical career.

"It's in a tricky spot, but I'm comfortable doing this surgery," the doctor said. "And regardless what you decide, you're going to need a second opinion. There are a lot of really good children's hospitals not too far away. There are a few in Chicago, and of course, there's the Mott Center at the University of Michigan."

"What about Cincinnati?" Denni inquired. "That's where we're from and we have family there."

"Cincinnati has a great children's hospital," replied Dr. Hopkins. "In fact it's one of the best children's hospitals in the country, and one of the best pediatric neurosurgeons you'll find anywhere is there, Doctor Kerry Crone."

Dr. Crone, Cincinnati, brain tumor... it all was too much for me to process. All I could think about was Amber Sorensen's claim and her tragic fate. It was a good thing the medical focus was on Katie, because if Dr. Hopkins would have checked my heart rate, he would have found it going through the roof.

"Doctor Hopkins, do we contact him, or do you?" Denni asked.

"I'll reach out to Doctor Crone's office," Dr. Hopkins offered. "But it's getting close to the weekend, so it might be next week before we hear anything. I'm going to give you the CAT scan films to take with you to Cincinnati or wherever you end up. In the meantime, try not to think too far down the road. I'll be in touch as soon as I hear. I promise."

We went to lunch in Kalamazoo to try to get our minds around what was happening. At four and a half years old, it was clear Katie had no idea what was going on, and we didn't talk about it with her. There was no use getting her alarmed when we knew so little. Katie sat on her mom's lap and Denni braided our daughter's long and beautiful hair as we sat in silence in the restaurant. That evening, Katie's CAT scan films lie in a large envelope on the dining room table. We pulled one of the film sheets out and started to hold it up to the light, but quickly put it back in the envelope. After all, what good would it do?

We knew that our next task was to make phone calls to family members. Even though we didn't know all the details, we did know the awful piece of information we had to share. The hardest call for me to make was to my mom. She knew Katie was having the radiology test as did the rest of our family, but just like Denni and me, my mom wasn't prepared to hear the news.

"Hey, Mom, it's Rob."

"Hi, honey. How is everything? Did Katie's tests go OK? You probably haven't heard yet, huh?"

"Actually, we have heard," I said. "And no, things aren't OK."

"Oh? What's the matter?" she asked.

I took a deep breath. "The scans showed a mass on her brain. Katie has a brain tumor."

My mom was stunned. "Oh, my God! No! Oh, honey! I'm so sorry!"

"Yeah, I know. We are, too." I didn't know what else to say, and there was long pause.

"What are you going to do?" my mom asked, her voice cracking as she tried to maintain her composure.

"We saw a neurosurgeon in Kalamazoo today, and we need to get a second opinion" I replied. "The doctor here is reaching out to a surgeon at Children's in Cincinnati, so we may be going there."

"You know," mom said, "St. Jude's is awfully good too, and they take every patient free of charge." My mom had worked for years as the Director of Volunteers for St. Rita's Hospital in Lima, Ohio, and was familiar with many hospitals around the country.

"I know they do, Mom. But if they'll see us, we're planning on heading to Cincinnati and go from there. We have insurance, and this isn't about getting free care." I knew that sounded harsher than I meant it to, and hoped my mom didn't take it wrong.

"Oh, honey, I didn't mean it that way," she said. "I just want Katie to get the best care possible." After she spoke, I felt bad about my curtness.

"So do we, Mom. So do we." I hung up the phone.

Denni then called her family, and the news was met with equal shock and sadness. Denni's parents were divorced and both lived in the Cincinnati area. For the last ten years, her father, David, had been married to Holly, and they offered their home should we decide on Cincinnati Children's for Katie's surgery. Denni promptly took them up on the offer.

Another call I made was to Dr. Jeff Acker, my high school friend, and the oncologist whom I'd contacted years earlier with questions about brain tumors. But this was an entirely different conversation. This wasn't for information about some obscure medical condition for an insurance claim. Now it was personal, as the brain tumor didn't belong to a stranger, it belonged to my daughter. Jeff said while the neurosurgeon in Kalamazoo was certainly competent, he felt strongly that it was important to get Katie to a major cancer center for treatment. He said that doing so could improve her chance of survival. The phrase "chance of survival" caught me off guard, and I hated the sound of it. I was still in information overload, and processing the words "brain tumor," I couldn't conjure up anything that was remotely positive. I wasn't in denial; I was just in shock.

Early Tuesday morning, Dr. Hopkins called. Dr. Crone agreed to see Katie, and his office could get her in on Thursday. But they wanted her at Cincinnati Children's Hospital the very next day so they could take another series of pictures of the tumor for Dr. Crone. The pace of everything seemed fast. For the past few months we were used to the word "wait" when it came to the medical community. Wait for appointments, wait for tests, and wait for results. But now we were in an entirely new realm, and clearly one with an abbreviated timeline and a sense of urgency. It made me feel special and concerned at the same time.

We reached out to a few close friends as well as our bosses to fill them in on the situation, and to inform them that we'd be leaving for Cincinnati later that afternoon. The reactions were similar, disbelief and offers of prayers of support.

In a frenzy of activity, we completed a whirlwind packing session and made arrangements for the neighbors to care for our dog, Rocky. Then Denni, Katie, and I made the six-hour drive to Cincinnati. Katie seemed oblivious to all the fuss, and spent most of the trip playing with her dolls and coloring. She traveled to Cincinnati several times a year to see her grandparents, so although she knew she had to see a doctor, it really didn't seem to be that big of a deal to her.

At the MRI appointment Wednesday morning, the anesthesiologist did her best to put everyone at ease.

"I understand you had some pictures of that pretty little head taken last week?" the doctor said, as she bent down to be on Katie's level. Katie nodded.

"Well these pictures are kind of like those only they'll be a lot clearer so it'll take more time. Let me show you something." She took Katie by the hand and led her into the MRI room, and walked her around the large machine.

"It's really just a big camera," the doctor continued, trying to put Katie at ease. "I call her Bessie. She takes great pictures, but boy, is she noisy! Since she's so loud, and because it'll take a while we're going to let you go to sleep. When you wake up we'll be all done."

Denni and I were impressed with the bedside manner of the doctor. Her demeanor had worked wonders, right up until the needle came out.

"Honey, to give you the medicine to help you sleep, we need to put a needle in," said the doctor. "It'll sting; I'm not going to lie to you. But it only stings for a few seconds, I promise."

That logic helped everyone in the room except the patient. Denni held Katie's hand as she cried while the nurses got the needle in successfully on the second attempt. The first attempt resulted in a blown vein, and by the time the needle was inserted correctly, there were two people crying in the room, Katie and Denni.

Two hours later, when Katie awoke in recovery, she reminded us of a drunken sailor. She wobbled from side to side, and her head bobbed up and down with little control. Interestingly enough, when the nurse came to assist, Katie asked her why she had two heads. The nurse just laughed and said, "You gotta love Nembutal."

"What do you mean?" Denni asked.

"Nembutal is a pretty common anesthetic. It works great and gets out of the system pretty quickly, but it can make for some doozy hallucinations."

"Should we be worried?" Denni asked with the tone of a concerned parent.

"Nah, it'll wear off and in a few hours or so we'll all have one head again." Sure enough, as the afternoon turned into evening, drunken sailor Katie returned to her normal state, much to our relief.

The next day, with access to much clearer pictures of the tumor, Dr. Crone performed a variety of neurological tests. Some were the same as Dr. Hopkins had completed in Kalamazoo. When he held his index finger in front of Katie and moved it from side to side in the "follow my finger" test, as soon as his finger crossed in front of Katie's nose, her right eye shook violently. He had Katie stand on her left leg, which she did easily. When she tried to stand on her right leg, she tumbled over. Katie could walk fine, but somehow in just a few days she'd lost the ability to skip. I couldn't help but feel like somehow we should have noticed the things we were now witnessing.

"I can't believe we all missed this stuff," I said. "I'm so glad Denni pushed for those hearing tests. Denni kept telling the pediatrician that something was wrong, but she kept telling Denni everything was fine. Shouldn't they have asked for a scan or something when Katie was hospitalized a few months ago?"

Dr. Crone said, "Don't be too hard on yourself or your pediatrician. I talk to lots of parents in your shoes, and sometimes everyone feels guilty for not catching things sooner. The reality is that lots of Katie's symptoms are likely pretty recent, and even though she's had morning sickness for a little while, we usually don't start off looking for a brain tumor. You start with the simple stuff and work your way up, which appears to be what happened in Katie's case."

"I guess," I said, still feeling angry at myself, the pediatrician, and the allergist. And especially the lab tech who'd so boldly declared, "I don't see anything." I wanted to find that guy and punch him.

CHAPTER 5

Get a Hold of Yourself January 27, 2000

§

Dr. Crone placed the MRI scans on the bright white screen like the ones on the TV medical shows, and as he talked Denni and I focused on the gray spot that wasn't supposed to be there. It was larger than the rubber sphere inside a golf ball. We had no idea what we were looking at, but we could tell Dr. Crone seemed to be focusing his attention on one spot in particular.

"This is a concern," Dr. Crone said, pointing to a small spot on the scan. "I can't tell if it's stuck on the brain stem like gum, or growing into it," he said. "Neither is good."

"What do you mean?" I asked.

Dr. Crone looked away from the screen and spoke directly to us. "The tumor is in the area of the fourth ventricle of Katie's brain where it connects to her brain stem. It's situated where her cranial nerves come together, and many of her major body functions are controlled by this area. I don't want to overwhelm you, but they include swallowing, her vocal cords, balance, muscle coordination, use of her facial muscles, blinking her eyes, and hearing."

"Can you tell what type of tumor it is?" I probed. I recalled some of the research I had done for Amber Sorenson's claim years before, and although some of that information had escaped my memory, I was keenly aware that that the type of tumor was very important. It could literally mean the difference between life and death.

"No, I really can't," Dr. Crone responded. "I'm somewhat encouraged that it looks to be a self-contained, spherical tumor. The more solid and contained it is, the better chance we have of getting all of it. But as far as what type it is, I can't tell from the scan. We'll need to have samples of the tumor analyzed in a lab, and that will be done during the surgery."

Dr. Crone's assistant gave me a brain tumor primer containing information about many of the major types of brain tumors. There are over one hundred types of brain tumors, and while there's no such thing as a "good" brain tumor, clearly some are far worse than others. Dr. Crone cautioned against reading too much at this point. He reiterated that the most important part of determining the type of tumor would take place in the lab. He then described the surgical procedure he planned to perform.

"There will be a team of us," Dr. Crone said. "I'll have several neurosurgical doctors with me, anesthesiologists and a full surgical nursing team. We'll prep her and lay her on the operating table in what we call a park bench position. She'll be on her side, like when you see people lying on a park bench. We'll open the skin over a fairly large part of the back of Katie's head and remove a piece of her skull as well as the cervical disc closest to the bottom of her skull. It's called the C1 disc, and the procedure is called a C1 discectomy."

In my years of handling auto injury claims, where neck and back injuries were common, I had reviewed hundreds of medical records involving disc injuries. The procedure and the terminology were familiar to me, but it was still unnerving.

"After we remove the piece of the skull and the disc then we'll go after the tumor. We'll incorporate a surgical microscope to try to remove the tumor a piece at a time, known as debulking, with the goal of removing all of it. I hope that when we get in there, we'll find that the tumor is contained and doesn't have a good blood supply. We'll cauterize any bleeding, but I don't expect much, based on where it is."

Denni and I just looked at each other. The whole conversation seemed surreal.

"Are you going to shave her head?" Denni asked, thinking of our daughter's beautiful hair. Katie had beautiful, brown hair that flowed to the middle of her back, and Denni had always loved Katie's hair. I had assumed they would shave her head, as when I thought of kids with these conditions, I recalled most of them seemed to have no hair.

"We try to not do that anymore," Dr. Crone said. "We'll need to shave at least the back of her head, but we'll leave what we can. We've learned that we really don't need to take it all off, and both the parents and the kids seem happier. I can't promise, but we'll try to leave as much of Katie's hair as we can. Deal?"

"Deal," said Denni.

"We need to talk about the risks," said Dr. Crone. "Every surgery has risks. Our goal will be to remove the tumor without doing further damage. Even if the surgery is successful, there are very real possibilities that Katie might have some level of facial paralysis, deafness, and sensation loss, blindness or vision issues, or worse. My intent isn't to alarm or scare you. I don't think I'm telling you anything you don't already know. This is a delicate surgery."

Dr. Crone ended the appointment by informing us the surgery would take place early the following week. They needed time to secure an operating room for at least six hours, and to assemble the team of doctors, anesthesiologists, and nurses. He wrote a prescription for a steroid medication, and told us the swelling in Katie's brain was likely causing some of her symptoms, so he wanted to keep things in check until the surgery. Then he gave us the same advice that Dr. Hopkins did.

"Don't get too far ahead of yourselves," he offered. "We take things one step at a time in these situations. I know we give everyone the brain tumor primer, but I'm not so sure reading all of it is helpful right now. If you have any questions, my assistant Mimi can help you or get you in touch with me. I'll see you in a few days."

Mimi handed Denni one of Dr. Crone's business cards with her phone number written on the back. Shortly after the consultation with Dr. Crone, Denni went off to relay information to her family, and I found myself alone in the doctor's small conference room. I called my best friend Brian Clark. The gist of the conversation was that, in what I was sure was a very unbecoming show of emotion, I admitted I didn't know if I was strong enough to handle everything that was going on. Brian had been my best friend since elementary school, we were roommates in college, and lived together in Cincinnati after graduating, up until the time Denni and I got married.

Brian and I talked about some of the major things we'd been through together. When Brian was eleven years old he was struck by a car on his bicycle and was hospitalized for most of the summer. He recovered, but it was the most serious medical situation either of us could personally relate to, and I remembered it well. My medical history amounted to several self-induced knee surgeries due to racquetball, and a broken ankle from playing tennis. Aside from those minor incidents and being in the delivery room for Denni's C-section, the only hospital rooms I'd seen had been on television. We agreed we'd never been through anything like this, but Brian offered comfort as only a best friend could. I made my next call to my boss.

Bob Butler had been my manager at State Farm for two years. He was a Marine in the 1960s, and although himself on the cusp of his sixties, he looked as though he could still be a boot camp drill sergeant. Bob offered comfort, but also gave me a dose of tough love I wasn't expecting. As I complained about my current situation and began to lose control of my emotions, Bob spoke up.

"I can only imagine how tough all of this is," he said. "But you need to get a hold of yourself. For you, for Denni, and especially for Katie. You need to do some quick and deep soul-searching to figure out how you're going to approach this."

Bob continued with his advice. "You need to be strong. You're the man of the family and Denni and Katie need you. You need each other. None of us is built for handling things like this alone, but you're not alone. You have each other, your family, and your friends. You have all of us, and we'll give you all the strength and support we can. And you have something far more important to lean on than us."

"What's that?" I asked.

"Faith," he responded. "This is in God's hands, and He is with you. I can't promise it's going to turn out like you want, but I can promise He's with you, Denni, and Katie. I promise that is the truth."

"I know that," I replied, although at the time I really wasn't sure it was entirely true, and even if it was I couldn't get my head around it. In all honesty, I was pretty angry and disappointed with God at the moment.

"You need to find whatever strength you can, and hold onto it. And you need to be strong for Denni and Katie. Can you do that?" Bob asked.

"I think so," was the best I could come up with.

Alone in the conference room, I thought silently for a few minutes, came to terms with the emotions I was feeling, and then had the first of what would be many conversations with God. If God was listening, He certainly wasn't sending any signals my way.

In the following days, we passed the time as best we could while staying at David and Holly's house. We tried to act as normal as possible, not even sure what that looked like. A few visitors came by to see Katie and offer their support. My wife's family was scattered around the greater Cincinnati area, and her brother and sisters came by for brief visits. Denni's mom, Darlene, and her fiancé, Don, came over to offer their support as well, as did a few other friends. Denni and I were grateful for the support.

Brian Clark and his wife Jill came over with their girls Lesley and Annie to play with Katie. Our families visited several times a year, and just a few weeks earlier, the entire Clark family had come to Allegan for our annual ski trip. Lesley and Annie presented Katie with a small stuffed animal. It was a gray and white husky with black marble eyes whose nametag said "Dakota." Katie quickly declared Dakota her favorite stuffed animal, and it became her new constant companion. From the kids' perspectives, it seemed like just another visit. For the rest of us it was anything but.

Against Dr. Crone's advice about reading ahead too much, I read the brain tumor primer that the hospital had given me. I wanted to know as much about brain tumors as I could. I relearned some of the information that I'd seen previously when I was researching the obscure condition to assist with the evaluation of a claim for work. Now it was much more personal. My research also led me to the Internet. There I quickly discovered information regarding brain tumors that ranged from credible and medically-validated, to downright frightening and lacking any foundation in science. There were sites offering everything from hope and promises of a cure, to total despair, and everything in between.

Denni took a different approach and was only interested in knowing what Dr. Crone and the staff told her. To her, the reality was that we wouldn't know what we were dealing with until Dr. Crone did the surgery and the pathology lab tests were completed, so what was the point in speculating? Regardless of the information in the primer, or on the Internet, it was becoming clear that what we were dealing with was of a magnitude we could hardly grasp.

I wasn't surprised that Denni brought her Bible from Michigan and had read from it every night for weeks now. Through the years, she often read her Bible, and highlighted passages that provided special meaning. I felt a number of emotions concerning Denni's faith, which I deemed to be much deeper than my own. I admired her for it, and in some ways envied the comfort, strength, and discipline it provided her. Although I'm ashamed to admit it, I also found it a bit off-putting, as sometimes I felt subjected to a certain "holier than thou" attitude under the guise of religion. Not specifically from Denni, but from church-goers in general.

From the time I was old enough to think for myself, I believed in God and Jesus and Heaven and Hell. I figured although I was no saint, I hadn't done anything that would be considered a major violation of the Top Ten list. I gave myself bonus points for obeying the "Thou shalt not kill" and

"Thou shalt not commit adultery" ones, and rationalized that, outside of a few stray office supplies, I really hadn't stolen anything. Could one actually go to Hell for a few pens and a couple of pads of misappropriated Post-It notes?

Overall, I figured I had as good a chance as most at getting into Heaven. And for me, throughout my adult life, that had been good enough. Or so I thought.

As evening waned on the night before our daughter's brain surgery, while Denni read her Bible, I combed through the pages of the brain tumor primer. Then I took a few minutes to send out a brief email message to some of our co-workers, friends, and my high school Internet chat group. Lots of friends and acquaintances were concerned, and wanted to offer whatever support they could. Considering the circumstances, we would accept all the support we could get.

From: Rob & Denni Proctor
Date: Monday, January 31, 2000
Re: Katie Proctor
As some of you know, Denni and I are with Katie in Cincinnati at Children's Hospital. Last week Katie had some tests and the doctors discovered a brain tumor, so Katie is having surgery tomorrow. The surgery should take about six hours. We sure can use all the positive thoughts and prayers you'd care to send.
Thanks,
Rob & Denni

CHAPTER 6

The Longest Day February 1, 2000

§

IN THE PRIOR FEW DAYS, the unbelievable turn of events had caught Denni and me so off guard that we really didn't have much of a chance to connect with each other. Denni had always been very communicative and liked to talk through events and feelings and emotions. We're a perfect example of the Women are from Venus; Men are from Mars concept. I don't naturally gravitate to the emotional, soul-bearing type of conversation. I'm a problem-solver, because as a man, it's what I do. But in this instance, both of us were so overcome with the shock of the news that we hadn't had much conversation on the matter.

"Are you ready for this?" Denni asked me as we lay in bed just after midnight. It was clear neither of us could sleep.

"No, I'm not," I said. "This whole thing is so unfair. I just don't get it. It's one of those things that make me so mad and so sad at the same time. I feel like God is punishing me for something. And if that's the case, I wish He'd take it out on me and not Katie."

"I went through that thought process, too, but I really don't think that's how it works. All I know is that I can't lose my little girl," Denni said, through tears. "I just can't."

"Me, neither," I said as I closed my eyes, and tried in vain to find the sleep that would never come that night.

With all of the activity over the past week, I wasn't certain how much of the entire brain tumor situation Katie was able to comprehend. As we waited for the surgery, two nurses from Children's came to the house and used a doll to gently, but accurately, show her what Dr. Crone would do. Both Denni and I talked about the surgery with Katie, and she'd performed a number of medical procedures on all of the family members and most of the guests that week, as there had been a clear focus on the topic. But at four and a half years old, how much could she possibly understand?

Apparently, she understood more than I thought. On the morning of her surgery, Katie woke up at four o'clock and crawled into her mommy's lap… and began to cry. And for a time I couldn't even measure, mother and daughter held each other and wept. There are points in everyone's life when it seems that things can't get any darker. For me, this was one of those times. I tried to find a place in my mind that offered some sense of comfort, but at that moment I couldn't find any.

It was a cold February morning in Ohio, and as we drove off through the pre-dawn darkness, I could see David and Holly standing in the driveway, holding each other and wiping away tears. Denni and I would have given anything not to be in this spot. But here we were, and both of us knew that no matter what, our lives would never be the same again.

The surgical prep area was a hub of activity. I looked up and down the hallway at over a dozen rooms filled with nervous parents and scared children. I wondered for a moment what other procedures were being performed that day. But that curiosity quickly left me when the anesthesiologist walked in. As far as I was concerned, there was only one patient at Children's that day - Katie Proctor.

The anesthesiologist explained the process; considering Katie had been sedated the week before, it seemed a bit redundant. Today's procedure was much more extensive than just a scan, and on this morning, Katie would get a jump-start on the anesthesia by inhaling some gas to make her groggy, hopefully making it easier for the nurses to insert the necessary I-V lines.

"Katie, what flavor do you want?" the anesthesiologist asked, referring to the veritable Baskin-Robbins menu of flavors of the gas that would start the anesthesia process.

"Bubble gum," was Katie's reply.

The room smelled of bubble gum and disinfectant. The nurses searched for a good vein, and as was the case the week prior, it took the nurses two tries to find a suitable one. Katie held on tightly to her new friend, the stuffed husky named Dakota, and cried for just a minute before the drugs started to take effect. Denni and I walked alongside her gurney to the operating room door. As the door opened we could see Dr. Crone and a number of other doctors and staff surrounding him. Over his mask we met his eyes for a few seconds and he nodded his head up and down once as his way of giving a positive signal. A brain surgeon's pre-game fist pump. As the gurney started to roll forward into the operating room, Denni held on to Katie's hand and couldn't let go.

In her groggy voice Katie said, "Don't worry Mommy, I'll be OK."

After the door closed, Denni and I stood in the cold corridor for a few minutes while we tried to compose ourselves. Denni tucked her head in my shoulder and sobbed uncontrollably. As she held on to me, my boss's words of encouragement came to mind.

Be strong, Rob. For Denni. And Katie.

At the moment, I felt a number of emotions. Panic and worry I had plenty of, but strength? I wasn't sure. I said a very brief prayer, not even sure what to say, other than something to the effect of "Please, God, make this go away, and make Katie all better." Denni was saying a prayer of her own, certainly more eloquent and well-founded. We eventually pulled ourselves together and headed through the doors into the waiting room for what we both knew would be the longest day of our lives.

We settled into place in the waiting room. It was a large area broken up by stereotypical-looking hospital furniture, fake plants, the obligatory aquarium, and pictures on the wall made by previous patients. It could easily accommodate up to seventy-five people along with all of their anxiety. Families camped out in groups around the large room while little brothers and sisters played board games, scribbled in coloring books, or watched TV as the adults had conversations or read magazines. After all, this was the year 2000, and the first few weeks of the new millennium. There were no such things as smartphones, and the first iPod wouldn't be introduced for over a year.

Katie's surgery was to begin promptly at 8:00 A.M. and was expected to last roughly six hours. Just minutes after eight, the receptionist passed a message to us from the operating room nurse that the surgery had started. An hour later a nurse came into the waiting room and told us that Katie was doing great, that the doctors had removed part of her skull, and they were preparing to remove her cervical disc. Then they could access the tumor. At 11:00 A.M. the same nurse told us that things were going fine, and that she'd be back at 1:00 P.M. with an update.

We passed the time with family and some close friends and tried to stay focused on positive thoughts, while other patient's families came and went as the morning surgeries ended. Denni and I wandered down to the cafeteria, but even with dozens of food choices, neither of us could find anything that looked appetizing. We hurried back to the waiting room in plenty of time for the next update.

1:00 P.M. passed without an update. As did 2:00 P.M., when Katie's surgery was originally set to be over. A few minutes after 2:30 P.M. the waiting room phone rang, and I could hear another family discussing that their child's surgery was being delayed because of complications with a current one. Denni was talking with her family and hadn't heard the exchange. I debated for a moment about not telling her, but thought I better pass on the information. Although we couldn't be sure it was Katie, we suspected it. We were both numb.

I discovered the mind is both a friend and an enemy in times like this. My mind was in a battle of good versus evil. I told myself Katie was doing fine and surgery was just taking longer than planned. Dr. Crone was one of the most gifted brain surgeons in the country, and he would make sure that the process was done one hundred percent right. To get the entire tumor, which was his plan, was just taking more time.

At the same time, evil thoughts about all the bad things that could be happening fought for space in my mind. What will Katie be like after the surgery - physically, intellectually, and mentally? What if the worst had happened? Is Katie still alive? I said another prayer, or, more accurately, begged God to fix things. I wondered whether God was listening, and hoped so. Then I thought about what I'd heard at countless business meetings at State Farm – hope isn't a strategy. It may not be a strategy, but at the moment it seemed like hope was all I had.

Just before 4:00 P.M. the waiting room phone rang, and we were told to meet with Dr. Crone in a small conference room down the hall. As we walked into the room, Dr. Crone rose and came towards us in his surgical scrubs with his mask hanging around his neck. He looked tired, but he smiled.

"First and foremost, Katie is alive!" Dr. Crone said.

Thank God!

"I couldn't remove the entire tumor as some of it was growing through her brain stem," he said. "But I removed most of it and although there are still a few more lab tests to run, everything points to a low-grade brain stem glioma."

"How does she look?" Denni asked.

"All things considered, pretty good," he said. "She's got quite a bit of swelling, and we'll need to watch her closely over the next couple of days in ICU to see what improvements she can make. For now, we'll just take things one at a time."

"Thank you so much! I'm a hugger - can I hug you?" Denni asked.

"You sure can," Dr. Crone said as the two embraced. "It's been a long day for all of us."

Denni and I weren't sure what we'd see, and my mind had another battle between good and evil as we rode the elevator to the Intensive Care Unit on the sixth floor. When we saw Katie, the entire right side of her face was swollen and distorted and there were tubes and needles sticking out everywhere. Denni held Katie's hand and kissed her forehead through the germ mask she'd been asked to wear. She carefully climbed into the bed with Katie, making sure not to disturb any of the protruding I-V lines. Even though she certainly did look worse for wear, we agreed with Dr. Crone that Katie had weathered the storm pretty well. I couldn't help but notice that Dakota, lying close to Katie, had a spot on its leg. As I grabbed a closer look the source of the stain became obvious. It was blood.

We would come to find that Dr. Crone had a gift for telling us what he thought we could handle in the moment. We'd learn later that as he tried to remove the tumor from her brain stem, Katie's heart rate dropped to almost nothing and she stopped breathing on several occasions. The call to the waiting room about the surgery with complications? Yes, that was Katie.

I knew there were lots of friends, family, and colleagues who were concerned about Katie and wanted some news. For simplicity's sake, I clicked on the email addresses of individuals I thought would want to know. I decided to label the distribution list "Friends of Katie."

> To: Friends of Katie
> From: Rob & Denni Proctor
> Date: Tuesday, February 1, 2000
> Re: Katie Update
> Way to go folks - those thoughts and prayers paid off! Although we're not out of the woods yet, today's surgery was as good as can be expected.
>
> Katie's tumor is in her brain stem which is not good, but it could have been much worse. As it stands, Dr. Crone got most of the tumor. He sent samples of the tumor to the lab on several occasions to make sure, but according to Dr. Crone and the radiologists, the diagnosis is a low-grade brain stem glioma. At least we know what we're dealing with. We're meeting with the Oncology

team later this week to look into chemo and radiation, but there is a chance if everything goes well Katie might not need any of that. Dr. Crone says the survival rate is very encouraging.

The next twenty-four to forty-eight hours will be pretty crucial. Katie has some swelling and as you can imagine she's pretty uncomfortable. They are monitoring her closely for seizures and the like, but so far so good.

Please keep those thoughts and prayers coming. We can't thank you enough for your support. It means the world to us.

Rob & Denni

As the evening dwindled, Denni and I were both exhausted and needed to decide what to do about the sleeping arrangements. In the ICU, a chair beside the bed was the only place for a guest. Denni was several months into her pregnancy and today had been long enough for her. There was a small bedroom at the end of the hallway with a bed and the nurse said Denni could have that room if she wanted it.

"I really want to stay with Katie, but I'm wiped," Denni admitted.

"I know you are and you really need to get a good night's sleep. Katie's pretty drugged up and I'm not sure she'll remember I'm even here." I said.

"OK, but you'll come get me if anything comes up?" Denni said, making direct eye contact with me.

"Of course I will," I said defensively.

"Promise me - I know you!" Denni said adamantly. Based on my past track record, she was less than confident.

"Promise," I said, and heard my boss's voice in my head again.

Be there - for Denni…

Dammit Bob, will you leave me alone? I thought to myself.

CHAPTER 7

Top of the First February 1-3, 2000

§

OVER THE COURSE OF THE night Katie and I experienced just what "intensive care" really meant. As was the case with each occupied room on the floor, a doctor and nurse were stationed just outside our room. Every sixty to ninety minutes the pair came in and measured Katie's vital signs, looked at her incision, and checked all of her I-V lines and medications. For the first few hours of the new day Katie was pretty out of it, but as the morning hours progressed, she seemed less and less comfortable. As dawn turned into daylight, and fresh off of at least seventy-five minutes of cumulative sleep, I was concerned about Katie's post-operative appearance.

"Is she okay?" I asked. "She actually looked better last night."

Dr. McBride, the ICU doctor, responded. "She's doing fine. Yesterday and into the early morning hours she was still under the positive effects of the anesthesia. Those have worn off now, but trust me, she's doing well."

"Hi, honey," Denni said as she came into the room. "How did she sleep?"

"Better than I did," I replied. "She was pretty out of it but they came in to check on her about every hour. She actually looked better last night. I was talking to the doc..."

"Hi, sweetie," Denni said, interrupting me. Katie had noticed her mom in the room, and through her tubes and needles made eye contact. I became a fifth wheel. Sometimes only a mom will do, and it was clear this was one of those times. Denni carefully crawled into Katie's bed, again making sure not to disrupt the I-V lines.

"Mommy," Katie said, but we could barely hear her.

Denni looked at me with an inquisitive look.

"That's the first she's said anything," I said. "It sounds like a whisper."

"Katie, honey, how are you feeling?" I asked.

"My head hurts. I want Dakota," Katie said, and I noticed Dakota had fallen on the floor under the bed. Katie's voice was barely audible. To Denni and me it sounded very much like Katie was whispering.

Just then the ICU doctor came back in the room.

"Doctor McBride, Katie's voice is hard to hear and it sounds like she's whispering," I said.

"Well, it could be temporary due to the tube that was in her throat for so long yesterday. She still has quite a bit of swelling, too. That should go down over the next forty-eight to seventy-two hours. Doctor Crone will be by later and maybe he'll have some more thoughts around that. Now we need to take Katie down to Radiology to get some new MRI scans."

At that moment Katie vomited. No one was prepared for it, and Katie looked at her Mommy and frowned. Denni was trying hard to maintain control, as she was way too close to the vomiting action. It was all she could do to not get nauseated, so she left the room for a moment to catch her breath.

"Do you feel better now, honey?" I asked. Katie just shook her head back and forth, indicating she did not. A few minutes later, Katie threw up again, and Denni and I were alarmed.

"Just like with her voice, this very well could be from all of the anesthesia and the effects from the tube in her throat," the ICU doctor offered, trying to calm our nerves. "Let's give her some Zofran and Tylenol 3 to see if that helps." Fortunately, Katie had four I-V lines, two in each arm, which allowed the nurses to give her the medicines intravenously. The vomiting stopped, and a few minutes later Katie fell asleep.

"Let's get those pictures now," the doctor said. "She's already pretty out of it so they won't have to use much anesthesia for the scan."

An attendant came to transport Katie for her MRI scan. There were a considerable number of medicines hanging from the I-V pole attached to the bed, and the bandages around her head left no doubt as to where her surgery had been. Most of the medical staff that passed us on the way to Radiology ignored us, but I noticed that the non-medical pedestrians passing by couldn't resist looking at Katie and the pole full of medicines. The ones that made eye contact with us showed concern or pity, I couldn't tell which.

At that moment, I first realized the new world we were living in. I consider myself a pretty compassionate person. Growing up, I felt sorry for people who had difficult challenges, especially medical ones. I had watched the Jerry Lewis Labor Day telethons for years, and was moved to tears countless times when I saw children suffering from terrible diseases. I felt sorry for them and their families. Now, here I was on the other end of things, wondering if people looked at us in the same light.

A few hours later, Dr. Crone sat on the edge of Katie's bed holding the new set of MRI films. Several neurosurgical residents surrounded him. Cincinnati Children's Hospital Medical Center (CCHMC) was a teaching hospital affiliated with the University of Cincinnati Medical School. Founded in 1883, it's one of the oldest Children's hospitals in the country. It was the benefactor of large donations of funds from Cincinnati philanthropists including William Procter, of Procter & Gamble fame.

In the 1950s CCHMC propelled itself into a world famous medical facility with the introduction of the polio vaccine, conceived by one of its own physicians, Dr. Albert Sabin. US News & World Report ranks pediatric hospitals annually and Cincinnati Children's routinely places in the Top 10 in the country in almost every category, and at times has ranked #1, above Dana-Farber Hospital at Harvard, the Children's Hospitals of Philadelphia & Pittsburgh, and St. Jude's, among others.

Dr. Crone was a Professor of Neurosurgery at the UC Medical School and was one of the most renowned pediatric brain surgeons in the country. With few exceptions, a group of neurosurgical residents accompanied Dr. Crone as he made his rounds. This morning the group was learning about a surgery performed yesterday on four-and-a-half-year-old Kathleen Proctor. I thought it was strange to hear the doctors talking about us in the third person while we were in the room. It was just one of the many things we would be getting used to in our new and surreal world.

"The patient presents with a posterior fossa brain stem glioma and initial lab results point to a low-grade tumor, possibly astrocytoma," Dr. Crone said, referring to Katie, who was laying in the bed right in front of him. This conversation was geared to the medical professionals and not so much to me or my wife.

"The parents suspected hearing loss and an evoked brainwave hearing test revealed complete deafness in the right ear. A subsequent CT scan revealed the mass. I performed a suboccipital craniotomy with C1 laminectomy and a subtotal surgical resection of the tumor with insertion of a Lapras shunt. We accomplished 80 to 85 percent removal at the lateral aspect of the medulla all the way up through the middle cerebellar peduncle, where the tumor was seen infiltrating the brain stem from cranial nerves seven through ten. The patient is status post-surgery in satisfactory condition."

Dr. Crone held up one of the new scans and pointed to a spot. Denni and I were still uncertain as to what we were looking at, but now Dr. Crone shifted the focus of his conversation to us and spoke in terms we could relate to.

"This white spot here is where the tumor was. It's showing as a void right now but it'll fill up with fluid. The fuzzy gray spot here is what's left of the tumor and it's going into the brain stem which is why I couldn't remove it."

Returning his focus to the residents, he added information past the comprehension of either Denni or myself.

"In the axial image here you can see where I inserted the Lapras shunt into the fourth ventricle through the aqueduct and to the third ventricle."

The residents nodded their heads and a few asked questions that were also beyond what we could understand. When it looked like they were done, I decided on a simpler question.

"Are you happy with the surgery?" I asked.

"I wish we could have removed all of it, but there was just no way we could," said Dr. Crone. "It's looking like a low-grade glioma and we got most of it. That said, I'm satisfied."

"So where do we go from here?" Denni inquired.

"In the immediate term we need her to recover," Dr. Crone said. "The brain perceives surgery as an attack on it, and considering the actual physical elements, it is."

Dr. Crone continued. "The body's an incredibly self-protective machine and it has a master plan to defend itself. All sorts of bodily functions adjust and shut down during the surgical process and in the aftermath. In the first forty-eight hours, most of our medical efforts are centered on assisting the body in a total reset. That's what we're focusing on now. As the swelling goes down then we'll concentrate on what we need to."

Denni was fixated on Katie's face.

"It seems like the right side of her face is swollen more than the left," Denni said. "I'm with Rob. I think she seemed much better last night, and it doesn't look like her right eye is closing."

"No, it's not, but she's still got a lot of swelling," Dr. Crone leaned in over Katie and touched her cheek. "Although I can't say with one hundred percent certainty, I'm pretty confident the nerves are still intact. I can't promise everything will come back, but I don't think the nerves are damaged. We'll just have to give it a while. The tumor affected things more on the right side, which we suspected from the fact that her hearing was impacted in her right ear as opposed to her left. But it's too early to come to any conclusions, and she has still a lot of healing to do."

Denni wanted to have Dr. Crone address another one of her major concerns.

"Katie, honey, can you say something to Dr. Crone?" Denni asked. Katie just looked at her mother.

"Just say something," I added.

"I don't feel good," Katie whispered. "And Dakota doesn't either," she said, referring to the stuffed animal lying by her side.

"I know you don't Katie. But you'll feel better soon," Dr. Crone assured her.

"It sounds like she's whispering," I said, pointing out the obvious to the renowned neurosurgeon.

"Yes, I know it does," he replied with a very patient tone. "She still has a lot of swelling and she's still recovering from the surgery. All in all, she's doing well. We'll help her body reset itself, which it should do over the next few days. Then, if everything continues to improve we'll move her out of ICU and begin some therapies. In the meantime, you two try and get some rest. Katie's going to need you more as she starts to feel better. I'll see you tomorrow."

Dr. Crone walked toward the door, but after a few steps, he turned around and looked at Denni.

"We're still in the top of the first inning," Dr. Crone said, gesturing at Denni's Cincinnati Reds sweatshirt. Denni was a huge Cincinnati Reds fan, and although still very concerned, the baseball analogy put a smile on her face. I was glad to see her smile. We been under constant stress for days, but finding the lighter side of things had always been a very important part of our lives. It seemed even more critical at the moment.

CHAPTER 8

All Choked Up February 3-5, 2000

AFTER THE DEBRIEF, DR. CRONE and his entourage left the room. Unsure of our new routine, Denni sat on Katie's bed and read magazines and her Bible, while I leafed through the brain tumor primer. Katie watched TV and drifted in and out of sleep. The ICU wasn't accessible to guests like the main floor, so we took turns visiting and relaying information. My mom and David and Holly came by as did Denni's mom, Darlene, and her siblings. It was a family reunion, without the fun part.

Like Denni, all of her siblings were adopted and their parents had given them names that started with the letter "D." In addition to her parents, the family consisted of her brother, David, Denebola (Denni's legal name), and her sisters Desiree, and Dana. The old joke about being too cheap to buy new monogrammed guest towels frequently came to mind whenever anybody rattled off all their names.

Denni had been close to her family, and the shock of Katie's situation rallied the family together. It's amazing how something like this can cause a few petty differences to evaporate. I was glad that Denni had this support system in place, and felt even better about the decision to come to Cincinnati where lots of things were familiar, including a large number of family and friends.

Since the surgery two days earlier, Katie hadn't shown any interest in eating. We figured with the trauma of brain surgery and all the needles and tubes sticking out of her, she just wasn't hungry. A nurse said this wasn't uncommon and that one of the I-V lines included a solution with sodium and potassium to keep her hydrated and to provide some basic nutrients.

As the morning shift nurse and resident completed their morning checkup, the nurse asked Katie if she was hungry.

"A little," she whispered.

"Well, let's try some Jell-O or peanut butter. How does that sound?" asked the nurse.

"OK," Katie said, and turned her head back to the TV, which was playing a videotape of *Winnie the Pooh*. In just a few days, both Denni and I would be able to recite most of the lines to the dozen or so episodes of *Pooh*, or another of Katie's favorites, *Madeline*, available through the video library.

Dr. Crone made his morning rounds, and we had another conversation about the facial paralysis and voice issues. He reassured us that Katie was doing as expected and that the swelling was going down at a sufficient pace. Dr. Crone deferred to the ICU pediatric medical team as far as the diet and eating went and said if she was up to it, it was OK for her to eat whatever she could tolerate.

The nurse brought a small packet of peanut butter, similar to the ones hotels provide in their complimentary breakfast areas.

"Let's just try a little bit and see how that goes," the nurse offered.

Katie was old enough to feed herself but with both hands constricted by several needles and I-V lines, Denni took the spoon and gave her a small spoonful. I couldn't help but think it looked comparable to when Katie was a baby, sitting in her pumpkin seat as Denni fed her.

Katie took the spoonful of peanut butter in her mouth and she immediately began to choke. The nurse quickly put her finger in Katie's mouth and swiped her finger to remove the peanut butter.

"I don't get it," Denni said. "It looked like she couldn't swallow."

"Yes, I know," the nurse said. "I'll be right back." In a few minutes, she returned with a glass of water and some red Jell-O.

"Let's try this and see if it would be easier," the nurse said.

"I want a cookie," Katie said. I smiled and thought, *that's my girl!*

"I don't blame you, Katie," Denni said. "We'll get you a cookie, but let's start with this."

The Jell-O ended in the same result, and a swig of water caused additional choking. The medical team decided to give Katie another day or two of giving her nutrients through the I-V lines to see if her swallowing improved on its own.

After the choking episode, Dr. Crone and the medical team examined Katie during the afternoon rounds. They looked over the nursing notes and then went in the hallway to discuss Katie and her recovery. Sometimes they'd slide the glass door shut, but at times they left it open, and we could hear most of the conversation anyway. The more we listened to Dr. Crone, the more in awe we were. Clearly the man was uber-intelligent; for God's sakes, he was a brain surgeon! Beyond that, he juggled an unbelievably wide array of complex medical questions from the residents. It wasn't just his intellectual capacity; it was the way in which he delivered the information. He veered back and forth between conversations that needed layman's terminology directly into discussions with medical peers that undoubtedly required extensive training, experience, and expertise.

Denni summed it up nicely. "Katie couldn't be in better hands."

Dr. Crone instructed the staff that in the next day or so Katie should begin moving around a bit. Nothing strenuous, although enough to get her arms and legs moving again. But for today it was another marathon session of *Winnie the Pooh* and *Madeline* videos, or coloring in one of the coloring books that Katie had received as a gift. Katie still had a number of I-V lines, and she used her left hand to pick up her crayons. I, being a left-hander, proudly pointed out the fact to Denni, who promptly rolled her eyes. The Holistic Medicine staff came by and offered their services including a full-body massage for Katie. I was skeptical and Katie wasn't interested. Denni, pregnant, and fresh off a night of trying to sleep in the hospital chair, begged for a massage. Much to her dismay it was for patients only.

More cards and gifts arrived and Denni taped up a few of the cards and pictures on the wall facing Katie's bed so she could see them. The plan wasn't to be in ICU very long, but she thought it couldn't hurt for Katie to see that some of her friends and playmates were thinking of her.

"Did you see the card from Katie's school?" Denni asked me. For the past year, Katie had been attending The Looking Glass pre-school in Kalamazoo. The brain tumor diagnosis had come as a complete shock to them, as they hadn't observed any signs that caused concern.

"Yes, and it seems like all the kids signed it. That's a nice touch," I said. "I sent a note to the director about us paying for Katie's spot until she comes back, and she said she wouldn't think of it, and that they'll hold it open for Katie for as long as we need it."

"That's sweet. I think a lot of people really just want to find ways to help in whatever ways they can," Denni said.

"I know," I said. "Judi and Michael are taking care of Rocky and the house, and folks at work are taking care of our stuff. I feel kind of guilty, but I guess it makes everyone feel better and we should probably let them. I'd like to think we'd do something if this happened to somebody we knew."

"I wouldn't wish this on anyone," said Denni.

"Yeah, me neither. Not even the Dallas Cowboys," I said, referring to my chronic NFL enemy. As a diehard Minnesota Vikings fan, I had just endured a recent Vikings playoff loss, although the events of the past few weeks had made the loss and the whole NFL season seem meaningless. On one level, I think Denni was somewhat relieved for my new perspective.

Suffice it to say up to that point in my life there had been only a few things that got me as passionate as did the Minnesota Vikings. It had been that way for years, and certainly since Denni had known me. It was so extreme my mood could swing for several days depending on whether the Vikings won or lost. And at playoff time, I was a basket case. Yet in a matter of a few weeks I had suddenly realized just how little pro football meant to me, or at least in the relative scheme of things. My daughter was facing a life-threatening illness, and the outcome of a game no longer registered on the scale of important things like it used to.

It's amazing how quickly perspective can change.

CHAPTER 9

Gag Me February 4-6, 2000

PASSING THE TIME IN A hospital setting was hard enough. Being in the ICU limited our activities even more. Our friends began to deliver care packages for Denni and me to help us occupy our time. Candy, paperback books, and assorted word games seemed to be the themes.

The first care package I opened included a John Grisham novel entitled *The Testament*. Anxious to read anything other than the brain tumor primer, I dug into the book. In the opening chapter billionaire Troy Phelan jumps out an office window and commits suicide, triggering the impending search for his now billionaire daughter, and setting the stage for the main plot of the book. The reason for his suicide? He'd just been diagnosed with a brain tumor.

I put the book down and took the opportunity to send out an update on Katie. Throughout the course of the last few days we were receiving more and more emails inquiring about the situation as word spread through the still freshly paved information superhighway known as the Internet.

To: Friends of Katie
From: Rob & Denni
Date: Friday February 4, 2000
Re: Katie Update

Considering the surgery she went through, Katie is doing very well. She is much more comfortable today and can move her hands and feet, stick out her tongue, and her eyes react to light.

She has already been weaned from the blood pressure medication, and they've been able to get her sodium levels up. Apparently, whenever you operate around the brain stem the body puts itself into a pure defense mode and does all kinds of things to protect it. Now everything needs to reset.

Katie still has some swelling and is having some issues swallowing. The volume of her voice is low, like a whisper, her right eye doesn't blink yet, and the right side of her face doesn't move. We are having a swallowing specialist work with her tomorrow, and hopefully it will help improve that function.

We'll probably be in ICU through tomorrow, depending on how the swallowing goes. Then the plan is to move Katie to the regular ward for a week or so - and then home! Thanks again for the prayers and we know you'll keep it up.

Rob, Denni & Katie

We settled in for our first weekend in Cincinnati Children's Hospital. Just like in the overnight space, weekends took on an entirely different dimension. As many patients as possible were discharged on Friday, so the floor was noticeably quieter. Fewer patients meant fewer staff and magnified the sense of isolation.

"It's Friday night, Katie. What are we gonna do?" I asked. I couldn't help but think of how Friday nights had changed since Katie was born, let alone with this development.

"Color!" said Katie. "Pooh." Still no volume in her voice. As evening wore on, I lost track of the pages and pages we'd colored. I caught myself reciting a line from Eeyore in advance of it being delivered in the video.

Eventually, Katie got groggy and drifted off the sleep. I moved on to the second care package and this time the book included was Stephen King's *The Green Mile.* Readers of that book may recall that falsely-accused death row inmate John Coffey had exceptional powers. In one poignant scene, the prison guards smuggle John out of the prison and take him to the warden's house, where he uses his supernatural skills to cure the warden's wife of her dreadful disease - a brain tumor.

"What the hell? I know everyone means well, but this is ridiculous. Does every book involve a brain tumor?" I said, as I vented to Denni. She was at her father's house and we would chat by phone at all hours since neither one of us was sleeping normally. "I think I need to take a pause from all these good intentions. Can I just have some gum and a non-brain tumor book, for Christ's sake?"

"Speaking of Christ," Denni said. "I could bring you Dad's Bible. It'll be more enlightening than *The Green Mile*, I promise you."

"I'm sure it would," I replied, although I didn't specifically acknowledge the offer.

Denni let it go. At least for now.

The weekend overnight ICU nurse and doctor team were on duty and came in to introduce themselves and to give me the briefing about checking Katie's vital signs. I half-listened and then pulled my chair into the corner and used the tiny night light as a reading lamp. It was strange; I was exhausted, but I couldn't go to sleep. Sometime after 3:00 A.M. and in between the intrusions for the check-ups, I finally drifted off to sleep.

In the few times that Katie had tried to eat over the past few days, something wasn't functioning correctly, making it difficult to swallow. Katie underwent a series of examinations related to her throat and voice.

"So what do you think about how Katie's doing?" the ear, nose & throat doctor asked, looking at us. Denni and I were impressed at how often the doctors and staff had involved us in conversations about our daughter.

I responded first. "I think she's making a pretty good recovery, but she's still not able to talk in more than a whisper. We tried to give her some peanut butter and Jell-O a few times, and she choked a lot. Sometimes it seems like she chokes on her own saliva. Her right eye doesn't seem to blink at all even though quite a bit of the swelling has gone down. You can tell her right arm and leg aren't quite in sync with her left side, and although *one* of us doesn't consider it to be a handicap, she's using her left hand to color with. Before, she used her right hand for almost everything. And half her face is paralyzed. Aside from that, she's fine," I joked.

"Seriously, all of these concern us," Denni added quickly.

"All of these concern us too," the doctor said. "As you know, one of the issues with brain tumors and surgery is that it's possible to damage the cranial nerves."

"Doctor Crone said he's pretty sure the nerves are still intact," I said as if my two-week exposure to the world of brain tumors gave me credibility on the matter.

"Well, we won't know for sure for a little while. They could just be stretched and not reacting properly now," he said. "We're still pretty close to surgery, but every day that goes by without improvement is a concern. So we need to see what's going on in there."

"Hold still, honey," the doctor said as Katie sat on my lap. "I'm going to slide this in your mouth and it'll feel strange for just a second but then you won't feel a thing."

I knew what was coming. The doctor had a scope to look at the damage to Katie's throat and vocal cords. He slid the tubed scope into her mouth, and in an instant, he pushed it past her gag reflex and down into her throat. I was doing my best to remain calm but the thought of what I was watching almost made me gag.

The doctor completed the scope inspection without saying a word, and then ordered a video X-ray. This required Katie to drink a small glass of liquid barium which tasted just as yummy as it sounds. With her choking, getting it down proved to be a challenge but Katie managed. During the X-ray, she was instructed to swallow, talk, and stick her tongue out, which she gladly did as she pointed her face towards the ENT doctor. The results revealed that the muscles on the right side of Katie's throat were completely paralyzed, including her vocal cords. This explained the whisper-like voice and the occasional bouts of choking. Katie's saliva and food were pooling in the back of her throat.

The doctor picked up Katie and set her on the examination table, careful not to pull on her remaining I-V lines. Katie held Dakota firmly in her grasp. The doctor looked at me as he spoke.

"We're going to need to put in a feeding tube," he said. "I'm not sure how long it'll be in, and I hope not too long. I think it's best if we avoid her swallowing food until we get a better handle on things." He returned his focus to Katie, who was now giving Dakota a similar examination.

"I know it's kind of hard for you to swallow, isn't it?" the doctor asked.

Katie nodded.

"Do you know where food goes when you swallow it?" the doctor asked, and Katie pointed to her belly.

"That's right. See this little tube?" the doctor said as he showed it to Katie. "I know this may sound a little weird, but to get to your stomach we're going to put the tube through your nose." Katie looked less than thrilled.

"It's going to feel kind of funny, but I promise it won't hurt, OK? We'll spray some medicine into your nose so you won't feel much, but if it starts to hurt at all you raise and hand and I'll stop, OK?" Katie nodded. *Man, this guy is good*, I thought.

In a matter of seconds, the doctor had run the tube up through Katie's nose, down her esophagus, and stopped when he felt it had landed in the right place in her stomach. As he finished he said, "Bingo," and poked Katie in the belly. She giggled.

I was amazed at not only how well the doctor was handling the matter, but also at how Katie seemed to take it in stride. She was quickly becoming my hero as the bravest little girl I'd ever seen.

After the ENT exam, Katie was visited by a cardiologist who listened to her heart. While I was initially confused, the exam made sense when I found out Katie's heart had stopped during surgery. That was followed by a visit from the orthopedist. After helping her out of bed the doctor asked her to try and take a few steps. Katie could walk but needed quite a bit of assistance. He asked Katie to move her arms and legs, and when she did it was clear that her right arm and leg was not in sync with the left side of her body. I felt a rush of sadness come over me.

That afternoon, Dr. Crone came by with his resident entourage, and as we sat on one side of Katie's bed with the residents lined up on the other, Dr. Crone performed his examination and Denni and I peppered him with questions.

"What do you think is going on with her eye? It doesn't seem to blink at all. How much longer until all of the swelling is gone?" Denni asked.

My turn.

"Do you think her voice is any better? It doesn't sound any louder to us."

Dr. Crone did his best to answer the questions, but freely admitted he didn't have a Magic 8-ball to forecast how some of the residual effects would play out for Katie. He reiterated several times that he didn't think the cranial nerves were destroyed and reminded everyone that Katie was still pretty close to the surgery.

"Don't panic," he said. "I know you want all of these things to go back to normal, and I do too. We'll just have to wait and see. But I do have a couple pieces of good news for you."

"I'm all ears," I said.

"First, I'm comfortable for Katie to leave ICU and head down to the main floor. That's a sign of a good recovery." It was a positive development, but ICU offered a one-on-one relationship with a dedicated nurse and doctor, and as intrusive as it was, both of us were a little concerned about losing that level of care.

Dr. Crone turned to Katie. "Katie, do you want to move to another room? You're getting better and we have a nice room waiting for you on the floor right below us."

"Can I bring Dakota?" Katie asked.

"Of course you can. We wouldn't forget Dakota. You two have been through a lot, huh?"

Katie nodded. Her immediate concern was alleviated. Her furry friend Dakota was now a constant companion. The blood stain was still visible, and for some reason, it was the feature I noticed the most. Katie was oblivious to it.

"Cool," I said. "You said there was more good news?"

"All of the tests have confirmed the low-grade glioma. We don't feel chemotherapy or radiation will be necessary. We'll just do MRI scans every six months or so to begin with, and see how it goes. How does that sound?"

"Can I hug you again?" Denni asked.

"Dang, you are a hugger, aren't you?" Dr. Crone said with a smile as they embraced.

"Tell me about it." I said. "*I* have to live with her." Sensing Denni's glare, I quickly tried to recover. "I mean I *get* to live with her." Too late.

CHAPTER 10

Momma Bear
February 6-8, 2000

§

WITH THE FEEDING TUBE IN place, it was time to get some additional nutrition into Katie's body. A pediatrician and dietician were in charge of monitoring her food. Actually, it wasn't food per se, but a bag of gray, liquid mush that hung from her I-V stand. From the very first feeding, Denni wasn't comfortable with the large amount of food being given to Katie. And from the start, Katie gave back a good portion of the mush, as it made her sick to her stomach.

Denni mentioned her concerns to the pediatrician and dietician as they conducted their daily assessments. Since her pre-school days it was clear she was much smaller than other kids her age. She registered in the bottom 5% in terms of height and weight, and as such, ate very little. Denni didn't hide her feelings about the feeding situation from either the pediatrician or the dietician.

"I can tell you, Katie eats like a bird. A baby bird – she always has. You can see she's throwing up a lot of the food that's being put into her through that feeding tube," Denni complained.

"Well," said the dietician with a tinge of condescension. "I'm comfortable with what I've prescribed. Let's just stick to the game plan. She'll get used to it."

The dietician had a chart she used to calculate how much liquid food Katie was supposed to take in, and while it may have made sense on paper, in Denni's mind it was too much for Katie. After each feeding through the tube, Katie would continue to give back a portion of what she was fed. Denni made several more comments to the dietician over the next few feeding sessions, but the dietician continued to assure everyone that she knew how much Katie should be getting, and that she wasn't going to change the amount. This was one of the first speed bumps we had run into in terms of care, and one of Denni's first lessons in being a patient advocate for our daughter.

"Can I speak with you?" Denni asked the pediatrician as they prepared another feeding. "Everyone can see Katie throws up almost every time she's fed through the tube. That can't be normal, but I can't seem to convince you that this is way too much for her." The pediatrician said that she appreciated the input, but that she supported the dietician so they were going to stick with the plan for the time being.

After another feeding with no changes in the process or the outcome, Denni hit her breaking point.

"Enough already! I'm her mother. I know how little she eats. You have this formula you're using and I can tell you that it's wrong!"

The dietician was about to square off with Denni, but the pediatrician relented. And what do you know? Katie stopped regurgitating food back the way it came in. Sometimes moms do know best. Stepping into the role of advocate is something all parents have to do, and it was just part of the hospital routine which made up our life at the moment.

There were a lot of things that were starting to become routine. At precisely five o'clock in the morning, the overnight nurse conducted the last of the vital sign checks for blood pressure, temperature, heart rate, oxygen levels, and I-V solutions. Then the morning doctors came for their rounds, and usually next it was Dr. Crone, then the therapists. Outside of Dr. Crone's chaotic schedule, it was like clockwork.

Katie would get daily visits from Dr. Crone and the neurosurgical residents who accompanied him. As the days passed, we noticed he was less precise as to the timing. Often his visits depended on what was going on with each patient at the moment. Sometimes we'd see him as early as 7:00 or 8:00 A.M., and other times not until after lunch, or even after dinner on occasion. I stopped trying to figure out if he was on a schedule, as it seemed like he'd pop in during any one of the twenty-four hours that made up the day, seven days a week. His work schedule seemed relentless.

Every so often, Katie would be weaned off another medication and another I-V line would be removed. Nearly a week out from surgery, Katie started a number of therapies. She had swallowing therapy for her paralyzed throat, occupational therapy for her fine motor skills and facial expressions, and physical therapy for her arms and legs. She took some assisted steps, and Dr. Crone was right. It was amazing how a week in bed could impact Katie's ability to walk. After a few tries, the therapist picked her up and set her back on the bed.

"A few steps at a time, that's all we need," the therapist told Denni. "We just need to get her body upright for a little bit each day, and even a few steps at a time will make a world of difference."

Denni and I continued to push the doctors for answers, and the medical staff, including Dr. Crone, were all very patient with our inquiries. Their responses all focused on a single theme.

"Let's wait and see."

CHAPTER 11

Hotel California February 7, 2000

NOW THAT KATIE WAS OUT of the Intensive Care Unit and on the main floor, friends and family came to visit and help us pass the time watching videos, coloring, and playing board games. It's amazing what adults will do to cheer up sick children, I thought to myself as I looked at my father-in-law David. He was a recently retired telephone company executive, and I was used to seeing him in custom-tailored pin-stripe suits with crisp white shirts, power ties, and immaculately shined shoes. At the moment, he was sitting on Katie's bed wearing gaudy plastic purple earrings clamped to his ears, had several shiny gold necklaces around his neck, and a plastic gold crown on his head: the most recent victim of Katie's domination in the game Pretty, Pretty, Princess. And in Go Fish, Katie showed no mercy.

In the afternoons, Katie's energy would start to wane and her pain would increase. She was on regular intervals for her medications and was connected to a machine that buzzed and beeped every so often to let the nurses know it was time for a new syringe of this or a dose of that. Evenings tended to lag, and by the end of most days Katie, Denni, and I were all exhausted. The doctors normally completed their rounds by seven o'clock, and after that the residents and nurses were the most visible medical staff on the floor.

As visiting hours ended, either Denni or I would head back to her Dad's house, and the other would settle in for the night in the incredibly uncomfortable chair-bed contraption in Katie's room. On most evenings, we spent time debriefing on the events of the day or just catching up. The topics of discussion were pretty narrow in focus and almost exclusively related to hospitals, medical procedures, and Katie. Sometimes we would force a conversation about something as mundane as work in an attempt to clear our minds of all of the medical issues of the day.

"I can't help but wonder why, with the thousands of dollars we're being charged each day for Katie to stay in this hospital, they couldn't have come up with a few bucks for some more comfortable furniture," I complained, as I stood and stretched after a long bout of sitting.

"How do you think I feel, I'm pregnant!" Denni responded, without much sympathy for my position.

"I think the hospitals get their furniture from the same place that McDonald's does. You know – the kind that's comfortable for about half an hour and then it's time to get up and leave! Only this is like the Hotel California – you can check out but you can never leave," I said, referring to the classic Eagles song.

Later that evening, it was time for another update.

"What should I put in the Katie Update?" I asked.

"I don't know," Denni said. "She's had a couple of pretty good days. She's out of ICU, and Dr. Crone mentioned that if things go well the rest of the week, we might be able to head back to Michigan soon. You could tell everyone that."

"Have you talked to Larry or anybody at work?" I asked Denni.

"Yes, he said everything is fine and not to worry - they have it under control." Denni thoroughly enjoyed her work and especially her new boss, Larry Wisner.

"Larry's sending me scripture passages and they're helping a lot," Denni said. I could tell she wanted to start a conversation, but at the moment I wasn't biting. While I was glad Denni found comfort in her faith, at the moment I just wasn't sure I was up for an extended conversation on the subject. As much as I knew I shouldn't feel that way, it was how I felt. I'd been struggling with my own faith for a while, and my head was so full of emotions I wasn't sure what to think.

"Good for you," I said, hoping it didn't sound too snarky. I fired up my laptop to begin the task of writing the latest Katie Update.

To: Friends of Katie
From: Rob & Denni
Date: Monday, February 7, 2000
Re: Katie Update
Katie is out of ICU and back with the rest of the hospital population! I am even happier to report that overall she is doing wonderfully! The lab tests have confirmed a low-grade brain stem glioma, which is good as far as the prognosis is concerned. The doctors don't feel radiation and chemotherapy is necessary, and instead, Katie will have several MRI scans a year to see if anything is happening.

Katie looks better each day. The swelling continues to go down and she had more of her I-V lines removed, so now she has her right hand free to color (and to hold Mommy's hand).

As thrilled as we are that she's doing better, she still has a lot of issues to deal with. She had an X-Ray video made of her swallowing (ever try to get a four-year-old to swallow liquid barium?). It revealed that the right side of her throat shows complete paralysis, along with her right side vocal cords. We're just going to have to wait and see how it goes over the coming weeks. They said this is not terribly uncommon, especially when the surgery involves a brain stem tumor. Since she can't swallow properly, they've placed in a feeding tube for now.

The right side of her face still doesn't function, and her right eye doesn't blink, but Dr. Crone doesn't think the nerves were damaged, and we continue to hope for improvement. She's moving around a bit, although walking is still pretty difficult.

Dr. Crone says if her recovery continues this week, we *might* be able to head back home to Michigan by the weekend, so hopefully, that will be the case.

Thanks again for everything you have done to support us. It means more to us than you will ever know!
Rob, Denni & Katie

CHAPTER 12

Ignorance is Bliss February 8-10, 2000

§

As evening approached the midnight hour, the overnight shift came on and the lights were dimmed. It was much quieter at night and the silence was broken only by the occasional blips and beeps of the machines in the kids' rooms. At first, when the machines beeped, we were a little anxious until the staff came in and took care of whatever needed attending to, such as a medication change. But after several days of the routine, we'd learned that most of the alarms meant basically nothing medically to the patient.

Oftentimes, the nurse would come in, hit the beeping buzzer, and walk back out. One night I decided to beat the nurse to the punch and I hit the button to turn off the alarm. Even though it appeared as the simple act of turning off the alarm, the nurse made it clear to me, in no uncertain terms, only they were to hit the buttons on the machines. *Note to self: don't upset the nurses!*

Now a full week out from surgery, Katie was well enough to be wheeled down to the children's common area where she could visit and play with the other patients. Sitting at the table next to hairless kids with needles sticking out of them, playing like nothing was wrong, was just another part of the surreal life we were living. Every now and then, as hard as they tried to be normal, one of the kids would get sick or have to go back to their room. A few were accompanied by a large number of I-V bags hanging from poles they pushed around with them. Some of the bags were sealed in larger plastic bags with yellow tape and warning symbols. These were the incredibly strong chemotherapy drugs whose aim was to selectively kill the cancer cells in the child without killing the child taking them.

By mid-week Katie had all but one of her I-V lines removed and she seemed to be improving steadily. The remaining line was for medications and blood draws. In addition, she still had the feeding tube inserted. None of the therapies were making much of an impact on the paralysis, but she looked and felt better each day. Dr. Crone said we'd take the next few days one at a time and if all went well, our family would be back in Michigan by the end of the weekend. We were all optimistic and feeling good about the direction Katie's recovery was taking.

The Katie Updates generated quite a bit of activity. Many of our coworkers and a number of family members were interested and concerned. What started as a handful of daily responses had grown to dozens. Katie was included on a number of prayer lists at churches around the country and people were sending positive thoughts, prayers, advice and work gossip. And as things continued to improve, sending the Katie Update was a more pleasant chore.

To: Friends of Katie
From: Rob & Denni Proctor
Date: Wednesday, February 9, 2000
Re: Katie Update

More good news with Katie! We got all but one of the I-V's removed so Katie's hands are free to color, paint, and the like. She's getting stronger each day and we're working with physical and occupational therapists to get her neck and shoulder muscles strengthened again. She can walk a few steps with some help, and they tell us this will continue to get better each day.

Katie is much less uncomfortable than just a few days ago. If all goes well, we might be discharged from the hospital and headed back in Michigan by the end of the weekend.

As you can imagine, Katie is not too thrilled with the events of the past week. But all things considered, she is doing very well. She's the bravest little girl we have ever seen. Hopefully, one of the next updates will be from Michigan!

We really appreciate your thoughts and prayers for Katie.

Rob, Denni & Katie

"Yep, from here on out it's going to be smooth sailing," I said, as I finished typing the most recent update.

There's a reason for the saying "ignorance is bliss." It's true.

CHAPTER 13

Spinal Tap - Not the Movie February 11, 2000

"SOMETHING'S WRONG, ISN'T IT?" DENNI asked Dr. Crone when he came in for Katie's morning examination.

"She looks worse than yesterday and she's lethargic. Dang it!" Denni said in a frustrated tone. "She was doing so well. We just want to get out of here and go home."

"I know you do," Dr. Crone said. "But we've got to make sure she's ready." Dr. Crone completed his usual examination of Katie, but something seemed different about the process.

"How do you feel, Katie?" he asked, and her response was simple.

"Yucky."

"Well, let's see what we can do about that," Dr. Crone said. He finished the exam and exited the room, sliding the door shut behind him. The debrief session in the hallway between Dr. Crone and the residents was longer and quieter than usual. There was a considerable amount of interaction, and occasionally one or more of the doctors would look at Katie through the glass. Dr. Crone came back in and gave instructions to the nurse.

"I want a full blood panel and let's get Doctor Carpenter in here to do a spinal tap." Then he looked at his beeping pager. "I'll be back in a little while and we can visit."

Denni and I looked at each other, confused. Dr. Crone had occasionally dropped in after he'd made his morning rounds, but the fact that he planned to come back was out of the norm. Within the hour, the lab results from the spinal tap confirmed his suspicion. Katie had meningitis.

"She was doing so well. How could this happen?" I asked, stunned by the news.

"It's a post-surgical complication," Dr. Crone said. "It's pretty rare, but it happens. We're fortunate to have caught it early and we're putting her on antibiotics. We'll use Cefotaxime and Dexamethasone to begin with. I've already put in the orders so they should be here soon. These are some aggressive antibiotics, but it's what's needed. I'll be back in a while to look in on her. We're going to keep a close eye on her, I promise."

Dr. Crone always possessed a calmness and confidence that reassured us. Those traits were some of the things we admired most about him. But we could also tell that his concerns were heightened. After Dr. Crone and his accompanying band of neurosurgical residents left, I entered the diagnosis on my laptop. I read the search engine result, which happened to be from a pretty reliable source: The Mayo Clinic.

> *Staphylococcal meningitis is a potentially deadly inflammation of the fluid that surrounds the brain and spinal cord. The possible complications of staphylococcal meningitis are severe, and include:*
>
> *Brain infections with residual damage*
>
> *Shock, which can damage organs and be life-threatening.*
>
> *The disease is fatal in 15 percent of cases. Those with the highest risk of death are young children and adults over the age of 50. Patients with suppressed immune systems are at particular risk of death. Most often, staph meningitis will occur after surgery or develop from an infection in a different part of the body that has been carried to the brain by the bloodstream.*
>
> *Symptoms of staphylococcal meningitis should be taken very seriously. It is vital to begin treatment as early as possible in the disease course; delay may contribute significantly to morbidity and mortality.*

"Can you imagine what would have happened if we'd have headed back to Michigan like we planned?" Denni asked. I shuddered to think about the consequences.

"Katie would probably have been dead by the time anyone would have figured out what was wrong," I said, and the thought almost made me sick to my stomach.

"A lot of our friends thought we'd be heading home. We probably need to let them know we're not. What should we say?" Denni asked.

"There's not much to say," I said. "It is what it is."

To: Friends of Katie
From: Rob & Denni Proctor
Date: Friday, February 11, 2000
Re: Katie Update

We wish we had a better update for you, but Katie has developed a serious infection – meningitis - so we won't be getting out like we planned. More tests, more needles, you can fill in the rest.

If everyone can say an extra prayer for Katie we would appreciate it.

Rob & Denni

CHAPTER 14

Class Act February 11, 2000

WITH THE MENINGITIS DIAGNOSIS CONFIRMED, Katie was hooked up to a larger amount of monitoring equipment that looked to us like it came right off the space shuttle. Katie felt horrible all afternoon and wasn't up for visits. Even *Winnie the Pooh* and *Madeline* videotapes did nothing to lift her spirits. Katie had a high fever, felt lethargic, and couldn't find a way to get comfortable. The lights hurt her eyes, so we kept them dimmed, and Denni and I took turns placing a cool washcloth over her eyes and forehead.

It was another Saturday at Children's, and we were now better accustomed to the difference between the weekday and weekend versions of the hospital. Katie was slow to wake in the morning and obviously was not feeling well. For most of the morning, she drifted in and out of an uncomfortable sleep. Denni had arrived from David and Holly's, and was answering emails while I read. There was a knock on the glass door and when I slid open the door, I couldn't help but smile.

"Hey Proc!" It was my best friend Brian Clark, and he wasn't alone.

"Dudes, what's up?" I said.

Brian, Todd Truesdale, Rod Apfelbeck, and Brad Keenan stood in the hallway. They were all classmates of mine from my Lima Shawnee High School class of 1981.

"Dang, Proc, you look like shit!" one of them said.

"Yeah, well I haven't showered in three days and have been holed up in this hospital," I retorted. "What's your excuse?"

"Did you get the Teddy Bear we sent from the Shawnee online group?" Brad asked.

"Yeah," I said. "It was butt-ugly and Katie hated it, so I sold it to the kid in the next room for ten bucks. But thanks anyway."

Denni just rolled her eyes and sighed. She'd been initiated into my high school class through her association with me. She accompanied me to Todd's wedding when we first were dating, and, in addition to Brian, she'd become friends with a number of my classmates.

Lots of high school classes think they're unique for one reason or another, but I believe mine truly was. I think what was most special was that the various demographic groups seemed to get along better than most classes. The jocks, the stoners, the band geeks, the losers, the brainiacs, rich or poor, white or black, it didn't matter, we co-existed as one happy class. There were a few fights and squabbles as one might expect of growing kids, but at the end of the day, it was a united class of '81. Through the years I've kept in in touch with as many of my high school buddies as I have my college friends.

Denni got me to think a little deeper about my philosophy on the matter, and I stumbled upon a conclusion I hadn't thought of before. For years, I had looked at my high school class through the lens of nostalgia, like we were all meant to be together in some big cosmic scheme. Filtering in reality, I decided there was a more practical reason.

We were all stuck in Lima together. Throughout the 1970s, the economy of the industrial Midwest, and especially Ohio, stumbled. Most folks were happy to have a job. There wasn't abundant opportunity to go anywhere else, and so everyone had stayed put in Lima. It's just that as kids, my friends and I didn't know any better. Our stability was fueled as the result of being in the same place at the same time – the newly tarnishing Rust Belt. And while Lima might not be a destination location, to me and my classmates, it was home and a great place to grow up.

My buddies had come to take me to lunch and get me out of the hospital, even if only for a little while. For the past week and a half Denni and I had rotated sleeping in the hospital room with Katie, but since Denni was pregnant, I had taken a few of her turns so she could go to her dad's house to get a good night's sleep in a real bed. That meant a number of days had passed since I had seen much of the outside world. Between the sleeping arrangements and the daily grind of the hospital routine, I was ready for a break.

Getting out of the hospital into the fresh air was liberating. Our group headed to a nearby restaurant in Clifton, the portion of Cincinnati that encompasses the University of Cincinnati and the hospital complexes. We talked about our families, classmates, and the good old days, like we always did. They asked how Katie was doing, but they'd seen the updates and they could see how she looked when they came to the hospital. It was a nice change to talk about something else.

While I was glad to see them and excited about the break, in just a few hours I was surprised at how ready I was to return to the hospital. My friends said their goodbyes and I found Katie asleep and Denni reading when I got back to the room. I was glad to be back. Back to what was, for now, home.

"Well, how's the gang?" Denni asked.

"Same as always," I said. "Pains in my ass."

"Yeah, right," Denni said. "If I didn't know better I'd think you guys would rather be married to each other."

"Could we do that?" I asked, meeting another eye roll.

Katie drifted in and out of sleep all afternoon and early into the evening. Denni and I walked through the tunnel between Children's and University Hospitals for a quick bite. After my high school reunion lunch, I wasn't very hungry but still enjoyed the walk, as it gave us a chance to catch up.

"Did anybody come by today while I was gone?" I asked.

"Mom and Don came by and we had a really nice visit. I'm so glad she's close and can come by. But Katie was pretty out of it, so they didn't stay long. Jill Clark called to see if they could bring us anything. She mentioned that Valentine's Day was coming and wanted to know if we could get out for dinner or something."

"Oh crap, Valentine's Day is coming up, isn't it?" I said in that insensitive male tone.

"Yes, it is, but I suppose you have an excuse for not doing much *this* year," Denni said with the necessary amount of sarcasm.

If I were to give myself an honest grade for my efforts towards gift-giving, I could go no higher than a C. Maybe a C+. The first Christmas after we were married, Denni acknowledged that since we had paid for our own wedding and didn't have much money, we should take it easy on gifts. Denni told me she wanted some cute Christmas socks and a few other little gifts, so I got her a pair of red socks and a pair of green socks. "Christmas socks, right?" I said, confused why she looked less than enthused about my creativity. That level of mediocrity played out several times over the years, although I had managed to score a few hits.

When Denni obtained her teaching position, I special-ordered pencils with the name "Denebola" on them. Over the years, Denni had given up looking for any personalized gifts with her name on them, as there aren't a lot of people with that name. OK, as far as we know, there are *no* other persons named Denebola. It comes from the ship her father was on in the Navy – the USS *Denebola*, and is a star in the constellation Leo. For such a seemingly insignificant item as pencils, Denni was thrilled, as growing up she'd never had the opportunity to have her name on anything.

Denni had told me many times, *it's the little things*. It is amazing how often that has proven true.

CHAPTER 15

"I've Got This"
February 12, 2000

AFTER DINNER, WE STROLLED BACK through the tunnels under the hospital to the fifth floor, prepared to settle in for an uneventful evening. Later, as the two of us sat in the room and made small talk, one of Katie's machines started to beep. By this time, we were both fairly used to the alarms going off and weren't immediately concerned.

What's that?" Denni asked Jenny, the on-duty nurse who happened to be one of Katie's favorites. Jenny had come into the room in response to the alarm.

"That's Katie's Pulse-Ox monitor and it measures the oxygen levels in her blood," said Jenny. "The level is supposed to be 100 percent or close to it. Katie's is approaching the low 90s."

"Is that bad?" I asked, hoping the answer was no.

"Well, it should be higher, and it's falling," said Jenny. Her pace and her tone caused us both to be more concerned. She took the oxygen cannula and put it up to Katie's nose and said in a calm but clear voice. "OK, Katie honey, I need you to take some deep breaths for me. Can you do that?"

Katie looked exhausted, but she tried to take several breaths. The machine was now registering 91… 90…. 89...

Jenny turned up the amount of oxygen flowing and waited to see if anything positive was going to happen. Seeing no upward movement in the numbers, she pushed one of the buttons on the panel over the bed and a speaker that sounded like a McDonald's drive-thru blared, "Room 540 - what's the issue?"

"We need Doctor Nesmith, now," said Jenny, in a voice that demonstrated more than a casual level of concern. By the time Dr. Nesmith arrived Jenny had replaced the cannula with a full oxygen mask, and she held it tightly over Katie's face. Katie's pulse-ox rate had dropped several more points. Denni and I looked at each other and felt helpless, not sure of what to do. And we were certainly not prepared for what was about to happen.

As her oxygen readings continued to lower, Katie looked even worse. When the pulse-ox level reached the mid-80s, Katie began to lose the pink hue in her skin and she looked beyond exhausted. Jenny and the doctor encouraged Katie to take deep breaths into the oxygen mask, but the pulse-ox rate still fell. 82... 81... 80...

"Come on Katie, breathe!" Denni said, failing to hide her now intense sense of panic. The doctor and Jenny, along with me and Denni, were all passionately encouraging Katie to take deep breaths. She tried, but she couldn't take in enough oxygen, and I saw in her eyes a look that told me she was sad that she was disappointing everyone.

I lost track of time as the downward spiral continued. 79... 78... 77. Katie's skin took on a grayish tint and I can honestly say I'd never seen another human being look so sick. And it wasn't just another human being. It was my daughter.

Denni was holding one of Katie's hands, and from across the bed I was holding the other. I looked over at Jenny, who was pressing the oxygen mask firmly on Katie's face, and my heart immediately sank. I could see that Jenny had tears streaming down her cheeks. *Oh, my God,* I thought. *She knows what's happening - Katie's dying!* I reflected back to that earlier moment on the morning of Katie's surgery. She had crawled into her mom's lap and the two of them held each other and wept, and I thought things couldn't get any darker. The anguish I felt at the current moment was so far beyond that. It was worse than anything I could have imagined in my worst nightmare.

It was at that instant I went to the most horrible place in my mind.

This is what it's like to watch your child die. This can't be real, I thought.

My head was spinning, and I could see and hear all sorts of thoughts and images. I saw Katie as a smiling toddler playing in her room, and with Denni at our house in Allegan, and at Lake Michigan. Those places felt like they were a million miles away at the moment.

I felt like I had a ton of weights pressing on my chest, and I wasn't sure if I was even breathing. Almost out of instinct I pleaded to God to save my precious daughter's life. I had made pleas to God before in my life, including several instances that at the time I considered to be "life or death" situations. But none of them involved death as a real possibility and to me, this truly felt like the intersection of life and death.

At the very darkest moment of my life when I found myself in the pit of the hell that I was experiencing, I felt the most incredible sensation I'd ever known. It was a soothing sensation like that of a warm blanket being placed around me. With all the chaos going on around me in the hospital room, including everyone shouting for Katie to breathe and the medical equipment beeping and buzzing, suddenly a sense of calmness came over me. In my head, it became totally silent, and the only thing I could hear were three words, as plain as day: "I've got this." I knew immediately it wasn't any doctor's voice I was hearing.

Katie's oxygen level bottomed out in the 70s, and over the course of the night, it eventually made its way out of the danger zone and back into the high 90s. Denni and I didn't sleep a wink and collectively we didn't take our eyes off the pulse-ox machine for more than a few seconds.

One thing became clear to me that night. In this journey, Katie was in God's hands and no one else's. I'd suspected it and had made some superficial comments to that effect, but it had never registered as real in my heart. For the first time in my life, I had truly felt the presence of God. Now what?

The next morning, I tried to decipher the events of the previous night. I had never felt such intense inner calmness, and certainly didn't expect it at such an incredibly dark, emotional moment. I was positive that I'd felt the presence of God right there in Katie's room. God had comforted me and saved Katie. He had this all right - and the *he* wasn't Dr. Crone or any of the other medical staff. The *He* was with a capital *H.*

One thing I knew was for certain - what I had felt was very real. But I wasn't sure how or what to share with anyone, including my wife. After all, for years I had measured Denni's faith as much stronger than my own. As I assessed my recent experience, I was amazed, inspired, comforted, confused, and embarrassed all at the same time. I wasn't even sure if anyone would take me seriously if I said anything. So I decided not to. At least not until I could sort things out.

CHAPTER 16

Penny for Your Thoughts February 13, 2000

§

THROUGHOUT THE EARLY MORNING ON Sunday, Katie was very uncomfortable. We all did what we could to keep her spirits up, but it was obvious this was going to be a rough day.

"Katie, honey, do you want to play *Pretty, Pretty Princess*?" Denni asked. When Katie's pain had been kept in check and she was feeling her best, that game was at the top of her list.

"No," she said and stared ahead with a blank look on her face.

"Would you like a massage?" I asked.

"No," Katie said in her whisper voice. Even attempts to include Dakota in the effort to lift her spirits failed.

It was just going to take some time, the doctors said. Meningitis was a very serious condition, but they'd caught it early and her body was on some powerful medications. In addition to the Cefotaxime and Dexamethasone, the doctors added Roxicette and Rifampin to the regimen.

As the medications ramped up, a new machine arrived to handle dispensing them. The Omnimax 3000 could dispense up to eight medications at once, delivering its contents with utmost precision in a chorus of bells and beeps. Regardless of the wonders of the new medication dispenser, in very short order it became clear that Katie was allergic to Roxicette. Within a few minutes of the drug being administered, Katie unleashed a torrent of vomiting. The nurse quickly turned off the medication and inserted a line of Zofran anti-nausea medication which alleviated the issue. Katie's oxygen levels dipped and she needed to be put on oxygen several times throughout the day.

The following morning Katie was fast asleep. Denni and I were reading when the nurse came in to check Katie's medical lines and the I-V machine. We were barely aware of the nurse's presence until she went to change Katie's pillow.

"Ewww," the nurse said as she lifted Katie's head.

At the same time Katie groaned. The nurse held her hand facing us so we could see for ourselves the slimy yellowish fluid on her hand. At first we thought Katie had vomited but we quickly realized it was much worse. The fluid had leaked out of Katie's head.

"What's that?" I asked, very much surprised by what I saw.

The nurse didn't respond and immediately hit the button on the bed. The McDonald's drive-thru speaker blared, "Room 540, what's the issue?"

"Page Dr. Crone and Dr. Ling - stat," she said.

I had seen enough medical shows on TV to know "stat" meant "NOW!" and my wife and I were in that place between panic and further panic.

Dr. Crone and Dr. Ling arrived quickly and examined their lethargic patient.

"Katie's leaking out of her surgical site, which is now showing outward signs of the infection," Dr. Crone opined. "It's definitely not a good development, but trust me, we know what to do."

We could tell he was concerned, but he again projected a confidence that comforted us.

"We need to put in a lumbar drain," said Dr. Crone as he discussed the situation with Dr. Ling. "And we need to do it now."

"What's a lumbar drain?" asked Denni. The last two weeks had provided us a lifetime supply of knowledge of medical procedures and terminology.

"It's basically a drainage tube," Dr. Crone answered. "We'll insert it in her lumbar spine and it'll help regulate her spinal fluid. I'm hoping it'll only be in for a couple of days and by then her body will figure out how to handle things. I'm really not thrilled about sedating her, and this surgery will take a couple of hours, but we really don't have a choice. We need your permission to operate, and you already know all the risks."

"Like you said, I don't think we have much of a choice," said Denni, as she looked at me. "Go ahead." I nodded in agreement.

"OK, I'll see you in a few hours," he said as he and Dr. Ling left to prepare for the surgery.

I fired up my laptop, anxious to know more about the lumbar drain. The first search engine response took me to the Johns Hopkins website.

> *A lumbar drain is a small flexible tube that is placed in the lumbar spine. The tube drains cerebrospinal fluid that fills the ventricles of the brain and surrounds the brain and spinal cord. In people with normal pressure hydrocephalus, assisted drainage of cerebrospinal fluid for a few days can also be helpful in determining if they will benefit from a shunt.*

Katie already has a shunt, I thought to myself. Reading on, I found this little nugget:

> *There is a 3-4% risk of infection with this procedure despite all safety measures. The infection, meningitis, is very serious and antibiotics need to be given intravenously for 14-21 days or more.*
>
> *There is approximately 1 death per 1,000 procedures associated with lumbar drainage.*

Well, isn't that comforting, I thought.

Denni and I sat alone in the waiting room while Dr. Crone reopened a portion of Katie's incision to drain the infection. He then installed the lumbar device in Katie's lower spine to regulate her spinal fluid. During the two-and-a-half-hour procedure, I hadn't said anything voluntarily, and in that time, most of Denni's questions were met with one word responses.

"Penny for your thoughts," said Denni. She knew me well and was always much more aware of my feelings than I was of hers. In the years since we were married, I know she'd hoped that my senses in this regard would improve. Denni, on the other hand, shared openly and could always tell when a lot was weighing on my mind.

"Just thinking, nothing in particular," was all I offered. Another of my predictable traits was that at times I'm very non-responsive and stubborn.

"Really?" Denni pushed back. "Our daughter is in surgery - again - and that's all you've got?"

I wasn't sure exactly what to say. Several options crossed my mind.

Oh, not much. I was just thinking about how God was in Katie's room the night before last, and threw a blanket around me to comfort me when I thought she was dying. God said, 'I've got this,' so we really don't need to worry. No, that wasn't going to work.

"Just thinking, that's all," I responded.

Denni leaned in and put her head on my shoulder. I knew that Denni needed some support and I put my arm around her. My wife was an incredibly strong woman, but all of this was taking its toll.

I held Denni, and after a while, I took my arm from around her, leaned back, and returned to the solitude of my own mind.

CHAPTER 17

Upgrade
February 14, 2000

WHILE WE WAITED FOR KATIE to be transported from the recovery area, one of the floor nurses found Denni and me sitting in the waiting room.

"Hey, when you go back up to the floor we're going to have you in a different room," the nurse said nonchalantly.

"Why?" asked Denni.

"You're going to need some more room. We're moving you into Room 502."

"Our room's not big enough?" I inquired.

"Katie's going to have some more equipment. And it'll be more comfortable," the nurse said. "You guys are going to be here a little while longer."

We were getting the deluxe accommodations on the fifth floor of Children's Hospital. Under normal circumstances we would have appreciated the room upgrade, but this wasn't the Marriott and the upgrade didn't include plusher towels and a wet bar. It was becoming clear - we were going to be there for the long haul.

After Katie returned from the recovery area, the Proctor party moved into Suite 502. The room came with a second fully reclining "bed" which would allow both Denni and I to spend the night with Katie, and not have to rotate back and forth between the hospital and David and Holly's house. The nurses had taken the time to rehang some of the get-well cards from friends, family, and Katie's playmates on the wall facing her bed so she could see them. It was a nice touch, but the hominess was offset by an incredible amount of medical equipment, the likes of which we'd never seen before.

Shortly after we settled in, Dr. Crone came by. Despite the million-dollar technology that surrounded Katie, he set a carpenter's level, a ruler, and a roll of duct tape on the table beside her I-V machine. He held the carpenter's level to her ear canal and carefully marked the spot on the ruler, now duct taped to the I-V pole next to her bed.

"The goal is to find the sweet spot for the lumbar drain and keep her as still as possible," Dr. Crone said, pointing to a mark on the ruler. "Raising Katie's head above this point will cause spinal fluid to drain; lowering her head will cause it to drain less."

I was amazed, and couldn't help but wonder in what part of medical school this was taught. Shop class maybe, but medical school?

Over the next twenty-four hours, the staff attempted to find the correct position for Katie so the spinal fluid would behave like it should. Too little drainage, and she'd get violently nauseous. Too much drainage, and she would be in agony. It was hard for us to watch.

We were stunned by the turn of events over the past seventy-two hours. We had tried to be as upbeat as possible on the Katie Updates, and we didn't want to make people panic, but clearly the news had changed. We were being inundated with "How's it going?" emails, and it was time for another update. But what to say?

To: Friends of Katie
From: Rob & Denni Proctor
Date: Monday, February 14, 2000
Re: Katie Update

We would love more than anything to be able to give a more positive update on Katie. Needless to say, it's been a difficult weekend.

> Katie has developed staphylococcal meningitis. She had a spinal tap on Friday, and had trouble keeping her oxygen levels up over the weekend. She had a lumbar spinal fluid drain placed in earlier today, because she's leaking infected spinal fluid out of the back of her head. There is no way to put a positive spin on that statement, as your body is simply not meant to do that. The lumbar drain is in place to help regulate the spinal fluid going into the brain.
>
> She's pretty miserable and right now, we are trying to make her as comfortable as possible.
>
> We thank you for your prayers and support. God willing, we hope and pray Katie takes a positive turn very soon.
>
> Rob, Denni and Katie

"I know you've got this under control, God. And I am thankful for that," I said to myself as I drifted off to sleep that night. I figured it was time for me and God to talk some more. Denni had been having a number of her own conversations with God. Seeing Katie on the brink had rattled Denni to the core. But it was clear that her faith had not wavered. She was shaken, but not deterred.

Although I tried to project a sense of confidence and optimism, I admit I was concerned my emotions were getting the best of me.

For most of my life, I had control of my emotions. Now, I felt like I was totally out of my league. I felt sad, scared, angry, confused, punished, and a whole host of other emotions, many of them simultaneously, which seemed to pile up on me. I gave myself a little credit, as I figured having a daughter diagnosed with a brain tumor registered pretty high on the stress scale.

I really didn't know where God fit into all of all of the emotional thoughts going through my head, but I knew I needed to talk to Him. And I really hoped He would talk back.

CHAPTER 18

Bedside Manner February 15, 2000

"Stop it!" Katie yelled in her whisper voice.

"Stop what?" her Mommy asked.

"Stop touching my bed!"

"Honey, I'm barely touching it. Can't I sit on the bed with you?" Denni asked, confused by Katie's new attitude.

"No! I don't want anybody touching my bed except for Dakota. Stop it!"

Denni's face expressed her hurt. She was trying to be understanding, but she just wanted to comfort her daughter. Apparently, Katie had other plans.

"She's not doing it to be mean," I said. "She's just miserable."

A few hours later David and Holly walked in, anxious to see their granddaughter. Shortly after Katie's surgery, they left for their annual trip to Hawaii. They had originally planned on being there for several more weeks. The trip was scheduled months ahead, and they went only after they thought Katie was fully on the mend. When they heard the news of the meningitis, they quickly changed plans and came back to Cincinnati.

"Nana & Bald-Bald are here!" Holly said with a big smile. David had been renamed *Bald-Bald* by Katie, since David was almost entirely bald. Holly chose her own nickname and wanted to be called "Nana." She was having none of the "Grandma" stuff, and she liked the sound of Nana, so that was the end of the conversation. Nana came over to the bed and leaned in to kiss Katie.

"Don't touch my bed, Nana!" Katie voiced her objection. "I don't want anyone to touch my bed."

"You don't mean that," David said, leaning onto Katie's bed.

"Yes, she does," I said. "Let's all give her some space. Clearly she doesn't feel well."

David and Holly weren't used to being given orders by a four-year-old, but they came to find that for the time being, Katie was very serious about her no-touching preference.

Many visitors couldn't understand why she didn't want her bed to be touched. Denni and I had to step in several times as patient advocate on behalf of our daughter to remind everyone that Katie's wishes in the personal space area needed to be respected.

Katie's condition could only be described as horrible. She was on the most powerful drugs her body could handle as the Omnimax 3000 I-V machine pumped the antibiotic drugs into her system. She felt lethargic, had a fever, and could never find a way to get comfortable for very long. This meant she was grumpy with a capital *G*. Family and friends came by to cheer her up, but she was beyond the cheering up stage. Outside of an occasional game of Go Fish, Katie didn't have much energy for play. Even her grandpa wearing purple earrings and a crown after getting walloped at a game of Pretty, Pretty Princess didn't seem to do much to lighten her mood.

"Do you see what she's doing?" Denni asked me. "She gets that from you."

Katie had begun to chew on her fingers. I'm a chronic nail-biter and will occasionally chew on my fingernails until they bleed. Now Katie's fingers looked as bad as mine. But Katie took it a step further: She began to pick at her forehead. The doctors couldn't find a lesion or anything that would have caused her to do this, but still she managed to create a raw spot on her forehead. Over the course of several days, it grew, first to the size of a pea, and eventually to about the size of a dime.

"She's stressed," one of the pediatricians weighed in. "Patients of all ages have to deal with stress, and when it gets bad it can manifest itself like this."

"So what do we do about it?" Denni asked. "That's got to hurt and she's going to give herself a scar."

"She's on antibiotics and strong pain medication so it probably doesn't hurt her as much as you'd think. But you're right about the scar and we certainly don't want her to keep digging at her forehead and chewing on her fingers. We'll get an antidepressant included in her medications. No big doses - just enough to take the edge off until she can find other ways to cope. And whatever you can do to distract her can't hurt. In the meantime, we'll put some antibiotic ointment on the raw spot and put a bandage over it to see if that keeps her away."

"Man, this kid needs a break," I said with a heavy sigh.

"I couldn't agree more," the doctor said.

"If there are any extra antidepressants that Katie won't be using, I'll take them," I said to the doctor as he headed towards the door. The doctor stopped.

"I can't say I blame you. In all seriousness, if you feel like you need to talk with somebody about all of this, we have counselors who could probably help."

"Thanks," I said. "But drugs are easier."

"I can neither confirm nor deny that statement," the doctor said, as he smiled and walked out of the room.

We tried to stay as positive as we could, but Katie's days consisted of treatments and activities that were pretty unpleasant. The Child Life Specialists and nursing staff, along with Denni and me and the rest of our family, did what we could to find ways to brighten her spirits. Playing the 100th game of Go Fish only went so far and Katie had watched the videos in the hospital library enough to recite them all from memory.

As Katie started her third week in the hospital, both Denni and I were becoming seasoned veterans on the floor. There were some extended-stay patients, but for the most part the population on the floor had turned over several times since we'd arrived.

"What are you in for?" one mom would say to another in the family lounge. The responses ranged from "tonsillitis" and "a touch of the flu," to "another round of chemo." In the room next to Katie's, the flurry of activity was hard to miss. The patient was a pre-teen girl who was receiving a kidney and partial liver transplant. Her father was the donor, and her mother and three brothers and sisters seemed to be ever-present. The mom was at least seven months pregnant at the time. The girl's bed was elevated about eighteen inches off the ground and the doctors attending to her stood on milk crates to gain a better perspective. Surrounding her bed were bags and bags of blood. I had never seen so many bags of blood. Frequently, the curtains to her room would be shut and it was clear that whatever was taking place behind them was something not for the faint of heart.

One evening Denni was standing in the hallway when another mom came outside and began to yell for the nurses, none of whom were in the immediate vicinity. Denni asked if everything was OK, and the mother told Denni her daughter had the flu and her temperature was over one hundred degrees. They'd hooked her up to an I-V, mostly at the mother's urging, as she insisted her daughter was dehydrated. Now, the I-V machine was beeping. And by God, somebody better do something about it.

Denni started to offer some words of consolation, but the mom would have none of it. In no uncertain terms, she told Denni she needed to back off and let the staff of Cincinnati Children's drop everything and take care of the only patient in the hospital that was truly in need at the moment - her daughter!

Denni did a better job of understanding the mother's perspective and showing compassion than I would have.

"Why didn't you tell her to calm down?" I said, tired from the day's events, and not having much patience for the drama taking place in the hallway.

"Because that wouldn't have been *nice*," Denni said, giving me a look.

"Did you tell her the beeping machine doesn't mean anything?" I asked, with my newfound medical background giving me authority to speak on such matters.

"She's just scared," Denni said.

"Aren't we all?" I said, as I drifted off to sleep in the more spacious but still uncomfortable lounge-bed in Suite 502. Another night in paradise.

CHAPTER 19

Genie in a Bottle
February 15, 2000

I GREW UP IN THE pre-attention deficit disorder-era of the 1960s and '70s, thank God. But I've always been restless, and even as an adult, I'm fidgety to a fault. It became so noticeable to Denni that after putting up with it for several years, she convinced me to go for ADD testing. After two days of tests the psychiatrist said I was a borderline case, although he said he'd probably diagnose me with impatience rather than a tangible medical condition.

Whether it was a medical condition or simply my impatient soul, the monotonous hospital routine was getting to me.

"I'm going for a walk. I'll be back in a while," I said to Denni, who was talking on the phone. She waved goodbye without looking up.

Occasionally, I would walk the halls on the floor or around the hospital when I needed a break. Cincinnati Children's was a massive facility, but Denni and I had learned to navigate most of it with ease. The color-coded tiles on the floor directed guests and staff to all of the various departments, and we even learned our way through the tunnels that connected Children's to several other hospitals located in the same area. The multiple facility complex included Children's, Shriners & Jewish Hospitals, the VA Medical Center, and University Hospital, where Denni had been born.

I walked through the hustle and bustle, past the cafeteria, the family resource room, and the gift shop. We had been there long enough that some of the security guards gave me nods of recognition as I walked by.

When I approached the stairway that led to the chapel, I thought about going up the stairs and having another conversation with God. I was still coming to terms with what had happened a few nights earlier in Katie's hospital room. But I decided against the chapel, and instead, turned and headed for the parking garage. After sitting in the car for a few minutes, I engaged the engine and pulled out of the lot.

I opened the windows of the Chevy Tahoe, and cold February air filled the cabin. I needed music. Music has been a big part of my life since my teenage years. I'm a horrible singer and have little musical talent, but to say I am "into" music is an understatement. I was even a DJ for several years in high school, and have always considered myself to have an encyclopedic knowledge when it comes to music trivia, at times to the annoyance of my wife.

Denni likes music too, although she has never been as concerned as I was with the background information. To me, it's a part of the equation and for years, we played our own version of *Name That Tune*. When a song would come on the radio, I'd ask Denni the name of the song, the artist, or the year the song was released. Denni politely obliged in the quizzing, and when in doubt, she would guess Abba, Journey or the Beatles, figuring the odds would eventually make her right.

I turned on the radio, which was set to my favorite rock station in Cincinnati, WEBN. My first exposure to WEBN had been in 1982 when I made the two-hour trip to Cincinnati from Eastern Kentucky University with some Phi Delta Theta fraternity buddies to attend one of the initial WEBN Labor Day Fireworks shows. The fireworks tradition grew, and for years several hundred thousand people lined the banks of the Ohio River to watch one of the most spectacular choreographed fireworks concerts in the country.

After a few songs, I switched over another rock station and was immediately transfixed by Manfred Mann's "Blinded by the Light." I have always judged the worthiness of a radio station by the cut of a song they chose to play. Good radio stations play the extended album versions of songs, not the condensed "American Top Forty" versions. The extended version of "Blinded by the Light" has a significantly longer middle section filled with almost incomprehensible lyrics. But this has always been one of my favorite songs, and I easily rattled off the words.

I hit the dial and the next station that came on was a Christian radio station. I listened to a few verses of whatever song was playing. Under normal circumstances, I would have flipped to another station up or down the dial until I found a song to my liking. But in this case, I took my hand off the scan button and listened.

"I don't know why you're listening right now," the DJ said, "But I do know God wants to talk to you."

"Let me guess," I said sarcastically. "God wants me to make a financial pledge to this radio station." I immediately felt guilty for being so cynical, especially in light of recent events.

"God doesn't promise us a problem-free life," the DJ said. "Your life may be going along swimmingly or you may have a boatload of problems."

I couldn't help but think, *Dude, its Ohio in February - swimming and boat references?* But I kept listening.

"Here's where we get into problems. We tend to think when everything is going along fine, it's because of us and that we don't need God. In fact, we really don't want God to look too closely sometimes, do we? We don't want him intruding in our lives. And when we run into problems, our turnabout in philosophy is amazing. We want God to come out and fix it and then go away again. Almost like a Genie in a bottle."

I looked at myself in the rear-view mirror. The last words hit me like a ton of bricks. I thought of my recent behavior. After years of a benign attitude, I reached out to God in desperation after my daughter was diagnosed with a brain tumor. I had called on God to "make this go away," but I hadn't expressed any interest in developing anything deeper. The realization of the truth was stinging.

I listened closely as the DJ continued. If God wasn't talking to me directly right now, the DJ certainly was. The words hit home and my head swirled with thoughts. I was actually relieved when the DJ stopped talking and a song came on. The tune was "True North" by Twila Paris and I turned up the volume and listened carefully so I could hear the lyrics.

We lost our bearings,
Following our own mind
We left conviction behind
Fear of the future,
Springing from the sins of the past
Hiding the hope that would last
How did we ever wander so far
And where do we go from here
How will we know where it is? True North…

I'd heard enough for one afternoon. I turned the Tahoe back towards the hospital, my head full of new emotions. Clearly there was more to think through. Much more.

I hadn't been gone very long and when I got back to the room, Denni and Katie were watching TV. Or more accurately, Katie was half-asleep and Denni was half-watching.

"I took the Tahoe for a little drive. It sounds kind of funny." I leaned over and kissed Katie on the head and did the same with Denni.

"Where'd you go?" Denni asked.

"To some new places I hadn't been to before," I said, thinking for a moment how deep that statement actually was.

Later that night, Katie had oxygen level issues. The doctors wanted Katie to stay awake, so she and I undertook a marathon goal to complete an entire *Winnie the Pooh* coloring book. I drew a few pages and then Katie drew, and throughout the night we talked and colored to our heart's content. One of the pictures in the coloring book featured Pooh, Eeyore, and Piglet on a beach. A thought came into my head.

"Katie, when you get better, what do you think about all of us going to Hawaii? How does that sound?"

"OK," was all Katie said. She was still stuck in a miserable state.

"Then it's settled. Hawaii it is, I promise."

"I heard that," Denni said, startling me, as I thought she'd been sound asleep.

The next morning's exam was a repeat of the day before.

"The main goal is to keep her sedentary," said Dr. Crone. "We need for her body to figure out how to regulate the spinal fluid in her system."

"Doctor Crone," Denni said. "Katie's miserable. And she's been miserable for days. Is she going to be OK?"

"Yes, I know she feels lousy. I think she's going to be OK, Denni. I'd like to get the lumbar drain out soon but it's still too early. It's working, although not entirely as we'd hoped. I don't like to leave those in for too long but her body isn't fixing itself like it needs to. We just need to keep her stable for a while. She needs to go three days, seventy-two hours, with no leaks at all. So far, she hasn't managed to do that and that's our main goal. We just need to take things one day at a time."

"I think one day at a time is our new motto for everything," Denni said.

To: Friends of Katie
From: Rob & Denni Proctor
Date: Wednesday, February 16, 2000
Re: Katie Update

Katie is holding her own today, although she just can't seem to catch a break. The lumbar drain is not functioning exactly as they'd like, and she is still having problems getting her spinal fluid under control. Our goal today is to stay completely sedentary to get the spinal fluid situation under control. Now that she has the heavy duty I-V line in place, they are adjusting the antibiotics. We're up to the "big gun" antibiotics, so hopefully they will do the trick.

They moved her to a larger room (i.e., a longer stay). Under normal circumstances, Denni and I would like the preferred-customer treatment, but as it is, we're not too thrilled about it.

We are at the wait and see stage. I know you are all praying hard for Katie, and we are, too.
Rob, Denni & Katie

Overcoming initial protests of being touched, Katie had been convinced to receive feet-to-neck massages from therapists in the Holistic Medicine department. I had initially been skeptical that a massage could do much for someone with a brain tumor suffering from meningitis. But sure enough, the therapists got Katie to relax as they gently massaged her from her feet to her neck. Every now and then, Katie would fall asleep by the end of her massage, and we would be grateful whenever that happened. Sleep seemed to be one of the very few places where Katie could find some sense of comfort.

CHAPTER 20

Memory Lane
February 16, 2000

Now in our third week in the hospital, outside of a long-term chemo patient and the kidney/liver transplant patient in the next room, Katie, Denni, and I were the most tenured residents on the main floors of Children's Hospital. Our family and some of our friends had visited often enough that the nurses easily recognized them.

Denni and I would still occasionally take turns to run to David and Holly's to get a real shower, and Denni would go there to sleep in a real bed to relieve some of her pregnancy aches. We'd long stopped caring about much beyond basic hygiene. Depending on what kind of day Katie was having, running a washcloth over ourselves and brushing our teeth might be the extent of the efforts exerted in that area. After all, it wasn't like we were getting much company who didn't already know our circumstances.

Katie had completed her early day therapies. She was still very uncomfortable and got an extra dose of pain medication which helped but made her sleepy. She drifted in and out of watching whatever kids' show was playing, and Denni and I went about our ritual of reading and visiting with friends and family, the doctors, and each other. We were simply trying to get through the day.

There was a knock on the sliding glass door. I stumbled in the dark to make my way over to it. Since the onset of the meningitis, Katie had demanded, in addition to no one touching her bed, the lights be turned off since they significantly increased her level of discomfort. The doctors said light sensitivity was pretty common with meningitis. We found it difficult to keep up our own energy levels after being in the dark all day, and then not sleeping well at night because of the endless parade of check-ins performed by the night shift nurses.

As I slid back the door, I was surprised by whom I found standing in the hallway. Sherry Jackson and I were high school sweethearts at Lima Shawnee High School. We began to date my senior year and continued the relationship through a portion of college. For a period of time we were even engaged. As I began my junior year at Eastern Kentucky University, Sherry enrolled at the University of Cincinnati, and lived in a dorm less than a mile from where we were standing.

But as often is the case with long distance relationships, the engagement was called off and we parted in an amicable fashion. I hadn't seen Sherry in a number of years. Now she stood in the hallway, holding a small teddy bear in her hand. I slid the door open further and we both entered the room.

"Honey, this is Sherry," I said as I made the introduction to Denni.

The look on Denni's face was priceless. She hadn't showered that day, nor had I, and she was wearing sweats, a ratty T-shirt, and hospital socks she'd borrowed from Katie.

"It's a pleasure to meet you," Denni said, trying to sound sincere. "I'm sorry I'm a mess but I've haven't gotten around to cleaning up for the day."

"Oh my goodness, don't worry about that. I understand," Sherry said. "This is for Katie," Sherry said and handed the bear to me. Katie was lying in bed, oblivious to the awkwardness taking place just a few feet from her. Katie, with her brain tumor and meningitis, was at the moment the most comfortable person in the room.

After a brief visit, Sherry left. I thought it was a very kind gesture and a great example of how people intersect in each other's lives at points not always of our choosing - but for a purpose. My wife did not share my appreciation for her visit.

"Well, that was lovely," Denni said. "Your ex-fiancée comes by looking incredible and I look like crap."

"I thought that was very nice of her, and you look fine," I said, knowing full well that answer wouldn't work out well. It didn't.

So much for the walk down Memory Lane.

CHAPTER 21

Houston, We Have a Problem February 18, 2000

§

THE NEXT MORNING KATIE'S CIRCUMSTANCES had changed again, only not for the better. The nurse came in for the morning sheet-changing ritual and rolled Katie over. This time she saw the pool of fluid not only by her head, but also at the site of the lumbar drain. It was clearly not a positive development.

Dr. Crone was summoned and the medical team gathered around Katie's bed in a matter of minutes. He spoke with the resident team, but he was aware Denni and I were standing within earshot and made time for a private conversation.

"I know there hasn't been much going her way lately, and this isn't the development any of us wanted."

"Is she going to be OK?" Denni said, which could be translated as, "Is Katie going to live?"

"I know it's a delicate time and you might be thinking she's hit rock bottom. We certainly don't want her to get any worse and we're going to do everything we can to get things under control. But as far as hitting rock bottom is concerned, believe it or not, there is still room to go. We just don't plan on letting her get there." We were as comforted as we could be under the circumstances.

"You know as well as anybody that Katie's in a weakened state," Dr. Crone said. "It's not safe to put her under anesthesia and reopen the incision again, or even remove the malfunctioning lumbar drain to try and install a new one. We need to figure out a way to make it work without having to do surgery. We're going to put our heads together to see what we can come up with. I'll be back before too long."

The group of doctors standing in the hallway looked like the engineers in the movie *Apollo 13.* One of them held a lumbar drain in their hand and the other doctors pointed to various parts of it. They would turn in unison to look at Katie and then resume their conversation. The solution they came up with was Extra Strength Tegaderm tape, a dressing that adheres to the skin so well the doctors called it "second skin." Using large squares of Tegaderm tape, they made a pouch that covered Katie's lower back. The plan was for Katie to leak spinal fluid into the pouch, and every so often they would drain the pouch and change the dressing.

The procedure sounded simple, but was far from it.

CHAPTER 22

Silent Screams February 19-21, 2000

IF THERE EVER WAS A time when Denni and I would have traded places with Katie rather than watching helplessly from the sidelines, this was it. Changing the homemade Tegaderm tape pouch involved creating a sterile environment and the staff wore outfits that resembled Haz-Mat suits. It took several nurses to perform the procedure, and we weren't allowed to do anything but watch.

"I hate having to stand out here," Denni said as we looked through the glass. "You can tell Katie is scared. I'm her mom and I should be there with her."

"Honey, I know you want to be there, but you can't," I said. "And the last thing she needs is another infection. She'll be OK …." I stopped mid-sentence and my jaw dropped with what I saw through the glass.

As they performed the procedure, Katie had a contorted look on her face that's hard to describe. It's difficult to watch any child in true pain, but this was the most unbearable thing either of us had ever seen. It was clear this wasn't just painful – Katie had already been through a number of painful procedures. This was excruciating. The staff was holding Katie down and pulling off the Tegaderm tape from her back. It took considerable effort to remove the tape and for all intents and purposes it looked, and obviously felt, like they were pulling the skin off her back.

The worst part was that this poor child couldn't even scream. With her paralyzed vocal cords, her screams of agony barely registered. We could see her pain, but could barely hear it. And the process had to be repeated. Again. And again. I pleaded with God – "Why? Why can't you stop this?" As thankful as I was God had spared her life, I was so mad that He allowed her to suffer this kind of pain. Where was that warm blanket feeling that I had felt a few nights earlier?

Dr. Crone continued to give reassurances that Katie would make it through this, but he was concerned that Katie could physically tolerate only so much. He went on to say that although it had been in longer than he'd wanted, the lumbar drain needed to stay in for now. In yet another procedure, Dr. Crone put several stitches around the lumbar drain and in Katie's original incision in her head in an attempt to curb some of the leaking and buy some time. Now everyone began another seventy-two-hour watch.

As I made one of my walks around the hospital, I headed to the parking garage once again. I started up the Tahoe and had planned on taking a drive. After a minute or two, I turned off the engine but left the key in the ignition so I could listen to the radio. The station was still tuned to the Christian station from a few days earlier. I leaned back in the seat and closed my eyes. I couldn't put my finger on the emotions I was having, but it felt like some gravitational force was pulling me in.

Several songs hit home and a few songs had better melodies behind the lyrics than others. But I did something that afternoon that was completely unlike me. I never changed the dial. Song after song, message after message, I listened for almost two hours and never once felt the urge to listen to what was playing on the other stations. Something was up. I just wasn't quite sure what it was.

After watching Katie eat her dinner, we headed to the hospital cafeteria and assumed one of our regular tables. I wasted no time in sharing my news.

"I think I'm going to head back to Michigan for a couple of days," I said, almost as if I expected no reaction.

"Seriously?" Denni asked, incredulous that I would even consider such a thing.

"Katie seems pretty stable and I think I'll just check on the house, the dog, and a few things at work, and come right back."

"OK, first of all, Katie's not really 'pretty stable' and you know it," Denni said, clearly upset. "I'm not sure how you're trying to convince yourself that she's doing so well. Every day it seems like she has something new she has to deal with."

Denni's rising volume indicated her rising anger.

"And second of all, this isn't about checking on the house or Rocky. Rocky and the house are just fine. Judi and Michael are taking care of everything there, and you know it. You said it was nice that everybody was taking care of all our stuff at home and at work? Remember that?"

I didn't have an immediate response.

"This is about work. You can't stay away. Bob told you not to worry about work, and every day you check your email like State Farm is going to fall apart if you're not there. You've got bigger things to worry about here."

"I do not think they'll fall apart if I'm not there," I said, in a voice that sounded like a teenager more than an adult. Then I realized I'd answered the wrong part of her statement. "Doctor Crone said Katie is pretty stable and now is as good a time as any. I won't be gone long and I just want to check in."

"You're rounding up if you think Katie is stable," Denni retorted. "You're a workaholic," she said flatly. "You've been a workaholic all these years and I really haven't said much and you know it. I can't believe you'd do this, but I'm not going to stop you because I know you've already made up your mind. If your precious State Farm is more important than your family, I can't help that. But it's pathetic."

"That's not fair and you know it." I countered. "We've been sitting here for days and now she's pretty stable so I figure this is a good opportunity to check up on things and come back. Is it really that big of a deal?"

"To you? Apparently not. Go have fun with your mistress," Denni said in a tone of disgust.

"Mistress?"

Denni looked me right in the eye. "State Farm is your mistress. It's beyond sad, but I guess you're in love with her more than you are with us." The disappointment was evident in Denni's voice.

"That's bullshit," I responded defensively, as I really had nothing else to support my case, and could feel myself moving into my stubborn lock-down state.

"Oh really, Proc?" Denni asked in a rhetorical fashion. "You need to do some serious soul-searching in all of this. If this hasn't conked you on the head about what's truly important, I can't imagine anything will. God has blessed you and us beyond belief. And right now, he's saving our daughter's life, but she's not out of the woods by any means. He's in charge of all of this. Whether you want him to be or not. He is."

"I know that," I said, thinking it sounded a lot like some of the messages I'd heard on the radio. Coming from my own wife, it made me feel guilty. But not guilty enough for me to change my plans.

For the first time, Denni co-authored the Katie Update and added a paragraph aimed not at the normal audience, but directly at me.

To: Friends of Katie
From: Rob & Denni Proctor
Date: Monday, February 21,
Re: Katie Update

Katie had yet another roller-coaster weekend. Saturday went well, and on Sunday things kind of crashed again. She had stopped leaking fluid Sunday morning, but after some vomiting episodes, the leaking started again. Then Katie had problems holding her oxygen levels up, so she went back on the oxygen for a while. There is concern that the paralysis with her swallowing and vocal cords is compromising her airway, so they are watching that closely. It looks like the lumbar drain will stay in place for now. Dr. Crone and his team are doing everything they can for her, but everyone has pretty much agreed that she has reached the maximum of what she can physically tolerate. She will be heavily involved in speech and physical therapy this week. Again, the thoughts and prayers are appreciated.

On a brighter note, Denni went to an OB/GYN in Cincinnati and heard an incredibly strong heartbeat, and the baby kicked at the ultrasound machine! It looks as though Denni will be due in early August so that will give Katie plenty of time to prepare in her new role of big sister. Katie has said if the baby is a girl, we should name it Kelly... if it's a boy, we should name it "stupid."

Thanks for keeping us in your thoughts and prayers.

Denni, Rob & Katie

PS. Rob plans to fly to Michigan later today although I'm not sure he'll actually be able to leave. He was hoping she would be a bit more stable before he takes off. Anyway, if he does leave, I am sure my updates will be even less frequent. Please bear with me.

CHAPTER 23

Guilt Trip
February 21-23, 2000

"WHAT ARE YOU DOING HERE?" my boss Bob asked as I peeked my head into his office.

"I just came back for few days to check on things, and then I'll head back," I said, trying to sound confident of my statement.

Bob looked confused and said, "We've been following the updates, but how is everything going?"

"OK," I heard myself say. "Katie seems to be holding her own and if all goes well they'll keep her on the antibiotics and we'll be heading home before too long."

What I said bordered on the truth and sounded plausible. I went to my desk and checked in on a few things, but no matter how hard I tried to concentrate, it was impossible for me to focus on work. The more I thought about it, it just didn't make any sense for me to be in Michigan while my daughter and wife were in Cincinnati. Denni was right - again. Checking in at the office didn't accomplish much and, even with my distorted lens, anything at work paled in comparison to what was going on with Katie. I wasn't sure whose voice I was hearing, but the message was clear; *Rob, you need to get your priorities in order.*

My desk phone rang, and I could see from the display panel that it was Denni.

"How's everybody doing?" I asked.

Denni wasn't going to let it be that easy.

"I should ask you the more important question. How is everything at work? Is State Farm still in business with you being gone a few weeks, what with your daughter's brain tumor and all?"

I let it go. I deserved that.

"Is she feeling OK? Is she breathing alright? How is her pain?"

Denni's frustration subsided and she eased off. But her news wasn't rosy.

"She's breathing OK," she responded.

I sensed there was something more.

"But?" I said slowly.

"But she's really in a lot of pain. I haven't seen her in this much pain for a while now. She can't get comfortable and you can just see how much pain she's in. And the lumbar drain still isn't working right so they keep doing the tape thing.

"I hate that," I said. I had images in my head of Katie being held down and trying to scream as they peeled the tape off her back.

"I feel horrible," Denni said. "I didn't even watch them change the lumbar drain dressing this morning. I couldn't bear it. I feel so bad but I just couldn't. Jenny came by and we went for a walk. When I came back, Katie was clutching Dakota, and she just looked so sad and mad at the same time. She's stopped digging holes in her face, but the stress must be incredible. I don't know how she's coping with all this. I couldn't handle it like she is."

"Don't be so hard on yourself. At least you're there," I said, realizing the guilt in my tone as I said the words. "Should I come back?"

"You should never have gone in the first place. But finish up what you've got to do and come back. She's really miserable but there is nothing any of us can do. It's just so hard to see her suffer like this." Her voice broke and the call ended with Denni bawling and me choking back tears.

I decided to take a walk around the office. The State Farm office in Kalamazoo was a remodeled Sam's Club warehouse and housed over 600 employees, with rows of offices and cubicles spread out over several acres. Directly across from the airport, it had an aeronautical theme, with propellers as wall art and aisles with street names like Runway Avenue and Landing Strip Drive.

As I walked, I was greeted by a number of colleagues and individuals who were unable to hide their concern. Some made eye contact and said "How are you doing?" with the descending pitch focused on the last word, highlighting a sense of pity. Some shook my hand and offered comfort. But a few interactions stood out.

The first encounter was from an employee who used to work for me. As I came within her view, she came up to me with a clear sense of purpose.

"I'm not a religious person," she said. "In fact, I'm not even sure what that means. But I have to tell you, I'm praying for Katie and you and your wife every day. I just want you to know that. There are lots of people, including legitimate 'Christians,' or whatever you'd call them, who are praying for you guys. I just wanted you to know that." And with that, she was off.

My next chance meeting was with a fellow member of leadership. We were acquaintances, but I wouldn't have said we were friends. She was involved in another conversation but gave me the signal to wait for her. I did, but only because I had nothing better to do and I thought it would be rude to ignore her.

"How's everything going?" she asked. I didn't even have a chance to respond before she continued.

"I couldn't believe it was a brain tumor when I heard it," she said bluntly, and kept right on going without taking a breath. "That's awful. I went to a funeral last week, and I was just thinking how tired I am of having to go to all these funerals."

I let the sentence sink in, not exactly sure how to answer. "I gotta get back," was all I could come up with. I thought to myself, *if Katie dies, we'll be sure to check with you to see if her funeral is convenient for you.*

After that conversation I needed to clear my head and catch my breath. I walked in a different direction and this time found myself passing by the office of one of my dear friends, Carla Orwin, who happened to be working late that night.

Since transferring to Michigan in 1994, I had worked closely with Carla. She frequently interacted with my leadership teams in Grand Rapids and Kalamazoo. Carla liked my straightforward approach, I respected Carla's common sense solutions, and we both shared a liking for sarcastic humor. We had remained professionally close and good friends through the years.

I walked in Carla's office and sat in the chair across from her desk.

When she asked how Katie was doing, I blurted out the first thing that came to me.

"She's suffering so much. I thought she was OK, but she's gotten worse since I left. Denni says she's in a lot of pain and nothing they do seems to make her feel better. Denni says it's so hard to sit by and watch her suffer. At least Denni is there. I'm not even there for her. I've got to get back."

"I can only imagine how hard this must be," Carla said. She came over and sat on the chair next to me.

"I feel so bad for her," I said fighting back tears. "She is so brave and she's put up with so much, but things just keep coming at her. It's not fair."

"She is so brave," Carla said. "No, it's not fair. None of this is fair. I can't help but think of how you and Denni feel. I think of how I'd feel if this happened to Ben or Audrey and it breaks my heart." I looked at the picture of Carla's toddler twins on her desk.

We talked for a few more minutes but I could feel a sense of being overwhelmed. I put my head in my hands and began to cry. It was the first time I'd cried in front of someone outside of my immediate family in a long time. But at the moment, I really didn't care. Carla sat in silence as I sat and wept. When I was finished and had regained my composure, I went back to my desk. Whatever work there was, none of it mattered. I was embarrassed that I'd ever made the trip.

Just as I was getting ready to leave, the phone rang. It was Denni again.

"Doctor Crone was just here. He doesn't like the lumbar drain issues but you can tell they don't want to operate. They gave her a numbing injection in her incision, and he put in another stitch to see if that would help, but her pain just won't go away. I can't stand that she's in this much pain." Her voice again choked with emotion and then she broke down.

"I'm coming home," I said. "I don't know how but I am." Home, as in the fifth floor of Cincinnati Children's Medical Hospital. Strange as it might sound, that was home. At the moment, as much as Allegan ever had been.

"I'm sorry, Katie. I'm sorry, Denni. And I'm sorry, God," I said to myself as I walked to my car in the parking lot.

I spent all evening trying to check the available flights from Kalamazoo to Cincinnati, and the few I found were already booked. Trying not to panic, I decided to take advantage of an old college friendship and contacted Don Bornhorst, a fraternity brother at Eastern Kentucky University. Don was Vice-President during one of the semesters when I was President of the Phi Delts, and we'd kept in touch a bit over the years. Don was President of Comair – the Cincinnati-based regional airline owned by Delta. Don put me in touch with an assistant who got me booked on a flight back to Cincinnati early the next morning.

In my absence, Denni took a stab at the Katie Update.

To: Friends of Katie
From: Denni Proctor
Date: Tuesday, February 22, 2000
Re: Katie Update

These are much easier to do at night after Katie is resting. The days are too busy. Katie was up early and wanted to sit up for the first time in a week. Sitting didn't last long as she began to have some pain management issues. I think the stitches are sore and probably the muscles too.

Katie received all her therapies today but wasn't as excited about them as on Monday. The pain was so bad at one point that not even the massage seemed to help. That is a first in a while.

When I asked Katie's neurosurgeon, Dr. Crone, if he thought Katie would be getting 'paroled' this week. He simply said "no." Katie needs to go seventy-two hours without leaking from her head or the site of the lumbar drain and she just can't seem to make it that long. That is still priority #1.

Rob did make it back to Michigan, but says it is hard to concentrate on work, and we expect him back in Cincinnati soon. He calls and emails several times a day. Family and friends are helping out in his absence so I can get my afternoon nap. For some reason, no one seems to bother you around here during the day when you sleep; it's just at night.

Now you know what I know. Thanks for your thoughts and prayers. We sure do need them.

Love,

Denni, Rob & Katie

As I lay in bed in Allegan that night, my phone beeped. I looked at the time – 3:30 A.M.

"Ugh" was all Denni's text said. She didn't need to say anything more. I knew that Katie had sprung another leak and that she had not made it through the seventy-two-hour window. Why did I leave them and come back to Michigan in the first place? While I scrambled to get back to Cincinnati, Dr. Crone and the medical team regrouped. The decision was to do another surgery to reopen the original incision from the procedure three weeks earlier.

In the days leading up to this, some of the neurosurgical residents who assisted with Katie's case had said that avoiding another surgery was a major goal. Now, she was leaking in a new place and her body simply wasn't fixing itself, so surgery was the only remaining option.

Sitting restlessly on the plane, I looked down over the dreary gray and brown countryside as the flight made its way into Cincinnati. I thought of the events of the past several weeks as one thing after another had piled up on Katie. The surgically induced meningitis which almost never happens, then the malfunctioning lumbar drain, which almost never happens, the continual leaking, the oxygen level challenges, the veins giving in, the Tegaderm tape episodes. Murphy's Law was becoming Katie's Law and it seemed like she just couldn't catch a break. I couldn't help but think that of all the people on the planet, no one deserved a break more that Katie Proctor. She was *owed* one.

When I walked into the room after my road trip, Katie looked at me and in the most excited tone her whisper-like voice could make, she said "Hi, Daddy, I missed you," and my heart melted.

I had left my seriously ill daughter in the hospital to check on some meaningless tasks with my job. Katie had every right to be furious with me. Instead, she gave me the unconditional love that only a child can. I felt ashamed. If only Katie knew better. She certainly deserved better, and so did Denni.

To: Friends of Katie
From: Rob & Denni Proctor
Date: Wednesday, February 23, 2000
Re: Katie Update - Third Surgery

Katie has had a number of issues this week, and the decision has been made for Katie to undergo yet another surgery. The doctors have weighed the risks and there are no other options.

Katie's still leaking out of her surgical site which is a major concern. They took the lumbar drain out today even though she is still having issues. They're normally only left in for three to five days, and Katie's was in close to ten. Dr. Crone felt the need to take it out to see if her body can regulate the spinal fluid on its own. The fact that Katie can't seem to go more than thirty-six to forty-eight hours without leaking is not good and she's been through a lot over the past week and a half, so the operation itself is a major concern.

Dr. Crone has scheduled surgery for 1:00 P.M. tomorrow afternoon, and they will assess her right beforehand to see if the surgery is still a go. The surgery may take two hours.

Your support has been so wonderful, and we hope we're not wearing out our welcome for asking yet again. Please pray with us for Katie to get over this latest hurdle. God will get Katie and us through this. We're still hanging tough - please hang in there with us.

Rob, Denni & Katie

CHAPTER 24

Third Time's a Charm February 24-26, 2000

KATIE UNDERWENT YET ANOTHER SURGERY, and Denni and I sat in silence in the waiting room, occasionally making small talk with family and a few close friends who had come by to offer support. The tension was so thick you could cut it with a knife, or more appropriately, a scalpel. We hadn't talked about it, but both Denni and I were as fearful for the current surgery as we had been for the original brain surgery over three weeks earlier. My mom was so upset she couldn't even discuss the topic with anyone.

It was Katie's third surgery in a month and a number of things went through my mind. I wondered how much more of this Katie could take. She was physically and emotionally exhausted, and over the preceding weeks not many things had gone her way. I wondered, too, how much more of this Denni could take. She was in the second trimester of her pregnancy with Brian, and had a miscarriage the year before. The stress of this situation certainly couldn't help.

And selfishly, I wondered how much more of this I could take. I recalled a saying I'd heard a number of times that a person is only given what they can handle. At the moment, I concluded, what a crock! I thought to myself, *Really, God? You know who you're dealing with here, right? It's me, Rob, the guy who can't find his keys two days a week, and who borders on tears when the Vikings lose in the playoffs.*

I quickly snapped myself out of that line of thinking as I realized that was not the direction I wanted or needed to go. Instead, I thought of the conversations with God I'd had over the past few weeks, and found comfort in the thought of a truly powerful and loving God who was in control. I felt like something was bolstering me up. So this is what faith is like. I wondered if this feeling was what people referred to when they say their spirits are lifted. No wonder Denni seemed to enjoy that feeling so much.

I reflected on some of what I'd been reading lately. Instead of novels and business articles, I had actually started to read the Bible that Denni brought from her Dad's house. Some of the stories were familiar to me, from my earlier church experiences, or just hearing them at various stages in my life. There were still many parts of the Bible I didn't understand, and there were pieces of it that bothered me. I was confused over parts that seemed to give seemingly absurd instructions. And I wasn't certain which parts were to be taken literally as opposed to those that were to be interpreted as metaphors. And it wasn't just reading the Bible that had captured my heart as of late.

Over the prior days and weeks, I had been listening to more Christian radio. I thought the name of the genre sounded odd. "Christian radio", like St. Peter was a DJ and Jesus was the producer. "And next up, Gabriel and his horns playing the soothing sounds of salvation. But first, a word from our sponsor."

Now the songs and bible verses were scoring direct blows to my heart and my mind. There was a change taking place within me, I could feel it. It felt incredible and unnerving at the same time. I still wasn't sure if God was punishing me, and rightfully so, for any number of sins, but I felt an inner comfort just knowing God was really there. If someone would have asked me before, I would have admitted God existed, as did Heaven and Hell, but that would have been the extent of it. I certainly wouldn't have felt comfortable digging much deeper than that. At the moment, I not only knew it went much deeper, I *felt* it.

Two and a half hours after the surgery began, we got the now-familiar call to meet with Dr. Crone in the conference room.

"She did well," Dr. Crone said. "For such a little thing, she's amazingly resilient."

"Yes, she is, isn't she?" Denni echoed.

"I reopened a large part of the original incision," he said. The infected tissue and spinal fluid seemed to be causing a lot of her issues. There were at least four separate leaks, so I added a mesh fabric that will serve as a barrier to protect her from additional infection. Then I overstitched the entire area."

"That sounds painful," I added.

"Very," Dr. Crone agreed. "She's on a strong dose of morphine and we'll keep her pain meds pretty high until she doesn't need them. She's been through enough lately that she doesn't need another episode of pain on top of everything. In many cases, morphine can have the side-effect of amnesia, so she may not remember a lot of this part."

"I wish I could say the same," I said.

"You know what I have to do now," Denni said as she rose from the table.

"Umm, a hug?" Dr. Crone asked with a smile.

"You know it," said Denni as they embraced.

"I'll settle for a handshake," I said. "But I can't tell you how grateful we are for everything you've done for Katie, and for Denni and me. God bless you."

"I think we can all feel pretty blessed today. Thank you," Dr. Crone said as he left the room.

Back in Room 502, Katie was out of it, blissfully numbed by the morphine that pumped into her body to prevent the pain nerves from connecting with her recently invaded brain. If all went well, she'd have little recollection of the surgery or the immediate aftermath. Denni and I wouldn't be so lucky.

As I plotted out the Katie Update, I decided to let more of my growing faith peek through.

To: Friends of Katie
From: Rob & Denni Proctor
Date: Thursday, February 24, 2000
Re: Katie Update - Third Surgery!

Thank you, God!!! Katie has made it through her third surgery! We just got back from recovery after about a two-and-a-half-hour procedure. As always, Dr. Crone continues to amaze us with his abilities, and no doubt, divine guidance! I think Denni and I were more nervous during this operation than we were for the first one three weeks ago!

Dr. Crone said Katie had an internal leakage of cerebral spinal fluid, a by-product of the surgery, as well as the bacterial meningitis. The surgical site was completely cleaned up, drained, and a man-made fiber was sewn into the area. Her own tissues will grow in with the fiber, and a sealant was used that will shore up the site enough to stop the leakage.

As you can imagine, Katie is very uncomfortable. Dr. Crone reopened a portion of the original surgical incision and over-stitched the entire area. She is on morphine tonight so we hope she gets some much-deserved rest.

When they are comfortable that there is no leakage exposure, they want to get her home! With everything that has happened nobody is brave enough to give us an estimated release date, but who knows - maybe soon?

Thanks again for your prayers and support - we know it's had a tremendous impact. Prayer works!!! And we are fortunate to have such special friends.

God bless you all. He certainly has blessed us!

Rob, Denni & Katie

CHAPTER 25

Katie & the Carpenter February 27, 2000

§

As we entered the weekend, another leak watch began. The procedure Dr. Crone performed had removed whatever infection he could, and in addition, he took out the lumbar drain. It was a fairly risky proposition in light of her weakened state. Everyone knew this was a critical point for Katie, and that this procedure needed to work. Over the course of the next forty-eight hours Katie was slowly weaned from the pain medication. As concerned as everyone was about the surgery, it's when Katie showed her true strength. She may have looked fragile, but her warrior spirit came shining through. Finally, she got that elusive break everyone had been praying for.

In the three days following the surgery, Katie not only stabilized, but also rapidly rebounded. It was almost scripted that as Katie's condition improved, the Ohio winter seemed to break and the temperature soared to near sixty degrees.

"Katie, do you want to go outside?" Denni asked. "It's beautiful." Katie was watching TV and didn't say "no," so Denni took that as an affirmative answer. She put a blanket over Katie, fit some plastic sunglasses onto her face to protect her from the bright sun, and wheeled her onto the patio. Cincinnati Children's Hospital had set up an outdoor play area overlooking a portion of the Clifton area and medical campuses. We enjoyed the view and embraced the warm weather. For a minute, things seemed almost normal, or at least more so than they had felt in weeks.

After the outdoor time, we returned to the room and I sat in my usual chair and took a moment to reflect. We were still in the large suite that had been our home during a lot of unpleasant events over the last few weeks. I looked around the room and thought of all that had taken place in the confines of that space. This is where the nurses had held Katie down as they peeled the tape from her back in the agonizing ritual that had become all too common. It's where, for a number of days, she'd had to remain still as the doctors aimed for the right position of the lumbar drain so it wouldn't throw her into a tailspin of nausea and pain. It's where the Omnimax 3000 pumped her veins so full of powerful medicines that they imploded, and the doctors had to insert a heavy-duty internal I-V line in to withstand the course of antibiotics. At one point the only usable vein was near her ankle, and over the course of the last few weeks she'd had needles coming out of every limb in her body. As I looked around the room, I could almost hear her silent screams as Katie endured day after day of her ordeal.

I looked at all of the equipment that surrounded us. Trying to imagine the price tag of the medical marvels that occupied the room, I couldn't help but notice the carpenter's level still sitting on the table by Katie's bed. Of all the modern medical tools available, the level just seemed so out of place.

Then it hit me. A carpenter! I thought of another carpenter, and there it was again, that warm blanket feeling. *Nicely played, God*, I thought, as my eyes filled with tears, and I was unable to contain the joy that welled inside me.

Later that evening Dr. Crone came by and gave Katie a thorough examination. Her head was wrapped in a similar fashion as her first surgery, but it was clear she was in better shape this time around.

"How ya feeling, kiddo?" Dr. Crone asked as he finished.

"Hungry," Katie said.

"Well, I have something I think you all will like to hear," he said as he turned to Denni and me, whose interest he'd peaked with that comment. His glance returned to Katie.

"I know you've had some difficulty with the whole swallowing thing, but I think we can take that feeding tube out. Would you like that?"

"Yes!" Katie said in her low-volume voice. "I want a cookie!"

"All right. Let's get you a cookie," Dr. Crone said and nodded at the nurse.

Then, in one of the most heartwarming moments of my life, for the first time in days, Katie smiled. It was uneven, as only the left side of her face moved, but it was the most beautiful smile I'd ever seen. I could sense Jesus the Carpenter smiling too.

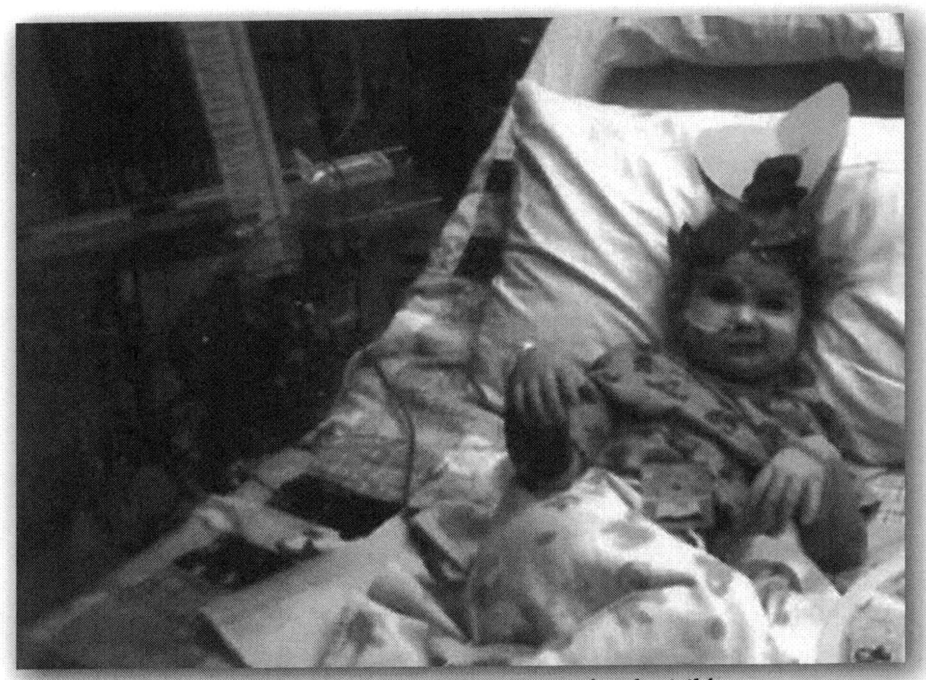

Katie Proctor with the carpenter's level, visible on the table next to her hospital bed.

CHAPTER 26

Conditional Release February 28, 2000

§

To: Friends of Katie
From: Rob & Denni
Date: Monday, February 28, 2000

We're sorry for the late update but Katie's room has been a hub of activity, and we wanted to be sure about a few things before sending another update.

We were all very concerned whether the third surgery would be too much for her to handle. Although we had some tense moments, Katie has shown us not only could she handle it, but also that she has recovered rapidly since then. Katie is doing much better. The roller-coaster seems to have smoothed out a bit. Katie has hit several key objectives in her recovery. The biggest and most important is that four days after the surgery still no leaks! Her dressing looks clean with no signs of infection. She has taken a few steps, but that is still a fairly painful process.

Another huge improvement is that they removed her feeding tube - YEAH! We still have some issues there, but Katie hated the tube down her throat, and Dr. Crone thought it would be good for both her mental and physical health to get it out. She was so happy to get that thing out and was even happier to be able to eat a cookie!

> As she enters her third week on the heavy-duty antibiotics, her temperature has returned to normal and she is much more comfortable. In fact, we got to see Katie smile, something she hadn't felt like doing for the past couple of weeks. She lit up the whole floor with the most incredible smile you've ever seen!
>
> This past week was especially rough, and we appreciate the prayers and support from all of you. We hope and pray that Katie has finally turned that elusive corner! We're so grateful – to God and to you guys. And please keep on praying. You are doing a great job!
>
> Rob, Denni, and Katie

From the onset, the Katie Updates had hit home with a number of our family and friends. And over the course of the past few weeks, the network had widened through the power of the Internet as the message spread. Katie's name had been added to countless prayer chains and church groups, and we were getting responses from almost every state in the country.

I appreciated the sentiments, and although it was impossible to answer them all due to the sheer number of emails, reading them helped me on several levels. It helped pass the time, as day after day in the hospital could be incredibly monotonous. Many people shared work and local news and gossip which allowed for a nice escape from our reality. In addition, the outpouring of concern was touching, and the sentiments showed just how much an ill child could pull at the heart strings of people, no matter how close or distant the relationship.

I could tell there was a difference in a few of the messages. Most all of them offered support and comfort. And some of the messages hinted at faith, but in a veiled message. They had phrases like, "The Big Guy is looking over you," or similar themes. But a few of the messages came from friends and colleagues who appeared to be deeper into their faith journey, and those had a different tone.

"I can only imagine how hard this is, but you have to trust that God is in control."

"The most important thing we can do is offer you our prayers and support. We're praying endlessly - please know that. But know that God has Katie and you and Denni firmly in His grasp. And as much as you love Katie, He loves her more."

"Keep looking up my friend; that is where the true strength lies."

"Praise the Lord... Kate is an awesome kid, you are awesome parents, but most important, God is an awesome God."

On Tuesday morning, Dr. Crone made his usual rounds. Katie's condition had continued to improve significantly. Every twenty-four hours marked notable progress, and her energy level, appetite, and mobility were all miles ahead of where they were just a few days prior.

"Holy smokes, look at you!" Dr. Crone said, as he gave Katie the once over. "If I didn't know better, I'd say you were ready to get out of here."

"Don't tease me," I said. "The last time we talked seriously about going home, I ended up having to buy more underwear."

"Not this time," Dr. Crone said, by now used to my random attempts at humor.

"I think she's stable and after over a month in this setting it would do her and you a world of good to get out of the hospital. I'll release her with one condition."

"What's that?" I asked.

"I'd like for you to stick around Cincinnati this week. You're still staying at your dad's house, right?" he asked, looking at Denni.

Denni nodded.

"Katie can come in for her therapies and we'll keep an eye on her through the rest of the week. If everything goes according to plan you can head back to Michigan by the end of the weekend. Is that a deal?"

"We'll take it!" I said.

"Oh, there is one other thing," Dr. Crone said. "You're going to have to give Katie her medicines through her I-V line. We'll give her a portable manifold and the nurses will come by before you leave today to show you how to do the Betadine scrub and how to administer the syringes. We'll try her on some oral versions of a couple of her meds and see how she does. We need her to finish out the entire course of the antibiotics, but you can do that from Michigan."

"Piece of cake," I lied. The thought of giving my daughter heavy duty antibiotics made me more than a little nervous.

Dr. Crone sensed the anxiety. "You'll do fine. Plus, I know Denni's in charge." Dr. Crone said with a smile as he headed toward the door to start the discharge process.

"Oh, no, you don't!" Denni said.

"What was I thinking?" Dr. Crone said, as he turned and opened his arms to await the impending rush of Denni, who was all too excited to give the good doctor a happy and heartfelt hug.

"I think I'm going to miss those," he said as he finally made it through the doorway.

To: Friends of Katie
From: Rob & Denni Proctor
Date: Tuesday, February 29, 2000
Re: Katie Update

You asked for more good news, and you've got it! Katie is being released from Children's Hospital! The doctors thought it would be good for Katie's mental and physical health to leave the hospital. The only condition is that we stick around Cincinnati awhile longer - at least through the end of the week.

Katie is leaving the hospital with her PICC line, and what appears to be enough medication for a small army. Nurses Mom and Dad will be administering the medications. Before you panic, we're receiving hands-on training prior to leaving the hospital. They even let us practice on a doll.

Katie did get one piece of news this week that she wasn't happy about. Much to her dismay, Katie found out that she'll be having a baby brother sometime this summer. She was so upset she cried! She really, really wanted a sister! But we know she'll love her brother, and that she'll make a great big sister when the time comes.

We appreciate the prayers and support. Thanks again to all of you and the biggest thanks to a wonderful and awesome God!

Hopefully, the next update will be from Michigan!

Rob, Denni & Katie

Back at David and Holly's house, Katie was settling into her new non-hospital routine, except for one thing. The oral version of Rifampin was so putrid that the first dose of the fluorescent red medicine ended up all over the white walls of the guest room. So did the second, and a quick revision to the program was made and that drug, too, was administered through the I-V manifold.

We made the daily ten-mile trek to Children's for Katie's therapies. Katie had physical therapy for the large arm and leg muscles, occupational therapy for the fine motor and facial muscles, and speech therapy for the vocal cords and throat. Like a trooper, Katie obeyed all of the commands of the therapists.

"Katie, close your eyes, honey," the therapist said as Katie stood in front of us, shoulders slumped and her left eye firmly closed.

"I see you!" I said to Katie as I poked her in the belly.

"I see you too, Daddy!" Katie said as her right eye remained almost completely open in spite of her efforts to close it.

It was a double disappointment, as Katie's voice was still whisper-like. I just looked at the therapist, who nodded and said, "It's still early." That was a small consolation.

Now that she wasn't confined to a hospital bed, Katie spent her time playing with some of the many toys and presents she'd received. Denni and I did our best to play nurse, and David and Holly enjoyed spending time with their granddaughter.

Katie took a break from playing and crawled up on Holly's lap for a back rub, her I-V in tow. Holly rubbed her back, careful not to disturb the I-V in Katie's arm, or come close to touching the large scar that ran from her neck up the back of her head. Katie drifted off to sleep as the adults carried on a conversation.

"We've decided a few things and want to share it with you," Holly said, looking at David as though they'd already had this conversation, at least with themselves.

"Before we got the news of Katie's diagnosis, we had planned the Hawaiian trip on the Big Island this year. You know Dave and I go there every year and the more time we've spent there, the more we like it. We hadn't shared this with anyone, but on the last trip, we looked at some property as a potential home base for at least half the year, and maybe longer depending on how things worked out."

"Wow, that sounds awesome," Denni said.

"Well, when we got the call about Katie's condition getting worse and we knew we needed to get back to Cincinnati, we realized just how far away Hawaii is. We've decided for the time being at least, we'll stick with our timeshare and leave it at that. You can come and visit us but we want to be here in Cincinnati, closer to you guys."

"I appreciate that, but I don't want you to give up something you love," Denni said.

"Oh, we're not," Holly said. "You know your father. He does what he wants. But things like this make you realize pretty quickly what is important and who you love."

"My goodness, I certainly hope so," Denni replied, and gave her Dad and me a glance. "And Rob promised to take all of us to Hawaii, so we'll take you up on that visit."

"I promised *what*?" I said with a tone of disbelief.

"You know you promised Katie you'd take her to Hawaii. And if you don't, there's a tidy little room in Hell waiting for you, mister."

"I suppose you're right on that one," I agreed. "Hawaii versus Hell. I think I'll take Hawaii."

CHAPTER 27

There's No Place Like Home March 2000

ON THE MORNING OF SUNDAY, March 5, almost six weeks after heading to Cincinnati, we said thank you and goodbye to Dr. Crone, the staff at Children's Hospital, David and Holly, and Denni's mom and siblings. We quickly loaded up the Tahoe with our luggage, a large amount of medical supplies, and a ton of gifts. And one special passenger, the toughest kid on the planet and my new hero, Katie Proctor. It was fitting that we went through a significant snowstorm on the six-hour trip home. I thought, *Oh, yeah, Mother Nature, that's all you've got? With what we've been through, you're gonna have to come up with something better than this.*

I felt incredible relief as I pulled the car into the driveway back home in Allegan. I wasn't sure who was happier to see whom, Katie or her dog Rocky. In any event, we were home at last!

"Rocky!" Katie squealed as she came through the door. The ten-year-old boxer turned into a puppy again, and his body wiggled with so much excitement that he peed on the floor.

I had been at the house just a few weeks earlier, even if only for a short time. But the house felt different somehow. Not better or worse, just different. Denni and I both knew that life from this point on would not be the same. It was the great unknown and though we had embraced the "one day at a time" philosophy, it was different now that Katie was out of the hospital. What it looked like from here was anybody's guess.

As we lay in bed that night, Denni brought up the trip home.

"I can't help but notice on the drive home you had some Christian radio stations playing," she said. "And once or twice, I could have sworn you mouthed the lyrics to a few of the songs. That's new, and I like it, but when did this come about?"

"What do you want me to say? Obviously, if something like this doesn't get my attention, nothing will," I responded. "You've had a strong sense of faith since I've known you. You don't just go through the motions. I know it's been real for you. I always believed, and you know that. But I haven't exactly been demonstrating the behaviors of a true Christian. I know God's had his hand in this from the beginning. I still need to find my way through it, but at least I think I'm pointed in the right direction."

I think Denni had sensed it, but I could tell she was happy to hear the words coming out of my mouth.

"I'm happy for you, and proud," she said. "God's wanted you to come to Him forever. In fact, He's always been there. *He* never moved, *you* did."

CHAPTER 28

Through the Looking Glass April 2000

BACK IN ALLEGAN, WE FOCUSED on getting into a routine. After only a few days of being home, Katie woke up one morning with a slight fever and pain in her neck. We took one look at her incision and rushed Katie to the doctor's office. It was one of our first forays into virtual medicine. Dr. Crone had us take a digital picture of the back of Katie's head. We had received a digital camera as a hospital gift and its whopping two-megapixel capability was state of the art at the time. We sent the picture to Dr. Crone who reviewed it and talked with the pediatrician in Michigan before proceeding.

The doctor pulled on a purple stitch sticking through the skin on the back of Katie's head, and out gushed the dreaded fluid again. It was a remnant of the meningitis infection that was still trying to attack Katie. Fortunately, Dr. Crone had taken the extra measure of sewing in the mesh that kept the infection outside of Katie's brain, so it was easily treated.

Friends and neighbors came by in a chaotic frenzy of joy and celebration. Our friends in Allegan were truly happy that Katie had come home. Judi McCall, our next-door neighbor, was beside herself. Several of Katie's playmates came by for short visits.

"Katie!" one of the children shouted as Katie and I made our way into the door of The Looking Glass, Katie's pre-school in Kalamazoo. Katie wasn't due to return for a few days, but Denni had reached out to the director and they agreed it would be a good idea for her to come for a visit to help her get reacquainted with the other children. Katie held my hand and smiled at the other kids. The teacher clapped her hands and said, "Let's get in a circle and we can share what we've been up to while Katie was out. And if she wants to share anything with us, she can."

The kids told Katie of the goings-on in their world: new games at recess, a rather graphic recap of one of the kids getting sick on the playground, and a new song they were learning. When the conversation lulled, the teacher looked at Katie and me and said, "If you want to share anything, that's fine, and if you don't, that's fine too."

"Do you want to say something, Katie?" I asked.

Katie did her familiar routine of melting into my side, tucking her head against my leg. She wasn't much for talking in these situations, especially about herself.

"You, Daddy," she said, pointing her finger at me as the prompt to speak.

"OK, as you know Katie has been gone for a while, hasn't she?" I asked, trying to channel my inner kindergarten teacher mode. "It's because she's been sick. In fact, she was very sick."

"What was wrong?" one of the kids asked.

"Well, you all have a brain inside your head, right?" I asked in a rhetorical tone as the kids nodded and some pointed to their head.

"Katie had what's called a tumor in her brain, and the doctors needed to get it out. A tumor is a lump that's not supposed to be there. And if you don't get it out of your brain, it can do really bad things. The doctor made a big cut in the back of Katie's head and took most of it out. Then she needed to be in the hospital for a while so she could get all better and come back to The Looking Glass with you."

"Did it hurt?" one of the kids asked and Katie nodded her head up and down. Katie had her hair in pigtails and one of the boys moved around the side of Katie so he could see the back of her head.

"Ewww," he said.

Katie looked at me, not sure of what to do.

"Does that look like it would hurt?" I asked the little boy, and he and a few other kids nodded.

"It hurt a lot," I said, "but the doctor had to do that to get the tumor out. And Katie had a lot of needles. Those hurt too, don't they?"

"They sting!" a boy said as he poked his finger into his leg.

"Yes, they do," I agreed. "But hopefully Katie's all done with surgeries and needles and all that stuff. Katie's hair will grow back and after a while you won't see much of it," I said as I patted her shoulder and she looked up at me and grinned.

"Have any of you had surgery?" I inquired, thinking it might help the kids relate to Katie.

"I had my tonsils out and I had to stay overnight in the hospital," a little girl said.

"Were you scared?" the teacher asked.

"A little, but I got to go home the next day and my daddy got me a big playhouse."

"To her mother and me it seemed even longer, but Katie was in the hospital over a month," I said. "I can tell you she's been through a lot. But now she's home and she wants to come back to The Looking Glass. Is that OK with you?"

"Yes," said Lindsay, one of Katie's playmates. "We missed you, Katie."

Katie tucked herself further against my side again and smiled. And that was it. The re-bonding session was complete.

"OK, let's figure this out," Denni said as she laid some papers on my desk. Denni was in her element when there were lists to compile and schedules to organize. Although I'm organized in my own way, my efforts pale in comparison to the robust systems Denni has developed. I readily admitted this was clearly one of those times to have Denni take the lead. Katie had physical therapy, occupational therapy and speech therapy four days a week at Bronson Hospital in Kalamazoo, thirty-five miles from Allegan. All things considered, it was the logical place for her to receive treatment.

"I've already talked to Larry," Denni said referring to her boss at Perrigo. "He's been incredibly understanding and I'm going to go part-time, at least while she's receiving so much treatment. I can take her to most of her appointments, but there will be times when I'll drop her off and you can bring her home."

"My boss has said the same thing," I added. "Bob said to figure out what worked for us and make it happen. I have no doubt you'll come up with the most efficient master plan in the history of master plans," I said wryly, never passing on an opportunity to comment on Denni's passion for organizing things.

"Yes, I will," Denni replied, knowing full well of my intended sarcasm, but internally beaming at the planning process playing out before her. The logistical ramifications of therapy appointments four times a week were significant, but I had to give Denni credit. We began to incorporate her plans into the daily and weekly routine and it actually became manageable.

The therapy sessions were intense. For her speech therapy, Katie was placed in front of a mirror and she would try to say different words and change the tone and volume of her voice. The physical and occupational therapy were far more interesting. In one exercise, Katie was placed on a hanging swing and the therapist would spin her - incredibly fast. Then the therapist would stop the swing and Katie would attempt to gain her bearings as quickly as possible. Initially, when the swing stopped, Katie's eyes would vibrate back and forth so fast it was clear she had no control over it. It made me dizzy just watching her. While her physical movements continued to make improvements that were visible to everyone, the shallow voice and facial paralysis remained unchanged.

To: Friends of Katie
From: Rob & Denni Proctor
Date: Tuesday, April 14, 2000
Re: Katie Update

Just like Dr. Crone said, Katie's recovery since coming home has been remarkable. She still tires easily, but walks much better and can even go up and down some steps by herself. Katie is writing, drawing, and painting with her left hand now. She was right-handed prior to the surgery.

She started speech, occupational and physical therapy four days a week at Bronson Hospital in Kalamazoo. We have to admit that juggling all those appointments and running back between Allegan and Kalamazoo has been a bit challenging. To all of you who've helped us with incredible meals or other acts of kindness, we thank you from the bottom of our hearts.

Katie and Rob visited her pre-school "The Looking Glass," and were overwhelmed by the greeting. Katie starts back school part-time this week, and we are very excited about that. Several of Katie's playmates have stopped over for short visits, and she enjoyed each and every one.

We have the first follow up MRI scan in Cincinnati on May 8. Obviously, we are praying that whatever remains of the tumor just stays put - forever!

Thanks again for everything! God bless you all!!!!!

Denni, Rob & Katie

With the hectic schedule of work and therapies, Denni and I quickly discovered that about the only time we could catch up was at bedtime. Denni had made a rule early on in our marriage; there was to be no TV in the bedroom. She used to tease me that this was the only place where she could get my undivided attention, and I have to admit, she had a point. The bedroom became the place we did a lot of our communicating.

"Have you noticed anything about the way Katie plays?" Denni asked.

"What do you mean?" I asked?

"I mean have you noticed anything in particular about the games she plays and how she uses her toys?"

"You mean that everything she does has something medical attached to it? Like the fact that every stuffed animal has a horrible disease and every Barbie doll is in need of brain surgery? No, I hadn't noticed," I added sarcastically.

"I know the staff at Children's said that it would take a while for Katie to figure out some things," Denni replied. "I'm just curious to see if it lasts. And it's one thing when she plays like that by herself, but it's different with her friends. So far the kids and even the parents have been really great about it, but it has been kind of intense."

"Ya think?" I said. "I thought Ashley Melvin was going to freak out the other day. Katie used her real stethoscope and reflex hammer to give her an examination. She wrapped up Ashley's arm with an Ace bandage and Ashley played along fine. Then Katie told her she needed a shot, and pulled out a real syringe. It took Ashley a couple of seconds to realize there wasn't a needle on the end of the syringe, but until then her eyes were as wide as dinner plates."

"And do you notice who her medical assistant is?" Denni asked me.

"Dakota," I replied. "It's always Dakota."

"I think that stuffed animal means more to Katie than anyone would ever imagine. She's told everyone that Dakota was with her in the operating room. And she knows I wasn't…" Denni's voice drifted off.

"You've got to stop doing that," I said. "Katie doesn't understand a lot of this, but she knows you were there. You know that, too, and beating yourself up isn't going to get you anywhere."

"I know," Denni said. "But I'm a mom. I'm *her* mom."

"Yes, you are," I interrupted, attempting to shut down the conversation once and for all. "You're the best mom she could ever have and Katie knows it. In a few more months, you're going to be the best mom to that little boy who'll be joining us. And if you're lucky, he'll be just like me!" I kidded.

"Oh God, that's *just* what we need," Denni said.

As May approached, the three of us were getting nervous for the big upcoming event. For me and Denni, it was nerves over Katie's first follow up MRI scan in Cincinnati. For Katie, it was something far more important - her dance recital.

A lot of thoughts were going through my head. In the car on my way to work, in the middle of meetings, and when I tried to go to sleep at night, I had Katie in my thoughts. I tried to remain positive, but sometimes it was difficult. A few times at work I needed to excuse myself from whatever was happening at the moment to gain control of my emotions. Sometimes

I won the battle, and sometimes I didn't. And for the first time in my life, at times I felt like crying.

I never really cried much growing up. Not because I was tough or macho, but simply because I didn't have a lot to cry about outside of my brother punching me, which I usually deserved. But now I found myself welling up with emotion. Sometimes it came out of nowhere and I struggled, as this was new territory for me. On the one hand, I felt a sense of embarrassment, as if I wasn't holding up my "head of the family" obligation. On the other hand, I thought that perhaps we really weren't built to handle all life throws at us, and considering everything that was going on, I was well within my rights to have emotional tantrums every now and then.

Either way, a part of me that I had not previously been aware of was now part of the new me. I wasn't sure how I felt about it, but in comparison to all that Katie had to deal with, I figured my issues were small potatoes. Tiny, tiny potatoes.

CHAPTER 29

A Little Communication May 2000

THROUGHOUT THE COURSE OF MY life I've been in a few stressful situations, but overall, I'd say my stress has been pretty minimal. In the fall of 1999 I'd begun to experience an increased sense of stress. I couldn't put my finger on it, but I had a feeling that something just wasn't right. I didn't tell Denni about it right away, but I could feel its presence.

In October 1999, my grandma Mimi Pritchard died at the age of one hundred and two. I was very close to my grandma, and I truly felt sad at her passing. But as I sat at her funeral, I suddenly felt a dull ache and a very strong sense of anxiety. I tried to focus and figure out its source.

"This isn't it," I said to myself, thinking of my grandma's passing. Whatever was causing my stress, her death wasn't it. Less than three months later, my daughter was diagnosed with a brain tumor. Dang those premonitions!

In my new world, complete with brain tumors and cancer and things that would normally make one feel bad and sad, there were also many times when I felt surprisingly at peace, although I never assumed it would be a guarantee that everything would work out in the end. Or at least not necessarily a guarantee that it would work out the way Denni and I wanted it to. But in spite of the stress that accompanied the situation, I felt a sense of peace and calm nonetheless. It was a sense of God in the form of a personal relationship that I'd never felt before. It was quite a feeling to say the least.

I found myself getting into a new spiritual routine. I had prayed at various times during my life but never daily, until now. Every morning as I started my commute and exited Allegan on the way to Kalamazoo, I'd recite a prayer. Oftentimes I would start with the Lord's Prayer and then frequently I'd ad-lib some material of my own.

"Dear God, thank you for today. Thanks for letting Denni, Katie, and me be a family. Thanks for saving Katie from her brain tumor, and please watch over her and keep her healthy. Or at least as healthy as one can be with a brain tumor."

My prayers added other bits and pieces depending on my mood, and extended from specific individuals such as family and friends, to large groups, such as the oppressed, poor and sick. I occasionally would throw in a political prayer - "Lord, please help our politicians not be idiots." Even though logic dictated God wasn't political nor did He show favorites, I was convinced if He did take sides, God would most definitely be a Conservative Republican and a Minnesota Vikings fan.

I had offered up prayers at various points in my life, but prior to my recently emboldened desire to have a personal relationship with God, my prayers were more about reciting the "right" words. It was almost like I was trying to get the Genie out of the bottle. But now it felt like I was talking with God. In some ways, my prayers certainly sounded like prayers, but over time they were just as much a conversation as they were a prayer. To me, it was overwhelming that God, who I firmly believe created everything - the Father of all creation - allowed me to have a personal conversation with him.

Whether it was a prayer or a conversation, it became a habit, and after a while it felt strange if I didn't talk with God at some point in the day. It felt like that was a big part of the relationship. My wife had said for years, "a little communication goes a long way." I guess that's also true in our relationship with God.

CHAPTER 30

Door Number Three May 2000

§

"ARE YOU READY TO GO to Cincinnati?" I asked Katie as we ate breakfast.

"I guess so," she answered. Katie was still too young to grasp most of what was going on, but she did grasp some of it.

"Am I going to get a needle?" Katie asked, and I could tell she was desperately hoping the answer would be "no."

"Yes, honey, I'm afraid you are," I answered truthfully. Denni and I tried to be as open and honest with Katie as we could. We figured she deserved it and often gave her just the basic factual information to see how that landed before going into detail.

Katie's eyes welled with water.

"I don't want a needle," she said in her still whisper-like voice.

"I know you don't, sweetie. They sting, don't they?" I asked. The conversations seemed healthier when we admitted some of the realities rather than glossing over them.

"Uh-huh." Katie added and pushed her cereal around in the bowl.

"I tell you what," Denni spoke up. "That's still a few days away, and in the meantime, you have your dance recital, and your grandparents are coming to visit. It's pretty cool that everyone is coming to Allegan for your recital and hopefully all that fun will make up for that stupid needle. OK?"

"OK, Mommy." Katie looked at her mom with her paralyzed face and did her best to smile. It was a crooked smile, but still a smile, one both her mother and I loved more than any other in the whole world.

What a trooper, I thought.

At Children's Hospital in the prep room, the doctors followed many of the same procedures as they did for the MRI scans several months prior. The nurse measured and weighed Katie.

"You're a peanut, aren't you, sweetie?" the nurse said as she recorded the numbers. Katie just looked at Denni.

"How much does she weigh?" Denni asked. Moms always seemed to be fascinated with weight - their own and their children's.

"Just under twenty-nine pounds." The nurse answered Denni's next question before she could even ask it. "That puts her in the fifth percentile," the nurse said. Ninety-five percent of kids her age weighed more than Katie.

The anesthesiologist arrived to explain the process.

"We'll sedate her with Nembutal and it'll keep Katie asleep for the ninety minutes or so that we need to take a full set of pictures of her spine and brain. About half-way through, we'll inject the contrast in the same I-V line so she won't have to get another needle."

"I think I know, but what's the contrast going to do?" Denni asked. A teacher at heart and by trade, her inquisitive mind and self-confidence made it easy for her to ask questions and she always wanted to learn. It's one of the things I've admired most about her.

The radiologist fielded the question.

"After we take some regular scan images we'll pull her out of the machine and inject the contrast dye into her I-V. We use gadolinium and it's very safe. We use it for patients who have a history of cancer, and it also can help us find infection."

"We know about infection," I said. "Katie got meningitis and it about knocked her down for the count."

"Yes, it'll do that," the doctor agreed. "I read her records and we have all of her scans, including the ones we took before Dr. Crone's surgery and the ones the day after." The doctor looked at Katie.

"All you have to do is lay there and go to sleep, OK?" the doctor said in a very comforting tone. We were impressed with Children's during the first stay, and we could see why they earned their reputation as one of the top children's hospitals in the country.

The nurse had given us a pager to let us know when the scans were completed. Two hours later it went off, and Denni and I returned from the cafeteria to the Radiology recovery room. Katie was still asleep, but the nurse was trying to rouse her as we approached the bed. It took several tries, and Katie came out of the anesthesia very slowly over the next thirty minutes. After trying to sit her up and failing, we tried to get Katie to respond to questions; easy ones with one word answers. That too, failed, and Denni asked the nurse if we should just let her sleep, although it was more of a rhetorical question from Denni's perspective.

"No, the quicker you can get her out of this, the better."

I recognized Denni's look of determination. It was the same look as she had a few months earlier, when the dietician was telling her about Katie's dietary needs in the initial attempts with the feeding tube process. Fortunately, there was no standoff and Katie awoke from the anesthesia.

I leaned over Katie and started to say something and in an instant Katie's hand shot towards my face and my glasses went flying to the other side of the room. Stunned, I went to retrieve my glasses and found them to be wearable, but the frame was broken.

"Didn't see that coming," I said and rubbed the bridge of my nose. "That kid's stronger than she looks!" I couldn't tell for sure, but I suspected the nurse seemed quite entertained by the sucker punch.

Several hours later, Dr. Crone came in with his assistant Mimi. He shook hands with us and we had some small talk about the trip from Michigan. Then Dr. Crone sat in his chair in front of the X-Ray screen and plopped a set of films in the machine.

"I think the scans are good," Dr. Crone said. "If there's any growth at all, I'd say it's negligible. The radiologist and I aren't in total agreement but I'd say the growth is less than three millimeters if that much."

"So that's good," Denni said in a tone that clearly required verification.

"Yes, it is," Dr. Crone replied. "Let me examine Katie, and then we can discuss these in detail."

What followed was an incredibly lengthy and thorough examination in which Dr. Crone had Katie complete a number of neurological and physical tests. In addition, he looked at the scar on the back of her head and examined her eyes and throat. He had Katie say a few words, which she did in her very soft voice. After the physical exam, Katie sat on the floor and dug into a coloring book. Dr. Crone turned his attention to us.

"I removed eighty to eighty-five percent of the tumor and I'm comfortable that what remains is stable. It's a low-grade solid tumor and it can do a few things. It can linger on indefinitely in this state, grow back, or shrink up and go away.

I had to chime in - "I'll take door number three - shrink up and go away."

He managed a smile and said, "Yes, we all want that. I'll see you in six months for another scan."

"Is that the normal time frame?" Denni asked, looking over her list of questions. Dr. Crone had answered many of them but in terms of thoroughness, the good doctor had met his match in Denni Proctor.

"Yes, six months is pretty typical with low grade brain stem gliomas. We'll keep our eye on it, and if it stays stable like this for a few years, we can probably extend to a year between scans."

"What about Katie's face and her voice?" Denni asked. She was pleased about the MRI scan, but she wanted answers about Katie's facial and vocal paralysis.

"I still don't think those nerves were destroyed," Dr. Crone said. "I've seen instances where it's been over a year before the function returned, so

I'm not giving up hope yet. I know you're doing the therapies in Michigan. In fact, she's had a lot of therapy."

"You could say that," I added dryly. "Four days a week."

"Well, keep at it. Time will tell," Dr. Crone said. "There's not much more we can do but have her go through the therapies and wait. All in all, I think things are about as good as can be expected." He looked at Katie. "I'll see you in six months, OK, Katie? You still like me, right?" the doctor asked his patient.

"Uh-huh," Katie said, and managed a crooked smile.

I shook his hand, and Denni gave Dr. Crone the now obligatory hug.

On our way out of the exam room, we took a different route to the lobby, and happened to pass Dr. Crone's personal office. In all of the time we were at Children's, we'd never seen it before. I froze in my tracks when I saw the sign directly over Dr. Crone's doorway. In big bold letters read the following: PRAYER CHANGES EVERYTHING

Denni and I smiled at each other and we made our way to the lobby.

In the car, Denni gave a sigh of relief and I assessed the situation.

"One down. I get the feeling we'll be living life one MRI scan at a time for a while," I said.

Denni agreed. We stopped at Izzy's, a delicatessen in downtown Cincinnati. It had been a long day, and we both craved one of Izzy's famous potato pancakes. They were a deep-fried heart attack in waiting, but both of us needed a fix.

As Katie sat and colored quietly in the booth, Denni took out her journal. Since the beginning of our ordeal, Denni made journal entries every so often. Some included her thoughts and observations, other times she wrote down medical questions to ask, and sometimes she used it as a way to write about her faith journey. As Denni wrote, I leaned over and looked at the notes she was jotting.

Nembutal - nurse woke Katie up too early. Broke Rob's glasses.

"Katie, I can't believe you broke my glasses. I'm going to start calling you Rocky because you're a boxer!" I said as Denni looked at me with scrunched up eyes.

"I broke your glasses?" Katie asked, clearly unable to remember. "I'm sorry," she said.

"That's OK, sweetheart," I said. "Now I can get a cool new pair. So really, I ought to thank you."

"You're welcome," Katie replied, and drank her milkshake.

"Nembutal," I said. "It reminds me of happy hour in college. You get all goofy and do crazy things. Then you can't remember it," I said.

To: Friends of Katie
From: Rob & Denni Proctor
Date: Wednesday, May 10, 2000
Re: Katie Update

Excellent news, folks! Katie has made it through her first follow up MRI scans with very little sign of growth in the remaining tumor! Dr. Crone feels the remaining twenty percent of the tumor looks pretty much the same as it did after surgery, with growth of three millimeters or less. We don't have to see him again until November! This was great news for Katie, who was not too thrilled with all of the needles and scopes she endured this week.

Her physical well-being is miles ahead of when she got out of the hospital. She goes to pre-school three days a week and has returned to dance class and gymnastics. She is excited about her dance recital later this month, and is also getting excited about her baby brother due this August. She does most things you would expect a four-and-a-half-year-old little girl to do, and we're trying to make things as "normal" as we can.

The swallowing and vocal cords continue to be an issue. She has frequent choking episodes and there are no signs of improvement in the vocal cord paralysis, so her voice is still faint. Katie has physical, speech, and occupational therapies four days a week. The right side of her face is still swollen and frozen, and her right eye doesn't close unless she is sleeping.

Our family and friends have been extremely helpful. Our neighbor Judi McCall has helped out in so many ways we can't even begin to thank her. Katie's pre-school and dance class have been fantastic about getting her back into their very caring environments.

The power of prayer has worked wonders for us so far! Thank you for your prayers and support. We really appreciate it.

God bless you all. He certainly has blessed us!

Rob, Denni & Katie Proctor

PART III
The New Normal

CHAPTER 31

The New Normal Summer 2000

IT WAS EARLY ONE MORNING when I heard the familiar sound as I walked towards Katie's room. By the time I entered the room, Katie was sitting up in bed with vomit all over the front of her PJs and on her bedspread. She was shaking.

"Oh, honey," I said, "Let's get you to the bathroom." I could hear Denni coming down the hall.

"I got it. I'll clean it up," I said. That was Denni's cue not to come in and see the mess. Denni's Achilles' heel was that when Katie, or anyone within ear shot, threw up, it often caused her to gag, and on occasion, get sick herself. She picked a fine family to have that trait.

Despite my character flaws, I do have one shining attribute that has proven to be incredibly useful in this family. Throw up, vomit, puke - whatever you call it, it really doesn't bother me. It doesn't bother me listening to the event, helping the person experiencing it, or cleaning up at the end. I have to think that I've been blessed with this special skill set for a reason. Maybe it's a God thing.

As was the case in a few of the episodes before Katie's diagnosis, the vomiting didn't stop. Every fifteen to thirty minutes, she would get sick to her stomach. Denni and I looked at each other, both of us with the "what should we do?" look in our eyes.

"I'm calling the doctor," Denni said. "I know we just saw Doctor Crone last month, but I'm tempted to take her back down to Cincinnati," Denni said.

"Why don't we call Mimi and talk through it?" I offered. Dr. Crone's assistant Mimi confirmed that while the vomiting was something to keep an eye on, it didn't mean there was anything going on with the tumor. Mimi instructed us to look for a fever, altered gait, and severe headaches in addition to the vomiting. We had seen none of those symptoms, which provided some relief.

Four hours and two doses of Zofran later, the vomiting subsided.

This was the first of several episodes over the course of the summer, and was apparently part of our new normal.

CHAPTER 32

Squirreltales Summer 2000

As I ATTEMPTED TO GET information on Katie's tumor, I found plenty of websites related to pediatric cancer. There were a number of groups and websites that offered support for patients and their families. I became acquainted with one website in particular, Squirreltales.org.

I logged onto Squirreltales mainly out of curiosity, but once I navigated through the site I was hooked. I found an abundance of information on all types of pediatric cancers - Leukemia, Non-Hodgkin's Lymphoma, Ewing's Sarcoma, Neuroblastoma, and of course, brain tumors. One side of the webpage had references for parents and patients, as well as links to hospitals and clinical trials. It was the other side of the screen that really caught my attention.

A "Scrapbook" section featured pictures of kids fighting cancer. Below that was a "Humor" section, where I found an article entitled "How You Know You're the Parent of a Kid with Cancer", and it included a list of things like "Your house looks like a Toys R Us warehouse." And, "You know there's no such thing as too many vomit buckets in your home." I related to many of the items on the list, and was glad to see other people trying to find humor wherever possible.

It was the "Caring Journal" section on the website that I wasn't prepared for. It's where parents of kids with cancers documented their child's journey. Often, the journal would include the child's picture. I noticed many of the children had a picture of an angel by their name, which meant the child had lost their cancer battle.

I started reading and lost count of the number of times I was moved to tears. All too often, the entries documented an up-and-down journey, further highlighting what a cruel disease cancer is.

"Yay!!! Jacob's in remission - his cell counts are normal. We're cancer free and home for the holidays!" The mother had written the entry in December 1997. In February 1999, there was another entry.

"My heart is broken. My precious Jacob's cancer has returned and it's much worse. It has spread and the doctors tell us it's just a matter of time. This is so unfair – he's only seven years old."

In June of 1999, there was a final entry.

"Jacob got his Angel's wings yesterday. I held him in my arms as he took his last breath. As his mother, I couldn't let him leave any other way. He was in so much pain, but not anymore. Now I am the one in pain. I will never recover from this. Ever."

I had to pause to wipe my eyes as I read. I thought of my most recent Katie Update. "Yay! Katie's tumor is stable…" I stopped myself. *I can't go down this path.*

I corresponded back and forth with several of the parents, mostly mothers. A few wrote back and we often exchanged messages of encouragement. A handful of fathers corresponded as well. This was new territory we had all wandered into. Everyone was searching for the same thing - comfort. Some days I found incredible comfort on the Squirreltales site. On other days, at least there were others who felt a similar despair, and in a strange way, even that notion I found comforting.

CHAPTER 33

Our Gang August 2000

In August 2000, Brian David Proctor was born. As if Denni hadn't suffered enough that year, Brian weighed in at ten pounds, three ounces. We knew Brian was going to be quite a handful. The first time we laid him on the changing table in the hospital room, Brian gave us a glimpse of just how different from Katie he was going to be. I removed his diaper and within a few seconds, Brian shot a stream of pee over his head and directly into my mother-in-law's new Coach purse.

At the end of August, Katie and I left Denni and Brian in Allegan and traveled to Ann Arbor, Michigan, to participate in a fundraising event. The Ride for Kids was a motorcycle rally sponsored by the Pediatric Brain Tumor Foundation (PBTF). I connected with the PBTF at the recommendation of the staff at Children's. The organization was founded in 1984 by Mike Trainor. A newspaper executive in Atlanta, Mike had felt helpless as his friend's son died from a brain tumor, and it motivated him to start the PBTF with the goal of increasing awareness and raising funds for research. The organization had grown throughout the 1980s and 90s to become the largest private funder of pediatric brain tumor research in the country. And since Mike was an avid motorcyclist, he focused on the motorcycle ride as the primary fundraising mechanism.

During a night when Katie was in the midst of her battle with meningitis, I had made a promise to myself to try and do something in the direction of finding a cure for brain tumors. After hearing of the PBTF,

I decided to try and help raise funds for the organization. In early May, Denni and I sent a letter to several hundred friends and acquaintances, mainly from our Christmas newsletter address list. The letter gave a brief synopsis of Katie's brain tumor journey and requested donations for the PBTF. Having never done anything like this before, we'd originally set a goal of $10,000. But by late August when the Ride for Kids event took place in Ann Arbor, donations to the "Gift for Katie Proctor & Friends" drive exceeded $21,000.

I had no idea what to expect as Katie and I pulled off the interstate in Ann Arbor. We noticed a number of motorcyclists in small groups as we neared the national headquarters of Domino's Pizza, the site of the event. A large PBTF Ride for Kids banner and balloons marked the entrance. As I pulled the minivan into the parking lot, we were greeted by a volunteer and a motorcycle policeman.

"Are you here for the ride?" the volunteer asked.

"Yes, we are." I replied. "We've never been here, so I'm not sure what to do."

"Who do you have with you?" he asked, peering into the window.

"This is Katie. Katie Proctor," I answered.

"Is she a Star?" the volunteer asked, who was now joined by another volunteer.

"A Star? Um, I'm not sure," I admitted.

"Is she a survivor?" A woman approached our car, and her name tag led me to conclude she was the wife of the original greeter.

"Yes, she is," I said.

The husband had a megaphone and he announced with great enthusiasm, "One of our Stars, Katie Proctor is here!" As we pulled down the lane, motorcyclists and volunteers clapped and waved.

"Katie, you're a celebrity!" I said, and Katie looked confused.

Several hundred motorcycles cluttered the parking lot, and a number of large tents had been set up for food and registration. More volunteers directed us to the family VIP tent, where we were greeted with equal fanfare. Katie received a green "Star" t-shirt differentiating the brain tumor survivors from the rest of the crowd, and we were both fitted for motorcycle helmets for the ride. Katie and I stood out as novices, as practically everyone else appeared to be an experienced and well-equipped motorcycle rider.

Katie and I walked through the crowd and noticed several other children around Katie's age wearing the green PBTF "Star" t-shirts. As we explored the grounds, we noticed the wide variety of motorcycle groups in attendance. Most of the riders wore full biker gear, with black leather pants, boots, and vests. Many of the vests were adorned with patches from their motorcycle clubs or other ride events. Their backgrounds were varied to say the least. I noticed a number of individuals who, frankly, scared me a bit. Although they may not have been Hells Angels, they certainly looked the part. At the other end of the spectrum was the Christian Motorcycle Club. They, too, had their vests adorned with patches, but most of them said things like, "Jesus rides with me."

In between the rough-and-tumble and Jesus motorcycle groups were a wide variety of motorcycle types. Factory workers, husbands and wives, and others who worked in Corporate America Monday through Friday, but on the weekends, took to the open road on their bikes. Most of the stereotypical biker breed had Harley-Davidsons, while the married crowd was made up of Honda Goldwings. I concluded the Goldwing must be the minivan of the motorcycle world. Honda was the national sponsor for the PBTF and their presence was demonstrated on practically everything connected with the ride.

The "Stars" were placed at the front of the parade. Our motorcycle escort introduced himself as a Vice-President at Domino's Pizza. The squadron of police motorcyclists turned on their lights and sirens and the ride was off and running. From our host's sidecar, both Katie and I looked like deer in the headlights as nearly six hundred and fifty bikers wound their way through the countryside surrounding Ann Arbor.

About twenty-five minutes into the seventy-five-minute ride, I noticed that Katie had leaned back against my chest and had fallen asleep. The required helmet was heavy and had been quite a burden for Katie, so she'd decided to use the ride as an opportunity to get in a nice nap.

Returning to the Domino's headquarters, the bikes parked neatly in rows to begin the "Celebration of Life" portion of the event. Tables of sack lunches donated by Subway were free for the taking, and the bikers devoured their food as classic rock and country music blared through the loudspeakers, and eventually everyone congregated under a huge tent.

PBTF Director Allen Hughes grabbed the microphone and took the stage. After some introductory small talk, a short prayer, and moment of silence for the kids who'd lost their brain tumor battles, he got to the heart of his message.

"We know why we're here. Take a look at these kids in the green shirts. They might be your neighbor's kid, or your nephew, or your own child. And they all share one thing; they've been diagnosed with a brain tumor. Brain tumors are the deadliest form of childhood cancers and we're here to do something about that. And who can tackle a deadly disease like this better than us motorcyclists? Nobody!"

A large "Whoop!" went up from the crowd along with a couple of "Hell Yeahs!" from the biker gang guys.

Allen passed the microphone to a neurosurgeon from the University of Michigan Mott Children's Hospital who spoke for a few minutes about some of the advancements they were making in brain tumor research. She thanked the bikers for their efforts and left the stage, again to much applause.

Then a mom took the stage. She didn't even get her first sentence out before she broke down. Her son had died just a few months earlier, and he attended the event in Ann Arbor the prior year. He was seven years old and fought his brain tumor battle for three years before succumbing. I felt my eyes moisten and looked around. I couldn't help but notice that the bikers, from the Hells Angels to the Corporate Vice-Presidents to the Christian bikers, were tearing up.

She thanked the motorcyclists for their efforts and asked them not to stop with the fundraising efforts until a cure could be found. She closed by saying she would pray for the day when no child or parent had to go through what her son and her family went through. I'd given up trying to stop the flow of tears coming down my cheeks. I really didn't know what to expect going into this event, but I hadn't counted on this.

Allen took the stage again and called all of the Stars to the stage. Katie felt shy and didn't want to go. A fellow Star named Ruth took Katie by the hand and said, "C'mon, you can go with me. It'll be fun, I promise." Katie just looked at me, and after I nodded my approval, Katie went up on stage with the other kids. Allen asked them each a few questions about what they were doing over the summer, how they were doing in school and the like. When he got to Katie and asked her how she liked her motorcycle ride, she just looked at the microphone, and then looked at Ruth and me. Allen quickly said something to try and put Katie at ease, and Ruth took the mic and spoke for several minutes.

Ruth was the senior member of the Stars and was several years older than the others. It turns out she was getting ready to go to college in Ann Arbor at the University of Michigan, and a portion of her tuition was being paid by the PBTF scholarship program. That drew another large "Whoop!" from the crowd.

For the next part of the program, Allen rattled off the top fundraisers in descending order, and as I listened to the second-place finisher's total, I knew what was coming.

"And the top fundraiser for the 2000 Ann Arbor Ride for Kids is Rob Proctor, father of one of our Stars, Katie Proctor. Rob and his family raised $21,575!"

The place erupted and practically everyone rose to give us a standing ovation. I was overwhelmed by a mixture of pride and happiness, but I also felt guilty, as a few feet away sat a mom I'd never met who'd shared her story of her son's death from a brain tumor.

The other Stars were called back on stage and lined up behind a large PBTF banner. The kids all held it up to show the grand total raised that day - $169,500, which brought another round of applause.

The celebration ended with a drawing for motorcycle-related gear. The grand prize winner would take home a new Honda Rebel motorcycle. I wasn't a motorcycle enthusiast, and wondered what I'd do if I won. Although I didn't win the bike, as the top fund-raiser I received a very nice motorcycle jacket with the PBTF logo emblazoned across the back. I wasn't entirely sure what I'd do with it, but it was a cool jacket nonetheless. I thought to myself, *who knows, maybe I'll get a motorcycle.* I doubted it, due to my fifteen years of experience in the auto insurance claims industry. All too often when motorcycles and cars met up, the motorcyclist lost. In my world, we referred to motorcyclists as "organ donors." But I have learned: never say never.

CHAPTER 34

Batman
Fall 2000

THERE WERE A NUMBER OF things Denni and I had to get used to when it came to living in our old house. Outside of the maintenance issues that could be expected, there were several things that not only fit into the "didn't see that coming" category, they were things we could have done without altogether. Bats, for example.

Since I was a kid, I remember having bats in the house. Just like our family, generations of bats made the Pritchard House their home. After Denni and I moved in, several experts came to look over the situation and they offered to build elaborate and expensive bat houses in the large trees outside the house. But they admitted the bats would likely use those as vacation homes while maintaining permanent residence in our attic. Denni *hated* bats, and for good reason.

One morning I awoke to a scream so loud I still can't believe it came from a lone person. A bat had found its way into the bathroom and brushed against Denni as she got out of the shower. By the time I made it down the hall to the bathroom, the poor bat was hiding under the antique claw-foot tub. Apparently, he too was in shock. He sat still under the tub and just stared at me with a look that said, "What did I do?" It was one of the few times I showed compassion for the critters. I put on a ski glove, scooped him up, and threw him out the window.

Another bat-fest occurred on a hot summer night, when I heard the unmistakable flutter of bat wings as Denni and I laid in bed. While the creature flew around our bedroom, Denni screamed and threw herself under the sheet, her go-to defense. In the darkness, I grabbed for my glasses, but instead, sent them flying. Undeterred, I jumped up and found the light switch. The bat and I were on pretty even terms vision-wise, as without my glasses, I am… wait for it… blind as a bat.

Seeing a blurry object swooping around the room, I stood in my skivvies and took wild swings with my pillow. I missed at least a dozen times. Miraculously, I finally made contact, and the bat went flying. Unfortunately, I didn't know where it landed.

Still gathering my bearings, I walked around the bed and noticed a black blob on the sheet covering Denni. Actually, it was on Denni's stomach. And worse yet, the bat wasn't simply lying there. The blow with the pillow hadn't killed the bat, but had just stunned it, and the bat flopped about, making an ungodly noise.

Clearly not using all of my intellectual capabilities, I decided to strike the bat with my pillow while it flopped on Denni's stomach. The combination of events sent Denni over the edge, and she made the head-swiveling girl in the movie *The Exorcist* seem calm in comparison. Eventually I knocked it off of Denni and onto the ground where I finished it off with my slipper. One might think that I would have scored some points as the brave husband protecting his wife from the evil monster. One would be very wrong. Let's just say I learned *numerous* lessons that night.

Several months after Katie's surgery, she went to bed at her normal time, and I was working on my computer when I heard her footsteps running down the hall.

"Dad, Dad," Katie said in her still whispery voice but with much enthusiasm.

"Go to bed, Katie."

"Dad!" Katie said again.

"Katie, go to bed - now!" I said in an impatient voice.

Katie went back down the hall to her room, although I could hear her muffled pleas.

After receiving one too many "Dad's," and having no patience that night for the extended bedtime shenanigans, I bounded upstairs and burst into Katie's room to let her have it, verbally speaking.

As soon as I entered the room I discovered Katie, in a fetal position on her bed and pointing upwards. I immediately saw the object causing the disruption. There, hanging from one of the blades of Katie's ceiling fan, was a bat.

Katie hadn't been saying "Dad" as I'd thought. She had been saying "bat," but the paralysis in her throat prevented her from creating sufficient volume and clarity for me to understand. I gathered Katie in my arms and took her into our bedroom in time to meet Denni, who had come upstairs after hearing all the fuss.

Leaving Katie and Denni in the safety of the bedroom, I returned to Katie's room to find the bat flying in a circle around the room. Eventually I timed my tennis racquet's medium-strength swing to catch the bat in flight and it fell to the ground. In the course of the several dozen bat encounters I experienced in the Pritchard House, I'd learned that anything more than a medium swing with the tennis racquet led to a much bigger mess. Another knock on the head for good measure and the poor bat was dead.

The next day I took off from work an hour early. At the Kalamazoo Toys R Us I bought the Grand Barbie Playhouse, and as soon as I walked in the door, I pulled Katie on my lap, apologized profusely for the night before, and presented her with my guilt-laden gift. To me, it still wasn't nearly enough. The following evening, the Grand Playhouse had a pink Barbie Mustang sitting in its driveway in Katie's playroom, and several days later, Barbie's friend Ken had a new motorcycle.

CHAPTER 35

Trick or Treat Fall 2000

§

Denni was a stickler about family photos, especially birthday photos. At the photographer's studio, Katie obliged all of us with a number of poses. We looked at the proofs and noticed that in the pictures where she smiled, her face was noticeably distorted. We'd taken a few pictures of Katie since her hospitalization, but for some reason, we thought professionally taken photographs might be different. In a few of the pictures Katie wasn't smiling at all, and her face looked much less distorted. We picked several poses and included one in which she wasn't smiling. On the ride home, I pretended not to notice the tears running down Denni's cheeks. I wanted to be supportive, it's just that I didn't know what to say.

When we got home, Denni vented.

"I'm so sad for Katie. Not because of how she looks - I think she looks beautiful. I'm sad because of how unfair this is. I know as she gets older she's going to have to deal with some things that are going to be very difficult. That's why I'm sad."

"It makes me sad, too," I agreed. "You and I think Katie is the most beautiful girl in the world. But, you're right. That may not mean much to Katie when she has to deal with this stuff."

On the morning before Halloween, I heard the unmistakable sounds of Katie vomiting. She had experienced several episodes since the MRI the previous May, and we had another appointment in Cincinnati coming up in a few weeks. It was none too soon for Denni or me. Several doses of Zofran failed to stop the vomiting, and Katie had to be admitted to Bronson Hospital in Kalamazoo for dehydration.

Denni and I had previously discussed what to do if Katie needed hospital care outside of Cincinnati. We had been pleased with the local hospital, Allegan General, for Katie's birth and my grandma's hip issues. But after our stint at a major center like Children's in Cincinnati, we decided we'd go to Bronson for some of the more routine things, or Cincinnati, if we felt it was something more severe. On this occasion, we went to Bronson, where they administered some I-V fluids and the vomiting eventually stopped. Katie was discharged on the afternoon of Halloween, just in time for a brief amount of trick-or-treating with her little pumpkin escort, ten-week-old Brian Proctor.

Brian was still an infant, but with each passing week he showed more of a very energetic and fun-loving personality. And nobody was more taken in than his big sister Katie Proctor. On a number of mornings, we'd walk into Brian's nursery to find Katie asleep with him in the crib. Considering her small frame, it was hard to imagine she was five years his elder. She usually had him curled up against her chest as the two slept soundly. It's moments like those where it's hard to capture the raw emotion. Just as Katie had showed me unconditional love when I returned from my ill-advised trip during her hospitalization, she was showing that same trait to her brother.

She's quite a girl, I thought to myself as I stood with Denni and we watched in silence as our children held each other. As far as I'm concerned, moments like this set the gold standard for memories.

The MRI took place in November, and while the vomiting episodes were a concern, the results of the MRI alleviated any apprehension and were cause for celebration.

When Dr. Crone came into the exam room, he had a smile on his face.

"Great news! Not only does everything look stable, but it looks like there is some shrinkage in the residual tumor. I think we can go eight or nine months between scans," said Dr. Crone.

"Whoot! Whoot!" I said to Katie as I pumped my fist.

Two down, I thought as we made our way to Izzy's delicatessen for another batch of celebratory potato pancakes.

To: Friends of Katie
From: Rob & Denni Proctor
Date: Tuesday, November 7, 2000
Re: Katie Update

Incredible news! The MRI scan showed that the remaining tumor has shrunk by about ten percent! We could not be more thrilled. Dr. Crone says Katie doesn't need to have another scan for nine months.

The video scope of her throat showed no improvement in the paralysis in her throat and right vocal cords, and although we won't throw in the towel, every month that passes without improvement is not a good sign. Katie will continue with occupational therapy for another six to eight months. Other than that, she has been cleared to return to all activities.

If you'd like to see an updated picture you can go to www.Squirreltales.org and click on the "Scrapbook" section under "Katie." This is a web site for parents of kids with cancer.

We are absolutely thrilled to have shrinkage in the tumor, and we thank all of you for your support!

And the biggest thanks to God - Thank you!!!

Rob, Denni, Katie, & Brian Proctor

CHAPTER 36

What a Difference a Year Makes Winter 2001

THE HOLIDAY SEASON CAME AND went and we celebrated the Martin Luther King holiday weekend with our traditional skiing event. Denni and I had taken up skiing a few years before moving to Michigan, and since then we'd hosted an annual ski weekend with a group of high school and college friends. It seemed to grow larger each year, and at its peak the Pritchard House brimmed with more than fifteen ski enthusiasts.

A short time after the guests left, Denni was unusually depressed. She always went into a funk when visitors left, but this time it seemed more severe. I noticed the heightened level of anxiety and asked her about it.

"You know what week this is, right? A year ago?" she asked.

"Yes, I get it," I offered. "It seems weird how we're measuring things now. Time and events seem to take on a whole new dimension."

"Well, plan on me being a wreck on the first of February," Denni said.

On Super Bowl Sunday, I woke Denni, shaking her shoulder.

"You need to come downstairs," I said with a clear sense of urgency.

"Katie? Brian?" Denni was up in an instant. "Is everything OK?"

"It's Rocky, he's dying. I mean *right now*, he's dying. Get Katie and bring her down to say goodbye," I said. I hurried out the door and headed downstairs, hoping he would still be alive when I got there.

Rocky, or Rocky III, as he was originally known, was almost twelve years old. Denni and I added him to our little family in 1990 when I was still in the "no kids" stage. Denni never had an indoor dog, let alone a big, drooling dog like a boxer. My family had boxers since the 1950s. They were all named Rocky, after undefeated world heavyweight champion Rocky Marciano. In the 1970s and 80s, with the release of the *Rocky* movies, it seemed logical to number our dogs like the movie series. Despite some initial concerns, Denni and Rocky hit it off. When he was a puppy, Rocky would sit in Denni's lap as she studied to complete her education degree at Bowling Green State University.

Even when he grew to over ninety pounds, he always believed he was a six-pound puppy, and would happily climb into any lap that would let him.

For reasons we never were able to figure out, Rocky grew into an incredibly aggressive dog. We managed to keep things in check for the first few years of his life. Then, just before the move to Michigan, a teenager was walking a small German shepherd on the sidewalk in front of our house. Rocky took off in full stride, broke through the electric fence, and hit the dog with enough force to snap the leash. He knocked the girl to the ground and blind-sided the dog like a linebacker.

Denni and I apologized to the girl and her parents and paid the vet bill to have the dog checked out. I took Rocky to our vet with the assumption that he would have to be put down. Having worked for an insurance company, I'd seen enough dog-bite claims to make me wary of owning an aggressive dog capable of attacking and hurting anyone, human or otherwise. It was not something I was willing to entertain.

Rocky III had been a frequent patient at the veterinary clinic, and the vet was fond of him. He knew that Denni and I had tried to work on Rocky's behavior at several obedience classes - all of which ended in disaster. But the vet wasn't ready to give up on Rocky.

"He's really a beautiful boxer. I hate to put a young and healthy dog down," the veterinarian said.

"I understand that, but we're lucky he didn't break that girl's arm when he hit that dog like he did. I'm not going to take a chance," I said.

"You say you're moving to Michigan?" the vet asked. "What's the house and yard like there? Are you in a neighborhood?"

"Actually, it's not really in a neighborhood," I replied. "It's a big old house with a huge yard. We have more than two acres and some of it is woods."

"Sounds perfect for a dog," he said, and I agreed.

With Rocky lying calmly at his feet, the vet said, "Why don't you get him to Michigan and see how he does?"

Fortunately for Rocky, that's exactly what I did.

Rocky loved Michigan. He chased squirrels and had the run of his large yard. Although they certainly wouldn't have been confused for friends, Rocky even allowed the two golden retrievers who lived next door with Judi McCall to venture into our yard without trying to kill them. At least most of the time.

When Katie was born, Rocky quickly assumed the role of security guard. Boxers were originally bred in Germany in the 1800s to guard meat houses, and their protective instincts are legendary. Always on duty, Rocky slept within a few feet of Katie, and followed her wherever she went. He even laid in silence as she cut her teeth on his loose skin. As he aged, he slowed down, but never lost his inner spirit, and Rocky and Katie were best buddies to the end.

In the last two years, his coal-black muzzle had turned to gray. Rocky's condition deteriorated to the point where he needed to sleep in the mudroom as he had an increasing number of accidents in the house. On this morning, when I went downstairs to let him out, it was clear Rocky wouldn't be getting up again.

I put Katie's hand against Rocky's nose and he sniffed it. He couldn't lift his head off the ground, and for several minutes Katie put her head on Rocky's chest as his breathing became slower. Katie said her goodbyes, and Denni took her out of the room. I put my own hand against Rocky's nose. He seemed comforted, and shortly thereafter, his breathing stopped and he lay completely still. After over eleven years as a big part of our family, Rocky III was gone. I relayed the finality of the event to Denni and Katie.

Katie cried as only a little child could. She went into the room where Rocky was laying and sat next to him. For a period of several minutes, she lay on his now still chest and cried inconsolably. Then, Katie looked up and through her big, brown eyes, said, "Now can I have a cat?"

So much for the grief cycle.

The sadness of Rocky's passing was tempered with the excitement of our upcoming trip. Keeping good on my hospital room promise, the entire Proctor family headed to Oahu and the Big Island of Hawaii for a ten-day vacation.

On February 1, 2001, one year to the day after her surgery, Katie Proctor soared four hundred feet over Kona Bay as she parasailed with her mom. Later that afternoon Katie swam with the dolphins. That evening, we ended the day with a beachfront dinner at Huggos, our new favorite restaurant in the entire world.

I admit the original promise of a trip to Hawaii was made in a panicked attempt to prod Katie towards a recovery. I enjoyed the beaches of South Haven and Saugatuck, but never fancied myself much of a beachgoer. To me, Hawaii sounded crowded, expensive, and touristy.

If any of those things were true, I quickly forgot them within several hours of landing. I became enamored with Hawaii. From the quaint shops and beaches on the North Shore of Oahu, to the black sand, rain forests, and volcanic landscapes on the Big Island. I understood why so many people called this paradise. And I certainly understood why David and Holly, along with so many others, wanted to move from the mainland to live there. That group now included me. On our last evening in Hawaii, I watched the sun sink slowly into the Pacific Ocean, my feet buried in the warm sand. The adults sipped their Mai Tais and Longboard beers and Katie nursed her pineapple smoothie, and I offered what I felt was an appropriate toast.

"Here's to my hero, Katie Proctor. I'm blessed beyond words to be her father. She's gone through so much and handled it better than I ever could have. I'd feel lucky to have just a fraction of the courage she's shown. And as we sit here today I think we'd all agree - what a difference a year makes." Indeed.

The trip ended all too soon and we made our way back to Michigan. The flight home seemed twice as long, and the reality of winter hit us the minute we stepped out of the airport to find our car amongst the other snow-covered vehicles in the parking lot of the Grand Rapids airport. I made a silent pact with myself as we waited for the icy windshield to defrost.

We're going back there again, I thought. *And soon.*

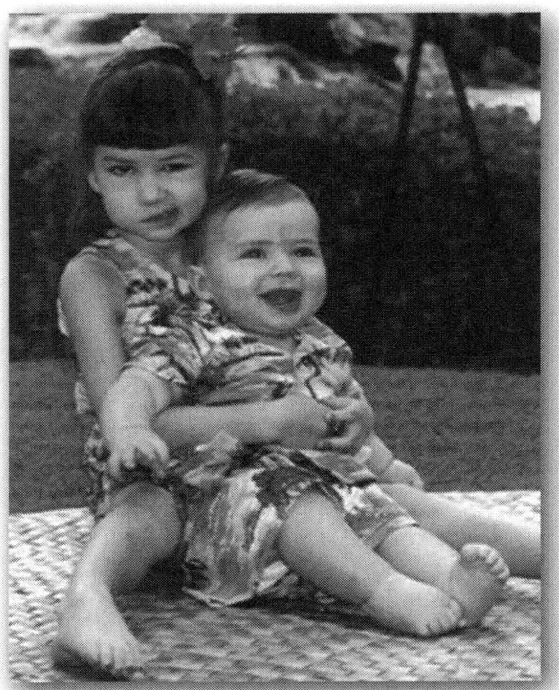

Katie and her six-month old brother Brian enjoying Hawaii.

CHAPTER 37
Popeye Summer 2001

KATIE'S THERAPIES WOUND DOWN TO a fraction of their original frequency. The eye and facial paralysis were visible, even exaggerated when Katie smiled. Her right arm and leg movements had improved greatly, although they were a bit weaker and just a tick out of sync. At first glance, Katie appeared to be like the rest of the kids on the playground, but there were also parts of Katie's appearance that looked different, and people noticed.

As we stood in line at a fast food restaurant, I asked Katie what she wanted. The cashier saw her respond to me and said to her, "Did you just go to the dentist?"

Katie just looked at the cashier, shook her head back and forth and leaned into my leg.

"No? Then what's wrong with your face, honey?"

I was stunned by the insensitivity of the comment, yet I could grasp that the cashier really hadn't thought through what she said or how she said it.

"Katie has a special smile, right?" I said, squeezing Katie's shoulder, and adding a smile of my own. Katie nodded her head up and down and smiled back at me.

"Huh?" was all that the cashier said. "What'll it be, sweetie?"

On the way home, I had a wide range of thoughts on how to deal with situations like the one we had just experienced. My heart felt sad to know it was likely that Katie would be dealing with comments like this her whole life.

"Katie, honey, when the cashier asked about your smile she wasn't making fun of you. You know that, right?" I asked.

Katie looked at me and nodded her head. That seemed to be her standard response.

"You know that the people who love you think you have the most special smile in the world," I said. "We love you and your smile just the way it is. And God does, too. You know that, don't you?"

Katie nodded again and looked out the window.

There would be so many of these situations that Denni and I would lose count. At Katie's dance recital after her surgery, I had come later than the rest of the family and joined the group in the auditorium.

As I sat in the vacant seat next to my mom, I could see she was upset.

"What's wrong?" I asked.

"I'm so mad I could spit," mom said. My mother was among the most passive people I'd ever known, so for her to react in this manner, I knew something significant must have happened.

She took a moment to calm down. "Denni dropped Katie and me off and went to park the car. Katie was so excited when she saw some of her dance mates, and she ran toward the door with a big smile on her face. There was a volunteer at the door, and as Katie ran up to her, the lady said in a very loud and gruff voice, 'What's the matter with you?' Katie just turned and looked at me. It was like someone took a pin and popped a balloon. You could see Katie's smile fade and her energy just totally changed."

Mom continued, still in a rage. "I walked up to the volunteer and said in the nastiest voice I could muster. 'She has a brain tumor.' The volunteer just said 'Oh,' in the most uncaring tone I've ever heard. I wanted to scream at her."

"It's hard to watch, isn't it?" I said. "There are some kids that ask, but most of them just don't know better. I'm stunned at how many adults do what that volunteer did. I can't believe they're that insensitive. I hate to think of all the times people are going to say stuff like that and we don't see it. I wish she could just shoot back with a comeback like, 'I've got a brain tumor – what's your excuse?' but that's just not her style."

Shortly after the recital we had the opportunity to travel to Sparta, New Jersey, to attend Denni's 20th high school reunion. Denni moved with her family to New Jersey her sophomore year in high school, when her dad transferred from the Cincinnati Bell office in Cincinnati to Parsippany. After graduation, Denni went off to college in Kentucky and by the time she'd finished her degree, her family had moved back to Cincinnati, and she hadn't returned to Sparta until the reunion.

Denni had a great time seeing old classmates and cheerleading buddies at the reunion. All the moms had pictures of their kids, including Denni. As she proudly showed off pictures of Katie and Brian, one of her friends flipped through the pictures and said, "That's the cutest thing ever."

"What's that?" asked Denni.

"How Katie is making that funny Popeye smile. It's dead on. What a riot. How'd you get her to do that?"

Denni looked at me and then her friend and said in a very matter of fact tone, "Oh, that. Katie has a brain tumor and half her face is paralyzed. But it does make for a cute picture, doesn't it?"

Without missing a beat, her friend bent down, took off her shoe, and put it in her mouth.

"Honestly, don't worry about it," Denni assured her. "A lot of people think she's making that face on purpose. You didn't know."

Finding the balance of how to react in these situations was a delicate dance that Denni and I were figuring out as we went. We just hoped Katie would eventually learn the moves, too.

CHAPTER 38

Making the Grade
Summer 2001

As I DID ON MANY nights, I logged onto the Squirreltales website. I perused the new entries some of the regulars had posted in the "Updates" section. Several caught my attention. Briana and Jack were two kids who appeared to be making some progress, when, as is the case all too often, the cancer came back.

When cancer returns, it tends to do so with a vengeance, sometimes as a more aggressive cancer, often spreading to different parts of the body. From what I could tell, both Jack and Briana were entering the final stages of what looked like would be a losing fight. The more I read, the more I hated cancer.

Between my prior research and my daughter's eighteen-month ordeal, I knew enough about cancer to be fluent in the basics. In addition to the type and location, the grade of the cancer is also incredibly important. Brain cancer is categorized into four main grades, and can be considered low or high grade as well.

There are technically five categories if one counts stage 0, which is an entirely benign tumor, usually curable by removal of the tumor. However, unlike lots of other kinds of tumors in the body, benign brain tumors can be life-threatening depending on their location. A tumor with cells that look more like healthy cells is called low-grade, while a tumor less healthy cells is described as high-grade. The prognosis is usually better for low grade tumors.

Grade I is the lowest stage in which the tumor has not invaded other tissues and is highly treatable. Grade II and III tumors have more aggressive cancer cells and invade other tissues to varying degrees. And then there is Grade IV. Grade IV is the most aggressive type of brain cancer, with high concentrations of extremely invasive cells which often metastasize to other parts of the brain. Grade IV cancers are associated with the shortest and lowest survival rates.

Even the names of the brain tumors sound ominous. Astrocytoma, named for its star-shaped cells; Ependymoma, Glioma, very familiar to our family as Katie has a Brain Stem Glioma; Medullablastoma, Primitive Neuroectodermal Tumor, better known as a PNET; and Teratoma, a rare brain tumor that has the ability to grow teeth. The thought of that makes my skin crawl.

Among the worst of all brain tumor types is the Glioblastoma Multiforme (GBM). While the Diffuse Intrinsic Pontine Glioma (DIPG) is the deadliest with a near-zero percent survival rate, the Glioblastoma is a much more commonly diagnosed tumor. GBM is actually a Grade IV astrocytoma tumor with an average length of survival from diagnosis at around twelve months. In 2000, the five-year GBM survival rate was less than five percent.

I vividly remembered an encounter I had with a fellow dad at Children's. I was riding in the elevator with the gentleman and couldn't help but notice he appeared upset. I asked him if everything was OK and he said that it wasn't. He said that his daughter had just been diagnosed with a brain tumor, and I replied that my own daughter was at Children's because of a brain tumor. I asked the father if he'd mind sharing the type of tumor his daughter had.

The man said, "I'm not sure how to pronounce it, but it has some letters."

In reading the brain tumor primer, I had come across several tumors that were known by abbreviated letters. PNET was one that came to mind and I asked if that was it.

"No," the gentleman said. "It's g-something."

"GBM?" I asked, fervently praying that this wasn't it.
"Yeah, that sounds right."
My heart sank.

Reading the stories on the Squirreltales website reminded me of the frail world we were living in. A few of the kids had been declared in remission, which sent spirits soaring. Others had to relay news of recurrence, and there were the heart-breaking entries of children who were losing their battle. Some of the hardest ones to read were from parents whose child had just recently succumbed to their cancer. It was interesting how parents shared different elements of the journey. Some provided little detail and tried to keep emotions in check. Others bared their emotions for the whole world to see.

One father shared a particularly detailed chronology of his daughter's final weeks. He shared the fairly common but difficult to watch progression as the cancer closed in for the kill. As the days passed, his daughter's pain became much more intense. So much so that significant pain medications had to be administered. Although alleviating the unbearable pain, the drugs made the child unresponsive and delirious. I tried to place myself in the father's shoes, not wanting to watch your child in pain, but wanting to spend the last moments on earth with them, and being robbed of the opportunity. There isn't even a way to describe that agony, I thought.

The father shared the girl's final moments up to a point. The point was when her brothers and sisters had said their goodbyes, and then he stopped. He said that the last few hours of his daughter's life were such a personal moment that he would never share it with anyone. He said he would cherish it in his heart until he saw his daughter again - in a place with no cancer and no pain. For him, that day couldn't come soon enough.

Every time I read one of those passages, I had the same empty feeling in my soul. *Damn I hate this disease*, I thought, as I wiped away my tears.

CHAPTER 39

One Step Forward, Two Steps Back Summer 2001

WHEN DR. CRONE ENTERED THE room, Denni and I sensed something was different. Dr. Crone greeted us and put the films onto the screen so we could see them. He'd done this ritual several times before. Katie was showing her stuffed animal friend Dakota some pictures in a book, oblivious to the adults in the room. We weren't sure what it was, but something was different.

"It's still a good scan but the tumor is a bit fuller and thicker than what it appeared to be in November," Dr. Crone said.

Denni and I looked at each other.

"What does that mean?" Denni asked first.

"We're not sure," he answered plainly. "The radiologist and I don't entirely agree, although I'm of the opinion the tumor doesn't appear to be any bigger than it was in November. But we do agree the image it is projecting is fuller and so is the cyst next to it."

He pulled up the scan taken eight months earlier. In comparison, the image was noticeably brighter. And the cyst that was barely visible in the prior scan could be seen without much effort on the latest scan.

Dr. Crone had mentioned the cyst in November, and said it was a benign object next to the tumor. He said the best course for treating the cyst was to simply monitor it as it could easily sit there Katie's entire life and do nothing. If it started to change, it could be treated, although it wasn't in a great spot to be accessed since it was deeper inside Katie's brain.

Dr. Crone gave Katie the now familiar, but incredibly thorough, neurological examination and afterwards the doctor addressed us.

"I'm inclined to do another scan in four to five months," Dr. Crone informed us.

"Four to five months? But we went almost eight months this last time." Denni said in a way that conveyed her disappointment.

Dr. Crone was looking at Katie when he spoke. "Yeah, I know, but I'd like to see her in a few months. If there aren't any more changes, we'll go back to a longer interval. We want to make sure what's left of the tumor is not trying to generate a blood supply again. We're not on a clock here."

"Oh, I know that," Denni said. "We'll do whatever it takes. We'll come back next *week* if we have to. It's just disappointing."

"I know it is," said Dr. Crone. "I have patients that go from a few months to two years and back and forth between scans. It just depends. I'll see you in a few months, OK, kiddo?" Dr. Crone said to Katie, who was now sitting in Denni's lap.

She looked up, nodded her head, and asked Dakota, her BFF stuffed animal friend and medical partner if that was OK, which, apparently, it was. Dakota was still Katie's constant companion on all of her medical appointments. The blood stain on its leg had faded but was still visible. To me, it was always visible.

One at a time, I reminded myself, thinking of the MRI results. *One at a time.*

Somehow, the potato pancakes at Izzy's delicatessen didn't seem quite as good that day.

To: Friends of Katie
From: Rob & Denni Proctor
Date: Tuesday, July 17, 2001
Re: Katie Update

After so many positive updates on Katie, it is a bit disheartening to give one that is more neutral. Katie's recent MRI scans show the remaining part of Katie's brain tumor is "fuller" than on the last MRI scan taken just a few months ago. Fuller means that the tumor showed up brighter and more clearly than on the previous scan but not measurably larger. Dr. Crone said he isn't entirely sure what's going on and doesn't want to speculate. Instead of lengthening the time between MRI's like we had planned, we will have another one in four to five months.

They also video-scoped Katie's throat and found no improvement in the right vocal cord/throat paralysis. Ditto for the right eye/facial muscle paralysis. As we're seventeen months out from surgery, there is not much hope left for improvement. We'll begin to consider plastic surgery options moving forward.

The good news was the return of an almost normal volume to Katie's voice. Apparently, yelling "Brian, get out of my stuff!" has been a very effective form of speech therapy.

We learned early on that the world of brain tumors involves steps forward, sideways, and backwards. Hopefully, at worst, this is a step sideways. We are optimistic that this is a blip in Katie's recovery.

Overall, Katie continues to do very well. She is playing T-ball, doing gymnastics, romping on the beach, having Barbie tea parties, and everything else you'd expect. She is a *very* happy kid... really!!!

Thanks again for your prayers, concern and support. We are very grateful. God Bless!
Sincerely,
Rob, Denni, Katie, & Brian Proctor

CHAPTER 40

Must-See TV
Summer 2001

§

"YOU'LL NEVER GUESS WHO CALLED me today," I said as our family sat down for dinner one evening.

"The President," said Denni sarcastically, with a wink to Katie.

"Well, he did, but I was too busy to take his call, so instead I talked with a news reporter in Kalamazoo!"

"A reporter?" asked Denni. "About what?"

"About the greatest hero in Allegan since General Benjamin Pritchard - Katie Proctor."

"That's cool!" exclaimed Denni. "Isn't it, Katie?"

She just smiled, not certain what was going on.

"They want to interview you about your surgeries and all you've been through," I explained. "Do you think you'd like to do that?"

"I guess so," Katie said nonchalantly, and shrugged her shoulders.

"I think it would be neat," I added. "You've been through an awful lot, and I think it might help other kids to see not only what you've gone through, but how well you're doing."

"OK," Katie said and went back to watching her one-year-old brother throw his food on the floor.

The following week, the six o'clock news in Kalamazoo aired the story. The video opened with Katie and Denni at a physical therapy appointment in Kalamazoo. The reporter interviewed the physical and occupational therapists who'd worked with Katie, and they raved about how incredibly motivating it was to work with a patient like her. They also interviewed the ear, nose and throat doctor who made the call to Denni when the brain tumor was discovered.

The interview included a visit to Allegan to show Katie playing in the yard with her brother, and a few screen shots of her recent trip to Hawaii. The reporter concluded the story with several quotes from her medical team that spoke to Katie's courage and positive attitude, and how they were such an important part of her journey. As the segment ended, the co-anchor chimed in, "What a remarkable girl. Truly inspiring."

"Dang, you're a celebrity again." I kidded. "First the Ride for Kids and now this. Can I have your autograph?"

"Oh, Daddy, you're silly," Katie said.

CHAPTER 41

Do You Feel Lucky?
Fall 2001

THE SCHOOL YEAR STARTED, AND Katie was off to kindergarten. I started a school year of sorts, as well. In addition to my responsibilities at State Farm, I began teaching Insurance & Risk Management in the Haworth College of Business at Western Michigan University in Kalamazoo. I was just learning the role, and in addition to everything else going on in our lives, it bordered on overwhelming. One thing was for sure, it certainly wasn't dull.

Katie was excited and nervous at the same time. Her pre-school experience in Kalamazoo at the Looking Glass had been a positive one, and we were hoping for the same in Allegan. We took the obligatory first day of school picture, outfitted her with a backpack, and off she went.

One evening a few weeks later, Denni came home to find me sitting on the couch staring at the television. Only the television wasn't turned on.

"What's the matter?" she asked.

"I just feel so bad for Katie. Sometimes I don't have the answers to help her." I couldn't hide my sadness.

"What are you talking about?" Denni asked, her concern growing.

"Katie wanted to know if I thought her smile was ugly," I said.

"What? What happened?" Denni said as she sat on the couch next to me.

"Tonight as we were getting ready for bed, Katie wanted to know if I thought her smile was ugly. I said of course not. Then she asked why God made her smile look the way it does. I guess one of the kids said something about it at kindergarten today. She's a couple of weeks into kindergarten and it's already started! I can't even imagine where it's going to go from here."

"Was the kid trying to be cruel?" Denni asked

"I don't know. I don't think so, but I don't know. Do you think Katie knows the difference?" I asked.

"It breaks my heart." Denni said. "How is she now?"

"I read her a couple of books and we talked for a bit. I tried to focus on some of the fun things she was doing in kindergarten. But when I left, I could hear that she started crying again. I didn't know what to do."

"This whole thing stinks," said Denni as she leaned in and put her head on my shoulder.

"Yeah, it totally sucks. And that's putting it nicely."

That night, I took my Bible off my nightstand and let it fall open. On several occasions over the prior months I'd started reading from the beginning, but found myself jumping around. I blamed my gnat-like attention span but also felt somewhat justified as frankly, I found it a difficult book to read at times. Every now and then, I just opened the Bible and start reading at whatever page I came to first.

The pages fell open in the book of Job. Job had been a godly man, and in a very short period of time lost everything. He lost his wealth and his health, and the text focused on Job's faith and perseverance. I couldn't help but feel sorry for Job, and like with many other stories I'd come across in the Bible, I pondered two things;

Why did people have to endure the things they did? And,

How would I react in similar circumstances?

Then I wondered if Katie's experience in life was going to be similar to Job's. What if her life was going to be one trial after another? Since the time of her original surgery a lot of people had told us how "lucky" Katie was. It was with good intentions, and they meant well by implying she was lucky to be alive. But of all the words we could use to describe Katie's situation, "lucky" didn't seem to fit the bill.

When I think of "lucky" people, I don't think of brain tumor patients. Lucky people win the lottery, or buy a five-dollar painting at a garage sale and find an original copy of the Declaration of Independence tucked in the back of the frame. Lucky is when an extra bag of Doritos falls out of the vending machine.

In the United States, about a dozen kids a day are diagnosed with a brain tumor. I doubt those kids and their families consider themselves lucky. As for Katie, she underwent several surgeries and as a result, was deaf in her right ear, had vision issues with her right eye, and had a number of other issues ranging from frequent choking caused by her throat paralysis to cyclical vomiting. Although she was over a year and a half out from surgery, her survival wasn't guaranteed. So, all that given, who would choose to call her lucky? Not me.

Denni and I preferred to use the term *blessed*. Katie was blessed to have survived her brain tumor and the surgeries so far. She was blessed that although she had issues, her life was pretty normal. She was doing well in school and her intellect didn't appear to be negatively impacted, and for that we were eternally grateful. Some other brain tumor kids we'd come to know weren't nearly as fortunate.

I remembered back to the time in the hospital when everything seemed to pile up on Katie and I pleaded with God that Katie really deserved a break. Well, in some ways, maybe she did catch a break. What if her break, or whatever you want to call it, was that she survived having a brain tumor? Although we didn't have a guarantee, it did appear Katie had a good chance for long term survival. While that is obviously the most important factor of all, what if that was her only break? What if her life was going to be a series of challenges – like Job – having to deal with these things over and over? How would she handle it? And why she should have to?

I didn't have the answers to any of those questions as I drifted off to sleep. At least not any good answers.

CHAPTER 42

Priorities
Fall 2001

With each passing month, it appeared more likely that Katie's eye, facial, and throat paralysis was permanent. During the MRI visit earlier in the summer, Katie had been referred to Dr. John Kitzmiller, a plastic surgeon at Cincinnati Children's. At the initial consultation, he advised us that there were several surgical options. It was his opinion that due to her young age the best course of action was to split the nerve under her tongue on the left side of her face and connect it to the nerve on the right side. The procedure was known as a cranial nerve reanimation. The surgery was set to take place the week of Thanksgiving as it aligned with her MRI scan to check the status of the remaining brain tumor.

Denni was tucking Katie in bed one evening about a month before the trip to Cincinnati, and Katie had questions about the upcoming procedure. We called it her "smile surgery" as it was much easier for Katie to say than "cranial nerve reanimation."

"What are they going to do in my smile surgery? Will I have a needle? Will they give me the smelly gas first?" Katie asked, without a break sufficient for Denni to answer her questions.

Denni was amazed at how much this six-year-old had to deal with and how astute she was. She did her best to answer Katie's concerns, but it was the last question that Denni couldn't answer.

"Will my smile be like it was before?"

"I don't know honey. We pray that it will, but we just don't know. You have a very special smile, no matter what. You know that, right?" Denni said, as she tried to reassure her daughter.

"I guess so," Katie sighed.

Several weeks later, I was attending meetings at State Farm's home office in Bloomington, Illinois. I came through the door of my hotel room at the end of the day and noticed the phone message light was blinking. The message was from Denni.

"Why didn't you answer your phone?" Denni asked when I returned her call. "Oh, I forgot – we can't be interrupted at work."

"Denni, I had it off – I'm sorry," I replied. We had plenty of these conversations over the years and they always ended in a stalemate. Denni raised very valid points about my workaholic nature and her perception that I put State Farm's needs above my own family at times. Apparently at times like this.

Denni sounded frustrated. "I've been trying to call you because Katie had a really bad batch of vomiting and I took her to the pediatrician in Kalamazoo. He sent us right over to Bronson Hospital and they've admitted her. I told the pediatrician she's supposed to have her smile surgery in less than two weeks and he thought it'd be best if they got an I–V in her to stop the dehydration before it got worse."

"I'm coming home," I said. "I'll see you as soon as I can get there."

I called the meeting facilitator about leaving due to my daughter's illness and was surprised at the response. The facilitator commented that the next two days of the meeting were going to be very important and that it was the essence of the week. When the facilitator asked, "Are you sure you have to leave?" I had to take a second to think before I spoke.

"My daughter is in the hospital – it's not like she has the flu. She has a brain tumor."

I hadn't shared that level of detailed information with the facilitator and to his credit, it changed the tenor of the conversation. Still, on the trip home I couldn't help but feel guilty, as Denni could point to a number of instances where I'd acted just like the facilitator when it came to State Farm.

Over the years I couldn't count the number of times I had rationalized why I needed to attend a particular work event. In most cases, I'd used the excuse that the issues Katie was dealing with were residual effects of the tumor and not life-threatening. The truth is, we really didn't know where Katie's tumor journey would lead to, and as much as I said many of the issues she faced weren't life-threatening, I had no idea.

The more I held up my arguments for scrutiny, the more they fell apart. I could hear myself saying, "Really Rob?" in the same tone Denni did. The mirror of self-assessment can be one of the most incriminating of all, showing character flaws in all of their ugliness.

For years, I'd been proud of my work ethic. From the time I was a teenager I had a job. I went to college with a plan to major in insurance and then work for State Farm, and that is exactly what I did. I have my fair share of shortcomings, but I've worked hard my entire life to build a reputation as a successful and intelligent leader. It's something I've always been proud of, so proud at times it clouded my vision when it came to my family.

Denni supported and encouraged me from the beginning of our relationship. She graduated a year behind me with a degree in Economics and took a job in the management trainee program at K-Mart in Cincinnati. Her reward for being one of the top students in the training class was to be assigned to one of the worst-performing stores in the country, a K-Mart located by the airport in Detroit, Michigan. She didn't enjoy it, and after a short while came back to Cincinnati, and she and I got engaged.

From the onset of our relationship, Denni accepted my passion for work. I put in long hours and often went in early and stayed late. After we were married and I was promoted into my first leadership position in Toledo, Ohio, she gave up her position at the phone company and went to Toledo with a positive attitude. The economy in Ohio at the time was still lagging, and Denni found a low-paying position as an office manager. She decided that wasn't satisfying and went back to Bowling Green State University, where she picked up another degree in Education. As she completed her degree, we were transferred to Cincinnati for another State Farm leadership promotion, and Denni gladly accompanied me back to a place she considered to be home.

Denni began her teaching career, and I jumped into my new leadership position with vigor. At times, she'd have to remind me that between work and extracurricular activities, I had a tendency to take on too much. In 1992 and 1993 things got out of hand. I attended a school board meeting in the district where Denni was teaching and made a public comment about a topic that apparently impressed the school's superintendent. He approached me after the meeting and asked if I'd be interested in running for the school board. I accepted the challenge, ran for the Kings Local School Board position, and won.

The public school board meetings were once a month, but the miscellaneous meetings were frequent, often requiring emergency sessions and lengthy conversations several times per week. Hectic as things were on the school board, I enjoyed it immensely. So much so that I accepted an invitation to join the Warren County School Board as the representative from our district, which meant even more meetings.

In addition to the school board activities, I had taken over responsibility for a new claims operation that was in need rebuilding. If that wasn't enough, as was often the case with people who wanted to move up the corporate ladder at State Farm, I was involved in several development opportunities. They were intended to give me exposure to some executives and to build leadership skills, but the other side of the coin was that a tremendous amount of labor was performed in the off-hours by a lot of aspiring candidates like myself. Between the school board, my regular State Farm responsibilities, and the development assignments, it was fair to say I was more than at capacity.

I decided to use this same time to ramp up my efforts towards achieving an insurance designation – the Chartered Life Underwriter (CLU). I'd completed another insurance designation, the Chartered Property Casualty Underwriter (CPCU) designation, several years earlier. For that, Denni helped me study at night, which was no small task, since to Denni and most of the rest of the population, reading about insurance is mind-numbingly dull.

Most individuals took one or two classes a year on a path to completion that lasted four to five years or longer. I would have none of that, and in a twelve-month period, I took and passed six CLU exams. I was on a personal mission to complete the designation as soon as possible, since to me it was a necessary building block in the foundation of the leadership track I was hell-bent on following.

One evening as I sat and studied my textbook, Denni came in and sat down. She didn't say anything at first, but I could tell something was up.

"I need to know something," Denni said after a while of sitting in silence. I knew enough to close my book.

"What's that?" I asked, having no clue where this was going.

"I need to know who you married."

"I married you, silly," I added wryly, hoping the levity would shorten the conversation and I could get back to studying.

"Are you sure?" Denni asked. "Are you sure you did?"

"I'm pretty sure," I replied. "I swore I saw you walking down the three hundred-yard long aisle at Hyde Park Methodist Church in your mom's wedding gown. Brian Clark had smelling salts in his pockets because we all thought I was going to pass out. Then Reverend Kumpf married us in less than twenty minutes, and we took a limo ride to downtown Cincinnati and had an awesome reception."

I'd given myself credit for providing such specific details about the wedding. All the while completely missing the point.

"I'm not sure you married me," Denni said. "I think you might have *married* State Farm, and I think you might have *hired* me."

The statement stopped me in my tracks.

"I'm not following," I said, still rattled by the comment.

"Oh, I think you are. You're smart. All the people I talk to at State Farm tell me you're one of the smartest people they know. Figure it out," she said as she rose and walked away.

There would be several more conversations on the topic, and eventually I did figure it out – or at least figured out the meaning in Denni's statement. Being married requires one to be committed without exception. It means putting that person above all others. It means putting them above a job, or a house, and especially any other person. As I thought through the multitude of examples Denni could lean on in our short marriage, her statement that night had rung true a number of times.

I was embarrassed and I knew Denni was right. Maybe not always, but almost always, I'd found a way to put State Farm first. It was sometimes disguised as a work crisis of some kind or another, but in reality, it fed my addiction. I found a way to make work the most important thing in my life. And Denni was in the role of good employee, dutifully submitting to me and whatever State Farm needed at the moment. I really had treated Denni like an employee, and she had called me on it.

When I looked back, I could see that it had started very early in our relationship. I spent our first wedding anniversary at a hotel in Toledo for State Farm. Denni mentioned it, but I had rationalized why I had to be in Toledo. After all, it was all about the promotion, and that would benefit both of us, right? There were a number of other examples. My trip back to Michigan when Katie was in the throes of meningitis was probably my most glaring example, but there were countless others that would score a direct blow to any defense I had.

As I drove the five-hour route from Bloomington to Michigan, I used the time to think about Denni's comment years before. I had married Denni, not State Farm, but she had a point. Years had passed and she still had a very good point. When was I going to change? Or more accurately, was I *ever* going to change?

Driving though the pitch-black Midwestern night, I scanned the radio hoping to find some sense of comfort in my thoughts. I went to the southern end of the dial and listened to a couple of Christian radio stations. Nothing I heard seemed to provide any assistance or direction for the issues that weighed on my mind. Apparently, God was exercising radio silence. It was a long trip home.

So I talk to the night,
I head for the light,
Try and hold it on the road...
Thank God for the man
Who put the white lines on the highway
"Lover," Michael Stanley Band

CHAPTER 43

Happy Holidays Thanksgiving 2001

For this medical visit to Cincinnati, we decided to take advantage of a program through the Children's Hospital Network. I felt guilty about using the Ronald McDonald House located about a block from Children's. I figured there were families who needed the free accommodations more than we did, so I decided on another option. Several hotel chains participated in the Children's Hospital Network and gave bargain rates to patient families. I booked the two-bedroom loft at the Residence Inn a few miles from the hospital for $40 a night.

During the week of Thanksgiving, the MRI scan to check the status of Katie's tumor was completed, and then the nerve surgery procedure was performed. The surgery lasted over four hours, and when Katie awoke in recovery, she was in a great deal of pain. It took several doses of morphine to get the pain under control and she went in and out of consciousness in the recovery room for several hours before being discharged to her room. Dr. Kitzmiller explained that he was able to split the nerve under her tongue successfully and that in his eyes, the procedure went "as smooth as silk." He said it would be at least eight to ten months before the results of the surgery could be assessed.

In addition to the nerve procedure, he made a small slit and stitched her right eyelid so it wasn't open as much. Katie's right eye fell partially closed when she slept, but aside from that, the paralysis prevented it from closing, and there was concern over residual damage to her eye, and especially her cornea.

After visiting with Dr. Kitzmiller, Denni and I left Katie with Holly so we could make a few phone calls to some other family members, friends, and co-workers. When we came back a short while later, we found Holly leaning over Katie's bed, crying.

"What's wrong?" Denni asked, afraid Katie was having issues.

"This whole thing just breaks my heart," Holly said through tears.

"It's not right. It's not fair. Katie shouldn't have to go through all these surgeries and have all this pain. I can't stand seeing her like this. I'd give anything to trade places with her."

"I know you would," Denni offered in support. "We all would."

From the time she was an infant, Katie had a special bond with Holly. Holly would sit with Katie on her lap for hours as they'd snuggle, and as Katie grew, so did her affection for her grandmother. Neither of them knew it at the time, but there would be a reason for the special bond that extended beyond any familial relationship. It just wasn't ready to be played out yet.

Katie was dismissed from the hospital on the morning of Thanksgiving, but she was still in a great deal of pain and we didn't feel comfortable driving back to Michigan. On short notice Holly did her best to make a nice Thanksgiving meal in the hotel kitchenette. As our family sat around the little table at the Residence Inn by Children's Hospital, one feeling became evident. Thankful as we were for lots of things, spending the Thanksgiving holiday at the hospital and hotel was about as depressing as it gets.

A few months later, Katie had a follow up appointment with Dr. Kitzmiller in Cincinnati. Although there was no sign of movement in Katie's face, the nerve showed signs of electrical activity, indicating a successful procedure.

On the night of the second anniversary of Katie's brain surgery, Denni felt someone tugging on her as she slept. Feeling awake, she looked up to a glowing object with white hair wearing a long flowing robe that was white with gold trim. She couldn't sense exactly what it was, but she sensed it involved Katie and assumed it was an angel of some kind.

Scared at first, Denni said, "You can't take Katie. Please don't take Katie!" The angel smiled and slowly disappeared. Denni quickly got out of bed and went to Katie's room to make certain everything was all right. The angel appeared to Denni on several occasions over the course of a few years, and Denni became convinced that this was Katie's guardian angel.

In the twenty-four months since Katie's diagnosis, our family had undertaken an incredible journey. Doctors, hospitals, tests, examinations, and surgeries had all become commonplace. We were living in timeframes measured between MRI scans. And Brian was an energetic and lovable addition to our family. Katie, despite her medical issues, was an incredibly happy child. As for me, I was exploring new areas of emotions, including my recently deepened faith.

Since the diagnosis and surgery, we'd known our lives would never be the same. But I had to give us some credit. We'd come a long way, and all things considered, life was good.

CHAPTER 44

The Island of Misfit Toys Winter 2002

Two days before his second birthday, Brian fell over a basketball in the driveway and fractured his leg. I felt like the character Norm from the TV show *Cheers* whenever we went to a medical facility in Allegan, Kalamazoo, or Cincinnati. Just like the tagline from the show's theme song, everyone knew our names: the receptionists, the doctors, and especially the nurses.

Denni and I had become accustomed to the monthly ritual of sorting out the medical bills, determining which were urgent, which were still being processed by insurance, and which bills we could try to negotiate. After thirty-six consecutive months of medical treatment of one kind or another, medical bills were a large and important part of our budget, and like the mortgage payment, they were due every month. On one occasion, I received a bill from Children's before it had been processed and it indicated we owed over $53,000. Thank God for health insurance!

Christmas was fast approaching, and in the Proctor household the ABC 25 Days of Christmas TV countdown had to be followed verbatim. We watched *Rudolph the Red-Nosed Reindeer*, *Frosty the Snowman*, *A Charlie Brown Christmas*, and of course everyone's favorite, *The Grinch Who Stole Christmas*. Katie was seven at the time, and the morning ritual included me helping her get dressed for school. She liked to wear pigtails, and didn't seem to be aware that when she did a six inch, L-shaped scar was visible on the back of her head.

One morning we were standing in front of the bathroom mirror, and I was on my third attempt to get the pigtails at least somewhat symmetrical when Katie looked up and said, "I'm a misfit too, aren't I?"

I stopped what I was doing and asked her what she meant.

"Like *Rudolph and the Island of Misfit Toys*. I'm a misfit, too, because of my tumor."

My spirit sank. I felt sad and wasn't sure exactly what to say. Sometimes there is just no good answer. I told her that she wasn't a misfit at all. If anything, she was extra special. I was pretty sure my answer wasn't convincing to either of us.

But in some respects, Katie was right. Along the way we had met a number of people who treated her like a misfit, and even at seven years old, she had picked up on it. Some were well intentioned and just didn't know any better. Others thought they were protecting her. And others were just cruel or thoughtless.

At Parents' Night at school that year, a teacher's aide said to Denni, "We don't expect as much from Katie, you know, with her condition," saying the word 'condition' in almost a whisper. In a response politer than I would have given, but in a way that couldn't have made her point clearer, Denni said, "Oh, no, that doesn't work for us. Her tumor has no impact on her intellect, and we expect every bit as much from Katie as any other kid, and you should, too." We wondered how many times in Katie's life she was going to face this kind of treatment.

The one-year anniversary of Katie's plastic surgery would be an important date. Dr. Kitzmiller had said the nerve regeneration process would take six to eight months and the success of the surgery would be fully determined at the one-year mark. For months, Katie had electrical stimulation therapy designed to generate electrical activity in the nerve, and thereby increase function in the muscle. We hooked up electrodes to her face and turned up the electricity until it would sting, and then Katie performed a number of facial exercises. Katie hated the therapy, but she had to do it four to five days a week.

Neither Denni nor I had noticed much of a change in Katie's smile regardless of all the therapies. The right side of her face, including her eye, seemed very much like it did over the prior year. Nonetheless, we were excited about the visit with Dr. Kitzmiller and looked forward to hearing some news.

During the exam, Dr. Kitzmiller asked Katie to perform a number of facial expressions, and he prodded and poked her face for a considerable length of time. Katie never liked the therapies that had caused her to focus on her face and today was no exception. Ultimately, Dr. Kitzmiller summed up the procedure as less than he'd hoped for.

"These surgeries have a high success rate – over ninety percent. And I know the procedure to split and connect the nerve went well. We even had some electrical activity when we checked a few months after the surgery. But it just didn't take. I'm sorry."

We returned to David and Holly's home from the hospital. Denni and I laid in bed and lamented the most recent surgical failure, but caught ourselves and changed the direction of the conversation.

"I know we're both upset about the surgery," I said. "But we need to put this in perspective."

"I was thinking the same thing," Denni agreed. "This trip seemed to be about the smile surgery, but she also had another MRI and the scan showed the tumor was stable. And Doctor Crone has said twenty times that the tumor being stable is the most important thing of all. This is a God thing," Denni continued. "The smile is the part *we* focus on and it's the part we sometimes confuse as being the most important. But it's on the outside and really doesn't define who Katie is. I know it's important to her and that makes me sad. I'll keep praying that God totally restores her smile. But, most importantly, God continues to heal Katie and protect her from the tumor. I need to focus on that."

"I need to do that too," I offered. "Her smile isn't going to kill her – the tumor could. That helps set the priorities really quickly."

"I hope Katie feels that way," Denni said. "It's easy for you and I to talk like this but this is going to be more difficult as she gets older."

"There are a lot of things about this that are much easier for you and I to solve in a conversation than for Katie to have to deal with in real life," I agreed. "I just wish we could make it turn out in a way she wants it to. I know its wishful thinking, but I still would like it to work out that way."

On the return trip to Michigan, we spoke quietly about the options. Katie was tired of all the medical talk, so she ignored us and played with her American Girl dolls the entire ride. Buckled in the seat next to her was the best stuffed animal friend anyone could ever ask for, Dakota.

At church the next week, the time came in the service for members of the congregation to share personal items, both good and bad. There were joys and concerns, celebrations of an anniversary, and pleas for a return to health of a loved one. Denni and I didn't always participate in this part of the service, but this time I felt compelled say something, so when there was a lull, I took a turn.

"As many of you know, Katie had her follow-up visit with the plastic surgeon in Cincinnati. I would love to be able to report that the doctor had good news, but he basically said the procedure didn't work." There was a slight groan from the congregation as I continued. "When we asked what we should do next, Dr. Kitzmiller said there are two things we can do. There is another surgical procedure that's an option to consider. It's much more invasive and she's far too young to have the surgery. But maybe later she can consider it.

"And he said the second thing we can do is even more important. Doctor Kitzmiller asked us to take her home and love her unconditionally," I said, and could feel myself getting emotional. "Denni and I promised him that is something we can do easily. A smile is only a small portion of who we are as people. It's unfortunate that Katie may have to deal with this her entire life. But she is so much more to us than a smile. Hopefully, we can all show Katie that our love for her is unconditional and that regardless of the shape of her smile, her heart and her soul are perfect in our eyes and more importantly, in God's eyes."

As I finished, a long-time member of the congregation came from her pew to the front of the church where I was standing. She hugged me, wiped her eyes, and went back to her seat. Over the years Katie had become an important part of their lives, and they had seen many of the ups and downs of her roller-coaster life. On that day, it was definitely one of the "downs."

CHAPTER 45

I Swear 2002

§

Our routine had settled down, and Denni, Katie, and I were regulars at the First Congregational Church in Allegan. Denni had attended since we'd moved to Allegan years earlier. I was the one who was frequently absent, but now even I was attending church on a consistent basis, and something about it felt very different. I was having feelings and emotions about spirituality that were still new to me and that continued to weigh on my mind.

Rather than change the radio dial as often as I used to during my forty-minute work commute, most of my time was spent listening to a few of the contemporary Christian radio stations in Grand Rapids and Kalamazoo. West Michigan had a large and varied Christian community, including Lutherans, Presbyterians, and a very large Dutch Reformed population. My grandpa Dudley was a church-going cynic. My mom recalls how Dudley used to make a public display of mowing the lawn on Sundays much to the dismay of some Dutch Reformed neighbors who considered any work, including yard work, done on Sundays to be a sin. Dudley would openly share his feelings about the Dutch Reformed Church, and when an opportune moment came to offer his opinion he'd say, "Dutch Reformed - they pray *with* you on Sunday, and then prey *on* you the rest of the week."

There were parts of my church-going past that had likely set the stage for my mixed feelings on church and religion. Attending church was something "good" families did and up until the time I was in high school my family was in church most Sundays. We put in our pew time at the Shawnee United Methodist church and brought casseroles to the pot-lucks and my dad was one of the head ushers. I served as an acolyte when I was in elementary school and as an usher through my middle school years. High school was another matter altogether, and my attendance dropped significantly. Frankly, my attendance was out of obligation and habit more than any spiritual reasons.

I also struggled to reconcile the conflicts I saw in my own family. Looking back, I'm sure my mom had tried to get the family to church for the right reasons. She'd taught Sunday school for several years, and if anyone in the family had the right heart around church and the spirit of worship, it was my mom. But she was outnumbered by a less-than-interested supporting cast. The Proctor family attended the 8:00 A.M. service, primarily so my dad could get in at least eighteen holes of golf every Sunday that there weren't more than a few inches of snow on the ground. I'll never forget his excitement in the 1970s when fluorescent orange and yellow golf balls came on the market and extended his golf season to the extremes of winter. His rationale was that they could easily be spotted not only in the rough, but also in the snow!

A lifelong golf addict, dad rounded up the family and we high-tailed out of church the minute the benediction was over. A quick ride home for a hurried lunch, a change of clothes, and he was headed out to the club to play his eighteen holes. Or, if possible, he'd play thirty-six holes, and as his frequent caddy, I can recall my dad being able to get in fifty-four holes on a single day a number of times during the longest days of summer. We'd tee off before the sun was fully up and finish as dusk turned into darkness. Golf was a religion to my father. In a way, it was a God-given right, in my father's mind, and Sunday was as much about golf as it was about God. At least it appeared that way to me, especially since I heard His name on the golf course a lot!

I was in the church youth group from my pre-teens through early high school. There was certainly an intention to have a faith-based program, and there were some biblical discussions and community "do-gooder" deeds like visiting nursing homes and raking yards. But truth be told, once us Lambs of God reached puberty, youth group became as much about dances at the church and the accompanying make-out sessions as anything else.

In high school, between sports, social events, and my job at a local restaurant, my church attendance evaporated, and by my senior year in high school I attended a few times at best. In college, I joined Phi Delta Fraternity, and one of its main tenants was to live a life based on strong moral values. My frat brothers were a great bunch of guys, and most of my extracurricular activities amounted to what I considered at the time to be harmless college stuff - booze and girls. But to say I experienced much spiritually in my college days would be an overstatement.

Unlike a large number of my high school classmates in Lima who attended Ohio State University in Columbus, I had decided to get out of Ohio to attend Eastern Kentucky University. It was twenty-five miles south of Lexington and in the heart of horse country and the Bible Belt. On EKU's campus there was a small but fervent group of Bible-thumpers who would frequently come to "Horny Corner," one of the main gathering spots in the center of campus, and an especially popular hangout with the Greek crowd. They would begin their fire and brimstone speeches, which I would watch disinterestedly. I didn't openly mock them like some others, but I didn't think their messages were bringing anyone into the fold. If that was religion, I'd prefer to be a silent believer.

From the time we first dated, Denni had not been bashful with me about her faith. She often encouraged me to go to church, sometimes with success, and talked me into several pre-marriage sessions at the church. She even persuaded me to complete the eight-week membership program at the Hyde Park Methodist Church in Cincinnati. As I'd done for most of my life, I went through the motions, as much out of ritual and appeasement as anything else. While I understood and even respected the boundaries of having faith, it did little to affect my day to day life. And as I had done in prior instances, I compared my behavior to other adults to rationalize that I had as good a chance as a lot of others of getting into Heaven, which was the ultimate goal of religion, right?

Among my daily struggles was my language. Growing up, on the rare occasion when I heard my mother swear, it was over something pretty big. My father added a few more words to my swearing arsenal, but for the most part his swearing occurred on the golf course. If his game was particularly bad that day, he'd bring out his religious side and put "God" in front of his damns. Apparently, God was more to blame for my dad's bad putting than his errant drives from the tee – something I never did understand. I remember him uttering the "f-word" only one time, and I was in college when that happened.

As for me, from the time I began high school and beyond, my language was pretty raw. "Damn" and "hell" were mild considering what came out of my mouth. First my mother, and later Denni, often reminded me those words really didn't help anything.

"Sure they do," I protested. "They make me feel better."

When Katie was born, I did try to make a concerted effort to watch my mouth. It was a constant battle and really didn't sit well with Denni. Complicating matters was that she had several family members to deal with. My brother Rick had taken swearing to an art form. Rick had a Ph.D. in Finance and Statistics and was a professor at Siena College in New York. And while he may have had a brilliant mind, he also had a potty mouth.

With good intentions, Denni implemented a practice she thought would help both Rick and me. On one of his visits to Allegan, Denni presented us with her new invention aimed at improving our behavior in the language department.

"This is the Swear Jar. Anytime somebody swears, they have to put a dollar in it," she declared one afternoon shortly after Rick arrived. "We'll donate the money to church or put it in the kids' college funds," she said with great pride, and then caught herself. "But the real goal is to keep the jar *empty*," she said.

First, I clarified the rules. *Dang*, *heck*, and *shoot* were OK. But *ass* was a cuss word according to Denni, and *crap* and *sucks* were on the fence, which I thought was total overkill on her part.

"This is going to be tough," I said with a sigh.

Apparently too tough for some. When Denni was finished explaining the new Swear Jar and the rules, Rick thought for a second, pulled out his wallet, threw two $20 bills in the jar, and said, "F-that. This ought to cover me for the week."

The Swear Jar remained a fixture in our household for years. Over time, I've made some progress as far as my language is concerned. That's as good an assessment as I can make. I'm self-aware enough to consider myself a chronically recovering swear-aholic. In some regards I'm better, but certainly not cured.

The upside of the Swear Jar was that it was a pretty good savings mechanism, and both Brian's and Katie's college funds benefited heavily from their profane father and uncle. And if Denni would have been able to enforce *crap* and *sucks* as finable words like she wanted to, Katie and Brian could attend any university of their choosing on a full-ride Swear Jar scholarship.

CHAPTER 46

Good for the Sole 2003

THE WEEKLY SCHEDULE AT OUR household included a number of medical-related activities, but many more were typical kids' stuff, and were driven by Allegan's Number One Mom, Denni Proctor. I joked that Denni would give General Pritchard a run for his money in the over-achiever department.

In the spring of 2003, as Katie was finishing second grade, Perrigo's business climate had changed. Denni had reduced her hours to a part-time schedule shortly after Katie's surgeries in 2000, and was presented with the option to return to full time status or resign. After prayerful consideration, Denni resigned. It proved to be a fortuitous move as Katie continued to have issues that required frequent trips to the doctors in Kalamazoo and occasionally Cincinnati.

Denni used her stay-at-home status to provide an opportunity for not only Katie and Brian, but also other children in the Allegan area. She reached out to a friend of hers who operated a mobile gymnastics program in Kalamazoo known as "Tiny Tumblers." The enterprising friend had converted a school bus into a gymnasium on wheels, complete with tumbling mats, bars, and an assortment of gym equipment. Denni arranged for the bus to come to Allegan, and since there was no location for it, for a time the Allegan Tiny Tumblers program was located in the driveway of the Pritchard House.

In addition to a wide variety of Allegan-based activities, Denni arranged for field trips for Katie and Brian to almost every conceivable attraction, whether tourist or educational. She and the kids took trips to Chicago to the Field Museum, the aquarium, and Navy Pier. Lake Michigan was a frequent destination, as were the museums in Lansing, Detroit, and Indianapolis.

It was during some of those trips that we were exposed to the residual effects of Katie's brain tumor we would have to deal with. Many of the more difficult effects weren't physical.

As Katie waited in line for one of the interactive attractions at the Indianapolis Children's museums, a child who was old enough to know better cut in front of Katie. Katie looked at us, not sure what to do.

"Don't worry about it Katie," Denni said. "Not everyone has good manners and waits their turn like you." She looked over at the boy's parents who likely had heard but didn't acknowledge the comment.

"What's wrong with your face?" the kid said as he climbed into the attraction and left Katie standing there, looking confused.

"What a punk," I said, loud enough that I was certain the dad heard me, but I still got no reaction.

On the ride home, Denni tried her best to tell Katie that although most of the people she'd come across in her life would be decent, there were a number of individuals who would be rude or even downright mean, and frankly, they weren't worth worrying about. Both of us were well aware that as much as we preached that gospel, it would be a harder sell as Katie got older and the social situations got more complex.

We attended the First Congregational Church, the same church that General Pritchard and his wife Mary attended one hundred and thirty years earlier, and where my parents were married in 1957. Katie was a proud member of Joyful Noise, the children's choir. She didn't sing a lot, but thoroughly enjoyed wearing the golden robe and frequently went on her own freestyle escapade, running around the choir as the other children stood and sang.

The congregation was led by Barry Lucas and his wife Denise. They were a delightful couple who had become good friends of ours. Barry was part pastor, part auto-mechanic and full-blown Green Bay Packer fanatic. He'd been a missionary, teaching English in Hungary when he met Denise, who was on the same mission as Barry, but from England. He convinced Denise to come across the pond to Allegan where she became a school teacher and he the pastor of the Congregational Church.

I loved hearing Barry preach, as his sermons incorporated just enough wry humor to keep my incredibly short attention span engaged. And the two of us had a great Minnesota Vikings-Green Bay Packers trash-talking rivalry. Even this man of God couldn't help himself but to pile on with Vikings jokes, because after all, it was clear, according to Barry that God was a Packers fan. Like me, he also enjoyed a nice cold beer every now and then. Occasionally I would buy a four-pack of Boddington's Pub Ale and drop it by Barry's house. After all, this was Mayberry, and from my perspective it wouldn't do well for Sheriff Andy Taylor's image to be seen buying beer at the local package store.

I found myself engaging in several church activities, including serving on the Diaconate and video-taping the service for viewing by shut-ins. I found another way to participate in the service that I particularly enjoyed, delivering the children's message.

"What do you see here?" I asked the dozen or so kids seated in a circle on the floor.

"Old tennis shoes," one child said, proud of his observation.

"That's right, old tennis shoes," I agreed. "And dirty. Just look at them. They used to be white and clean, and now they're scuffed and stained and ripped and have all sorts of damage, don't they?"

The kids all nodded.

"Well these shoes have been through a lot of stuff, some good and some not so good. And the not so good stuff we call sin. Sin is when we do things we're not supposed to."

I pulled a black magic marker from my pocket.

"Like sometimes, even though I know better, I tell a lie," I said. "Have any of you done that?" The kids looked around to see which of the guilty ones might admit such a thing in public. Blank stares.

"Well, I've told a lie, and when I do, it makes a stain of sin on me." I took the marker and made a smudge on the old shoe. "See - that's what sin does to us - it stains us and leaves us looking like this old shoe."

"And what do you see here?" I asked as I pulled a new pair of tennis shoes out of the box.

"New shoes!" several of the kids answered at the same time.

"Yep, new shoes!" I agreed. "If you look closely you'll see these shoes are really just like the other ones. In fact, they're the exact same type of shoes," I said, pointing to the colored star that every kid knows is the trademark of Converse All-Stars.

"Does anyone know the story of Jesus on the cross?" I asked. One of the older kids raised his hands.

"The Romans took Jesus and they nailed him to a cross. And it was so he could die for our sins."

"Couldn't have said it any better myself," I said. "That's exactly right. Jesus died on the cross for our sins. And when he did that, he paid the price for all of our sins. It's like he took these old and dirty shoes and made them into the shiny new ones. That's what he did for our souls. And not these soles," I said, pointing to the bottom of the tennis shoe.

"C'mon, that's a better joke than the ones Barry tells," I said, and the rest of the congregation laughed.

I got back to my message.

"Now that doesn't mean we can just sin and make ourselves scuffed and dirty just because we know Jesus died on the cross for our sins, does it?"

All the kids shook their heads.

"Alright then," I said as I concluded my presentation. "Be good this week, keep your hearts and your tennis shoes clean, and we'll see you next Sunday!"

CHAPTER 47

Chantilly Lace 2003

OUR FAMILY HAD GONE SEVERAL years without a dog, and while there were aspects of being dog-free that we enjoyed, we missed having a four-legged friend in the house. As was the case earlier in our relationship, the discussion between Denni and I centered not on what type of dog to get, but what type of boxer to get. The questions to consider were simple: male or female, fawn or brindle?

Male dogs were all I'd ever known, so I was counting on a male addition to the family. At least that was the plan until Chantilly Lace showed up. We'd gone to the local boxer breeder to look at a litter, but the pups were only four weeks old and not yet ready to leave their mother. Denni and I were fully intent on waiting for one of the pups, and we were standing in the barn where the dogs were when out of nowhere came a bounding bundle of energy. It was a small female boxer and she went right up to Katie and wiggled her body against Katie, knocking her to the ground.

"Oh, Tillie!" the breeder said. "Calm down!"

Tillie licked Katie's face and it was clear there was some serious kid-dog bonding taking place.

"I want Tillie!" Katie said, as the dog continued to wiggle its way onto her lap.

"Well, she is available," the breeder said. "She's three years old and the family that had her before returned her because their child became allergic to her. She's a nut, but a great dog and full of energy and love." The breeder left for us to have a conversation on the matter.

"I don't know," I said. "Every boxer I've owned we got when it was a puppy. I'm not sure about taking on an adult dog."

"And there's another reason you don't want her, just say it," Denni offered.

"She's a girl," I said, fully expecting Denni to point out that I was a male chauvinist pig or something to that effect.

"It's just that I've never had a girl dog," I said defensively. "I don't know if I can play with a girl dog like I did with Rocky."

"Well, it looks like you're going to find out," Denni said. "Just look at her and Katie and Brian." By now Brian had joined the mix, and the three of them were playing and laughing, and it was clear to me that the conversation was over.

So Tillie, or Chantilly Lace, as her AKA certificate read, came home with us. I can vouch that the breeder was completely honest in her description of the dog – she was a total nut job. Tillie was a fitting addition, and in short order she became a fixture in our family. After all, what was a little more chaos in the scheme of things?

CHAPTER 48

Ucky Bucky 2003

Although things with Katie were relatively calm at this stage of the game, we were frequently reminded of her brain tumor. Katie's tumor was originally the size of an egg yolk. Now, several years later, what was left after surgery was about as big as a lima bean. The residual effects included the lingering paralysis: her right eye still didn't blink, the entire right side of her face was "frozen," and Katie choked a lot. Over the course of the months and years, Denni and I, and even Brian, became used to Katie's choking, but for those who didn't know her circumstances, it could create quite a stir.

Occasionally, when we were dining out at a restaurant, Katie would start choking without food in her mouth. We'd check to make sure her airway was clear and knew that eventually she'd be fine. It was just something she had to work through herself. We'd seen it enough to know that it would stop and the rest of the table would go about our meal. Denni and I got used to the glares of the guests at other tables who would stare at us with a look that implied what horrible parents we were for ignoring our choking child!

Another residual effect that was hard to miss was the cyclical vomiting. Vomiting is one of those things most families don't seem to have to deal with much. In brain tumor and cancer families it's pretty common. And for Katie it was part of her new normal.

The tumor sat right near her throw-up button and every few months Katie would have periods of cyclical vomiting. She'd be sick as often as fifteen to twenty times a day. At that pace, she became quickly dehydrated, and when we couldn't get it to stop after using Zofran, as often as not, we'd have to put Katie in the hospital, where they'd hook her up to an I-V and wait for it to run its course.

As any parent knows, little kids have no concept of proper vomiting etiquette. More importantly, they totally don't grasp the idea of getting to the porcelain throne prior to the start of the festivities. They just look at you and then projectile vomit all over the floor. After a number of these episodes, Denni decided to try another approach. In order to encourage a neater process, Denni crafted designer "Ucky Bucky's" that were strategically placed around the house. We encouraged Katie that if that special feeling cropped up, to immediately grab a designer bin. For a long time, it was hit or miss, literally, but she eventually got the concept. Whenever we heard, "Where's my Ucky Bucky?" it was a call to action. And Brian found as he got older that when not in use they made excellent garages for his Matchbox cars.

CHAPTER 49

The Never-Ending Spiral of Doom 2004

§

NOTWITHSTANDING THE MEDICAL APPOINTMENTS, WE tried to do what we could to make life as normal as possible in our family. Katie and Brian had a fantastic relationship, and it was an absolute joy to watch them together. Brian idolized his big sister, and although they had their moments, they got along tremendously well.

We had turned one of the upstairs bedrooms into a large playroom, and Katie and Brian played together in that space for hours on end. Katie would have her American Girl and Barbie dolls arranged neatly with Dakota, her constant companion, tucked under her arm. She'd play house and decorate and redecorate her Barbie playhouse. Brian would have on his Bob the Builder tool belt and she'd instruct him on which projects needed undertaking in her own version of *This Old Barbie House*.

Though they spent a good amount of their time playing inside, we were glad that our kids enjoyed being outdoors. Michigan has four beautiful seasons, and we loved every one of them. With several acres to explore on our property, they played tag and hide and seek for hours. We set up a croquet course and made part of the yard into a ball field, and Katie and Brian challenged the adults to whiffle ball games several times a week.

Dozens of huge trees scattered around the house made a beautiful multi-colored canopy in the fall. I repurposed a former goldfish pond in the garden into a fire pit, and on many fall days we'd build leaf houses, and then make s'mores over the open fire. In the heart of the north, when the snow fell, we had plenty of it to make snowmen and have snowball fights. If it sounds like all of these scenes might make for Norman Rockwell prints, they could have. It really was an incredible setting.

Aside from Brian, Katie's playmates consisted of several girls in her class, and they formed a typical clique as girls do. And there was one little girl ritual I could have done without.

Katie continued with her dance lessons and the weekly classes were all building in a crescendo towards the ultimate experience in the dance universe - the dance recital, or, as I called it, "the Never-Ending Spiral of Doom." I really do like the concept of little girls enjoying dancing, and I appreciate the art and physicality of it. But for the life of me, I just cannot get my head around the dance recital. Being so fidgety myself, I never understood the notion of kids under the age of ten having to sit quietly for so long, and every few hours be herded onstage for a three-minute dance, which, especially at the youngest ages, although cute, looked more like choreographed seizures. All the while, parents seemed delusional that they were witnessing the next coming of Mikhail Baryshnikov.

I'm pretty sure it's state law that parents and grandparents must attend all recitals, along with any family members not currently incarcerated or hospitalized. Brian Proctor, therefore, endured countless recitals, and, to his credit, with fewer visible tantrums than his father.

As the months passed, Denni enjoyed having the time to focus on our children. She also became even more engaged in the community. She served as President of the Library Board in Allegan as I continued my teaching responsibilities at Western Michigan University. Both of us had also become more active with the Pediatric Brain Tumor Foundation. Whether by intent, accident, or perseverance, we had stumbled on our own version of comfortable. After several years now, the question that always stuck in the back of our minds was, "How long is this going to last?"

Both Denni and I frequently received inquiries from friends, acquaintances, and coworkers from all around the country, requesting a status update on Katie. It was heart-warming to know that so many people cared so deeply for Katie and were interested in her journey. From the time of the Katie Updates in the hospital, we'd decided to share Katie's journey. Originally it was more out of our need for support, but as the time passed, it had evolved into something more. Just as we were drawn to Allegan for the Pritchard House, we felt that Katie's story was somehow bigger than all of us.

From the onset, when Katie was in the hospital for her original surgeries, lots of people had reached out to express concern and support for Katie. People who'd never met Katie felt very close to her, and dozens of people were caught up in Katie's journey. It was especially heartwarming to hear from so many people who said how inspired they were by Katie. For a girl of such a young age, she was clearly having an impact on the lives of a large number of individuals. It gave us a sense of satisfaction that we were on the right course. Yes, it was bigger than us. I couldn't be sure of the details, but I knew this, too, was a God thing.

To: Friends of Katie
From: Rob & Denni Proctor
Date: Monday, March 15, 2004
Re: Katie Update

We've been getting enough "How's Katie doing?" emails that we figured it was time for a Katie update.

Katie is eight-and-a-half years old now and in second grade. She is very fortunate that her brain tumor has had no impact on her intellectual abilities. She's literally one of the top students in her class. She recently stunned the doctors by spelling "onomatopoeia" as they were getting ready to sedate her for an MRI.

Katie continues to study dance and absolutely loves it. She is trying out for her school's talent show by dancing a hula with one of her friends. She has developed a small circle of friends, and her classmates have been very supportive. Katie really does the best she can to fit in and just be a normal kid. We are very proud of her, as she is turning into such a neat young lady.

Katie had gone several months without any cyclical vomiting, and we were hoping that this would stop. But she's had two episodes recently, ending up in the hospital yet again. Another MRI scan was done just last week, and Dr. Crone said he is confident that the remaining tumor is showing no signs of re-growth, so the vomiting is just an unfortunate side effect. She has almost daily headaches, but controls them fairly well through medications.

The facial and eye paralysis will probably be a permanent condition and several plastic surgery options have been considered and ruled out. Her right eye is constantly covered in gel and drops and the doctors say she doesn't really use that eye so the degeneration will likely continue. Her throat paralysis will likely be permanent as well. But, as Dr. Crone points out, all of these are problems that Katie can *live* with.

Katie's neurosurgeon, Dr. Kerry Crone, recently gained national media attention as he has pioneered a new technique to make previously inoperable tumors now open to surgery as an option. In fact, there is a headline in today's edition of CNN.com on his developments. We feel truly blessed to have been directed to Dr. Crone for Katie's care.

We are eternally thankful to all of you for your love, support and prayers over the past four years. God Bless you all!!

Love,

Rob, Denni, Katie & Brian Proctor

-The Never-Ending Spiral of Doom Dance Recital, 2005 edition.

CHAPTER 50

Gu Gone 2004

§

In the years since Katie's diagnosis, our whole family had become involved with the Pediatric Brain Tumor Foundation. We initiated an annual letter-writing campaign to our friends and colleagues explaining Katie's current situation, as well as giving an overview of the Pediatric Brain Tumor Foundation and a request for donations. It was quite effective, and Team Proctor was one of the top fundraisers each year.

The Ride for Kids event was built around a forty-five-mile motorcycle ride through some of the more scenic parts around Ann Arbor. Prior to these events, I'd visited Ann Arbor a few times to participate in some court-ordered insurance mediation sessions at the University of Michigan. As fine a school as the University of Michigan was, I found the campus and downtown to be rather drab and figured the surrounding area would be the same. With my limited visits to the area, I had no idea Ann Arbor was home to some beautiful rolling hills and comprised a good number of horse farms and large country estates. Many of the estates were for higher-ups in the auto manufacturing world as Detroit was located about forty-five minutes away.

In 2004 Denni decided to put a new twist on our fundraising campaign. Early in the year Denni announced that she would *run* the forty-five-mile Ride for Kids course that August. It was a daunting goal and although she ran with a group of friends almost daily and had done so for years, most of her runs were fewer than seven or eight miles in length. In all her years of running, she'd never run anything longer than a half marathon.

But Denni made a pact with herself and committed to a rigorous training program. Her intent was to run the course in two intervals, two weeks apart. Her training regimen consisted of increasing lengths to eventually give her enough endurance to complete the two intervals, the first leg of twenty-two miles, and the last leg of over twenty-three miles.

Although I fully supported Denni in her endeavor, I had no intentions of joining her. I had dabbled at running a time or two in my life and concluded at an early age that I hated the sport. My father had jogged his way into the 5,000 Mile Club at the YMCA in Lima, running tens of thousands of laps around an indoor track. Several times during my youth, my dad dragged me and my brother along in the early morning hours to run with him, but I hated it. For years, my motto has been, "if it's longer than a few hundred yards, I'd rather drive." I had taken several more stabs at running during and after college, and was never good at it. After two knee surgeries for injuries I incurred playing racquetball, I figured I'd pass on the entire running thing.

Denni, on the other hand, loved to run. She ran daily, and over the course of months and years of running, had clearly become addicted to it. In fact, there was no guessing if Denni had run on any given day. Her mood was noticeably different on days when she couldn't run. My dad was the same way, and I've learned over the years that many runners get an adrenaline high from their sport, and when they miss their run, they miss that high. I've found comfort in the fact that I can get that same inner glow from the right amount of caffeine.

As August neared, Denni's training became even more rigorous, and I joined in on the campaign. Not as a runner, but as a pacer, driving the car a few miles at a time and giving Denni much-needed water and her "Gu." Gu (pronounced "goo") was a pudding-like substance that contained significant concentrations of amino acids and carbohydrates, geared to the serious athlete to be taken at crucial times during long runs. At least that was the intent.

On one occasion during an especially long and hot session, I was fulfilling my support duties, driving the Honda Odyssey minivan several miles in front of Denni and letting her catch up to get some water and then repeating the process. While it was helpful to Denni, I found it quite boring. In order to curb my boredom, I brought a newspaper to read. Waiting several miles ahead of Denni, I read the paper and mindlessly nibbled on a snack. I was engrossed in my paper, and was startled when Denni knocked on the window, out of breath and exhausted.

"Where's my water and Gu?" she asked through gulping breaths.

I opened the door and handed Denni a half-empty water bottle.

"Did you drink my water?" she asked. I just looked at her and then turned my head away to avoid further eye contact. And that's when Denni saw it.

"What the *hell* is on your chin?" she asked in astonishment.

"Nothing," I said, sounding like a six-year-old who'd been caught with his hand in the cookie jar. I wiped my chin and felt the chocolate Gu on my fingers. The empty packet lay on the front seat, now visible to Denni.

"You ate my Gu?" Denni said in a tone I hadn't experienced before.

"You owe me a dollar," I said in a badly-timed attempt at humor, referring to Denni's rare outburst involving a Swear Jar word.

There would be no more Gu on this day, and the ride home was not a pleasant experience for me. Another life lesson learned, this one entitled: *Sometimes Rob is an Idiot.*

On the day of the Ride for Kids, Denni finished the final leg of her forty-five-mile journey and made the entrance into the packed tent at the Washtenaw Community College, the new site of the event. The emcee announced what she'd completed that day on the loudspeaker and the place erupted in applause. Then Denni relayed her experience to the audience.

"Running the course was hard. I'd never been through anything like that in my life. There were times when it hurt and I felt like giving up. And when I got to those times I thought of these kids sitting in front of you. They're in a battle that's so much harder than what I faced. And I know sometimes they hurt. They must feel like giving up, too, but they don't give up - ever. Of all the kids we've met in the years since our journey started with Katie's diagnosis, I've never seen a single one of them give up. So I didn't either. These kids inspire me. They should inspire all of us. We need to keep the fight going. These kids deserve that from us, because they're running a race more difficult than any of us can imagine."

At first there was silence and as I looked around I saw a number of men and women wiping tears from their eyes, then there was clapping and in a few short seconds, people began to get on their feet and the applause turned into a thunderous standing ovation.

I could hear the voice in my head. It wasn't God, but it *was* the word of God. "Well done, my good and faithful servant." Denni had earned His praise.

CHAPTER 51

Streets of Heaven 2004

§

THE SUMMER OF 2004 WAS an emotional time for us. Katie's tumor appeared to be stable, which was the most important detail to the doctors, and, therefore, the most important detail to Denni and me. The residual effects of the facial and eye paralysis and vomiting were engrained into our daily lives, and as a family we'd become used to them. But a few things were happening around us that made us even more grateful for Katie's progress in her brain tumor battle.

Since moving to Allegan, Denni and I had formed a close relationship with Rick and Denise Grover. Rick was a lawyer at a firm that performed insurance defense work for my claim operation at State Farm. Rick and I connected from the moment we met, and the business relationship had turned into a social one. Rick and I went golfing, and occasionally he and Denise joined Denni and me for dinner. A deep friendship developed between Denni and Denise, in fact; Denise became Denni's best friend in Michigan. They had two boys, Richard and Warren, who were a few years older than Katie and Brian. The Grover boys became as close as any cousins our kids could have known.

Denise nick-named Katie "Katie-Bug" as an infant, and the moniker had stuck throughout the years. The Grovers became friends with David and Holly as well. They even traveled to Cincinnati one summer when

Katie had an appointment at Children's, and we all made it into a large group vacation, including a trip to Kings Island amusement park and a Cincinnati Reds baseball game.

We were all shocked in 2002 when Denise was diagnosed with breast cancer and had aggressive treatment and therapy. It shook Denni to the core as she witnessed the disease inflicting its cruel progression. Over the two-year period there were glimpses of remission, but in 2004 the disease returned with a vengeance.

It was during this time that another person's battle with cancer hit close to home for us.

Courtney Grauman was a high school freshman who lived less than a mile from our house in Allegan. We had first learned of Courtney's illness when we saw her at the Allegan County Fair parade and she was in a wheelchair, having been recently diagnosed with a brain tumor. Denni contacted Courtney's mom, Shelly, and the two arranged for Courtney and Katie to get together.

A five-year span separated them, but Courtney and Katie hit it off like gangbusters. On nice days, Shelly would bring Courtney over to our house and they'd sit on the covered porch or in the kitchen and talk. After Courtney went to Hawaii on her Make-A-Wish trip, she showed Katie the pictures of her with the dolphins and it was clear they had a fantastic experience.

Shortly after we'd met, I asked Shelly about Courtney's diagnosis.

"She has a glioblastoma, a GBM, but she's going to beat it." As I went about my daily prayer ritual, Courtney was on my list, and I begged for a miracle that would allow Courtney to beat the odds and beat the horrible tumor.

By the summer of 2004, Denise Grover's condition had deteriorated and the outcome became inevitable. Only the timing was unknown. For years Denni and I hosted a "Ribs Party" with half a dozen couples from Allegan and Grand Rapids. From the onset Rick and Denise had been included in the group, and in June we assembled the gang. The Grovers made a brief appearance, as Denise was exhausted. That night Denni cried herself to sleep at the thought of losing her friend, the finality of it seemingly much closer than ever.

We could see the decline in Courtney's condition as well. She and Katie got together and they shared a piece of Denni's homemade raspberry pie. Courtney loved the pie, the girls enjoyed a wonderful few hours together. It would be the last time the two would see each other, and Courtney died shortly after the visit.

The funerals of Denise Grover and Courtney Grauman were less than two weeks apart. Denise was forty-five years old when she died, leaving behind a loving husband and two incredible teenage boys. Courtney was fifteen years old and had been robbed of the opportunity to even finish high school, let alone live a full life on earth. A brain tumor had robbed her of that life just as breast cancer had robbed Denise of hers. It was beyond unfair. All I could think was that they were both too young for this to happen, and I hated cancer to the core of my being.

At Courtney's funeral, I looked over at Shelly and Leroy Grauman sitting in shock as they sat several feet from their daughter's coffin. My mind started to race. I thought of a phrase I'd heard a number of times throughout my life, "There but for the grace of God go I." Then I caught myself on the word grace. What kind of grace is it when a parent has to bury their child? What kind of grace turns a healthy teenager and a vibrant mother into cancer-riddled individuals in unbearable pain? Why Courtney and not Katie? As was often the case in these moments, I had to stop myself. After all, what was the point of it?

One of the songs playing on the radio at the time, Sherrie Austin's "Streets of Heaven," made me choke up, but I forced myself to listen to it in its entirety whenever it came on. The song relayed a parent's torment as their child lay in a hospital bed, and it wasn't certain if the child would live through the night. The mother begs God to spare her little girl, wondering who'll hold her hand when she crosses the streets of Heaven. I connected with that song on so many levels.

I'd been praying more over the past few years than I had in the several decades prior. Prayer had a different feeling now than it had in the past. It felt like I was actually talking with God, and it brought a sense of closeness that I'd never felt before. But I was learning another important lesson about prayer, as well. I was coming to accept the fact that sometimes the answer to prayer is "no."

CHAPTER 52

Find Your Happy Place 2005

§

SINCE OUR ORIGINAL TRIP IN 2001, our family had fallen in love with Hawaii. In 2003, Denni and I made a return trip without the kids and stayed at a resort on Oahu. In a move neither of us would have considered in our prior life, we bought a timeshare at Marriott's Ko Olina resort. It was a splurge, especially now that Denni wasn't working. But we rationalized it, since on the merry-go-round of life, you only go around once. Considering the obstacles we'd faced over the past several years, we figured our family had earned a little splurging.

We returned to Hawaii in 2005, this time as a complete family. Katie was almost ten years old, and Brian was nearly five. It was certainly a different trip compared to the one we'd made just a year after Katie's surgery in 2001. As we had done on the first trip, we visited Holly and David on the Big Island of Hawaii, and then they accompanied us to Oahu. From the black sands of Hilo on the Big Island, to the white sandy beaches on the North Shore of Oahu, I became even more enamored with Hawaii. To me, there was something so special about Hawaii. It truly was my "happy place."

During our visits to Ko Olina, we became acquainted with several of the staff members who worked there, and one in particular, nicknamed Izzy. He was a Samoan who'd been on the island for years, and was a popular fixture around the resort. As he passed Denni and me at the pool one day, he said, "Aloha, Mrs. Proctor. Have a blessed day."

Denni looked up from her book and smiled. "You too, Izzy. God bless you."

Izzy stopped. I wondered if Denni had said something inappropriate, but couldn't imagine what it had been.

"You know, Mrs. Proctor, we have a church service here at Ko Olina on Sunday mornings. It's on the lawn between the lagoons. We'd love for you to come."

"We'd love to come," Denni said. Izzy gave her details and was off.

I looked at Denni, and we both said at the same time, "It's a God thing."

Denni had used that phrase on a number of occasions since our marriage. She felt strongly that many events unfolded by divine design and not happenstance. I had never doubted what Denni felt, it was just that I didn't think too deeply about it. Since I've found a deeper meaning in my own faith, I at least understand the phrase better, and have to admit the feeling can be pretty strong.

Sunday morning Ko Olina church service became a family tradition for a number of years. And it turned out, Izzy not only attended the services, he led them. Sitting outside on the green lawn in Hawaii with the ocean breezes in the background, surrounded by picture-perfect blue skies and deep turquoise waters, I could fully embrace the concept of God's handiwork on earth. I loved the Congregational church in Allegan, but if there was another church I cared to attend on a regular basis, it would be this one. Paradise on earth leading to eternal paradise. The way I figured, it wasn't a bad deal any way you looked at it.

Denni, Katie, Brian, Nana, and Bald-Bald with a giant sea turtle on the North Shore of Oahu.

CHAPTER 53

Farewell, Dr. Crone 2005

"I'M VERY PLEASED WITH THE stability in Katie's tumor," Dr. Crone said, as he finished one of Katie's lengthy examination appointments. "As you know, the radiologists and I don't always agree, but we do agree on the fact that her tumor is stable. We're more than five years from her original surgery now, and outside of a few glitches, the scans have shown what's left is just sitting there. With that being the case the surgical component becomes much less important. In essence, you don't need me anymore. I think it's time we transferred Katie's care over to the neuro-oncology team."

Neither Denni nor I were sure what to say.

"So, this is a good thing? You're not just trying to ditch us?" I asked with a smile.

"No, trust me, this is a good thing," Dr. Crone replied. "A very good thing. I'll transfer Katie's care over to Doctor Sutton. Mary Sutton is a great neurologist and she'll determine the care path from here."

"For how long?" Denni asked.

"We have some patients who are now in their thirties that we've been following for years," Dr. Crone replied. "I'm not speaking for Dr. Sutton, but I imagine she'll want to keep an especially close eye on things during her teenage years. Teenagers go through an awful lot physically, so we want to make sure we're watching everything closely during that time period."

The appointment now over, Dr. Crone rose and Denni got up from her seat and came over to him.

"Doctor Crone, I can't thank you enough for all you've done for Katie and for us. We've said all along she couldn't have been in better hands." Denni became emotional as she continued. "I can't imagine going through what we have with anybody else. You were always there for us. You always took the time to answer our questions and it was clear you put your heart and soul into helping Katie. You've been a God-send. I'm going to miss you. We're all going to miss you. Thank you for saving Katie's life. Thank you for everything you've done. God bless you."

"It's been my pleasure," Dr. Crone said, as he looked at our daughter and smiled. "Katie is a very special girl. Hey kiddo, when you graduate college, I want an announcement – deal?"

Katie looked at Dr. Crone, smiled and nodded her head in confused agreement.

"Deal," I said. "And I thank you, too."

Denni and Dr. Crone embraced for one final hug. I actually took one myself. After five years, Dr. Crone and his staff had become like family. Saying goodbye was extremely hard.

After spending so much time in the care of Dr. Crone, none of us knew what to expect. When Dr. Sutton came in the room she had another doctor with her. Dr. Maryam Fouladi was a neuro-oncologist, and Dr. Sutton informed us that the two of them would be tag-teaming Katie's care. Dr. Sutton would manage the neurology end of things, including prescribing medications as necessary, monitoring Katie's daily headaches, and determining her physical progress and limitations.

Dr. Fouladi would oversee the MRI scans and monitor the tumor portion of Katie's care. Katie's tumor was stable, but there was a cyst sitting right next to the tumor. As Katie grew, Dr. Fouladi wanted to make certain everything was checked pretty closely. In fact, she preferred annual scans, and after one two-year period between MRI scans, Katie was put on an annual regimen.

Over time, Dr. Sutton and Dr. Fouladi became just as close to Katie and our family as Dr. Crone had been. Each appointment became an opportunity to build a bonding relationship, and over time we forged not only an incredible professional-patient relationship, but we'd become friends as well. It made sense, as in some ways the doctors at Children's were an extension of our family. They were great doctors for sure. The fact that they were such great people was icing on the cake.

CHAPTER 54

Life of Brian
2006

BRIAN WAS AN INCREDIBLE ADDITION to our family in so many ways. Just as with Katie, Denni devoted unbelievable energy to Brian. As soon as he was out of his infancy stage, he was mobile with a capital *M*. The bike trailer now held two kids in tow, and Denni, Katie, and Brian were among the most visible residents in and around Allegan.

Brian's personality was very different from Katie's. I'm fascinated by the research around birth order personality traits and believe there has to be something more to it than coincidence. First child Katie was thoughtful and approached situations with caution. Second child Brian, on the other hand, was a "jump first, ask questions later" type of child, much like his dad, who is also a second child.

Denni and I knew that things would be different when he uttered his first words, which were "I'm OK." That became his go-to phrase. When he ran headfirst into a tree in the yard, "I'm OK." When he tumbled down the stairs playing with the dog, "I'm OK." He was a rough-tough, rock 'em-sock 'em kid, and due to his huge size, his mom gave him the nickname "Chunk-A-Load-A-Buddha-Boy, as he reminded Denni of the plump statues of Buddha she'd seen.

Brian was a very happy child. Katie had been a happy child, too, but Brian combined happiness and energy in a way that I described as "the energizer bunny on steroids."

Mostly because of the logistics involved, Brian accompanied Denni and Katie on almost all of Katie's medical appointments. The frequency of Katie's medical attention varied, but overall it was a significant part of our lives, and Brian had known nothing different. As a toddler, on too many occasions to count, he packed up his Matchbox cars and headed off with Katie and Denni to therapist's and doctor's offices, as well as hospitals in Grand Rapids, Kalamazoo, and Cincinnati. And he tagged along with a remarkable attitude. He was always, or almost always, the happiest kid in the waiting room. And, undoubtedly, the healthiest kid.

Life with Brian was entertaining to say the least. In addition to his energetic personality, he developed a quick wit and just had a way about him that made us all feel like we were the straight part of the comedy team, while Brian filled the headline comic role.

His antics started at an early age. I described several of his more noteworthy events in the Proctor Gazette, the Christmas newsletter we sent to family and friends that had become an annual tradition for us. There were two stories involving Brian that stuck out in particular and both related to Mother's Day, oddly enough.

In 2003 the lead story of our Christmas newsletter featured Brian:

Scene 1:

Operator: "Hello this is 9-1-1, what is your emergency?"

Little Boy: "I can't find my Mommy."

Operator: "You can't find your Mommy? "What's your name?"

Boy: "Brian Proctor."

Operator: "Where's your Daddy?"

Boy: "Daddy's outside digging a hole for her."

Click.

Scene 2, several minutes later:

Rob was out in the garden, sweaty and dirt-covered, busily digging a large hole to plant Denni's Mothers' Day rose bushes. Imagine his surprise when a police car rushed into the driveway and the officer asked what he was doing with the shovel, where his wife was, and why his children were calling 9-1-1 to report their missing mother.

<u>The rest of the story:</u>

Putting Brian down for a nap, Rob informed him that he was going to dig a hole for Mommy (to plant the rose bushes). Brian had awoken from his nap and couldn't find Denni, as she had gone for an afternoon jog. Brian had been previously instructed that if something was really wrong he should call 9-1-1. Apparently, awakening from a nap without being able to locate her was serious enough to warrant the call. And at less than 3 years old, we were stunned that he could even dial 9-1-1!

Several years later Brian eclipsed the *9-1-1* story with his own Mothers' Day sentiments, which also achieved leadoff status in the 2006 Proctor Gazette.

It sounded like such a cute project. Brian's kindergarten class was making Mothers' Day cards. Each child had a list of things they liked best about their mothers. It was a question and answer format, posed to the children about their favorite things Moms made for them, did for, them, etc.

Everything seemed to be going quite well until Brian came to this fill-in-the-blank question; "My Mommy is prettiest when_______.

The other children provided answers like "when she wears her blue dress," or "when she gets her hair done," and other appropriate responses. Do you think Brian Proctor could have provided such a tame answer? Of course not. His answer to the question?

"My Mommy is prettiest when she is naked."

Denni was flattered and disturbed at the same time. We have a new rule that Brian is not allowed in our bathroom when Denni is getting dressed in the morning!

Such was life with Brian. Katie took most of the chaotic free-for-all in stride. After all, her life had not exactly been smooth sailing up until this point. And his addition helped our family take advantage of an important therapy we all could use to help us along the way. The secret weapon was humor. It had been a big part of our lives prior, but in our new reality it was downright crucial.

Brian adored his big sister. He was far too young to understand all of the issues she'd been through or was facing. But he had a special soul and an approach to her beyond description. His demeanor and energy brought a new dimension to our family, and was just what we *all* needed.

Watching Brian interact with his sister, I witnessed countless episodes of what I can only describe as unconditional love. He lifted us all up, and that is a pretty neat accomplishment for a kid who hadn't even started grade school yet.

CHAPTER 55

North Dakota, South Dakota, Lost Dakota 2006

TRIPS TO CINCINNATI HAD BECOME somewhat routine, and Katie's tumor had been stable for a while. The appointments at Cincinnati Children's were much less stressful, but even so Denni and I cautioned ourselves about getting cocky.

The ride to Cincinnati from Allegan was a solid six hours. Often, we'd stop at my mom's house in Lima to visit and then make the last two hours of the journey. We had made the trip so many times over the years that we knew which gas stations and rest stops along the way had the cleanest restrooms, and which exits were truly the "easy-off/easy-on" variety.

The rest stops were a chance for all of us to stretch our legs and for Brian to run off some energy. Both children were often reminded to check for their possessions as they were getting in and out of the minivan. And the kids could be counted on to provide the same auto-reply answer, "I did!"

On this particular trip, we arrived in Cincinnati after dark, and Katie and Brian were groggy. In addition to their suitcases, both kids had their most important worldly possessions with them. For Brian, it was a backpack full of Matchbox cars and his Christopher Robin stuffed animal. For

Katie, she had a tote full of dolls, but her most prized possession in the whole world was Dakota. Dakota and Katie had been through thick and thin, and the stuffed animal had accompanied her on countless medical visits. Over the years, the bloodstain had long worn off, but to me it was one of the things about Dakota that I remembered most of all.

I found myself surprisingly attached to Dakota as well. After all, it might have been a stuffed animal, but Dakota had been with us through it all, and Denni and I often had to carry or hold it. To Brian, it was practically a half-brother. For Katie, Dakota was family.

As I cleared the contents of the car, Denni came out of the house.

"Katie wants to know where Dakota is."

"I thought she had him," I said. "This is the last of the stuff and I haven't seen him."

"I'll go back inside and look around and you check the car again," Denni said as she scurried off.

Thirty minutes later, after tearing apart the car twice and looking through every personal belonging of all of the family members, we reached a terrible conclusion.

"Dakota's gone," I said. "When is the last time you saw him?" I asked.

"I don't know!" Katie said, now in tears.

"You didn't take him in to Gigi's. I called her and he's not there. We stopped at that rest area in Indiana. That has to be where he fell out. I've told you kids a hundred times to check for your stuff," I said as started with my usual lecture.

"Rob, not now. I think she understands, but that isn't the point right now," Denni said.

Katie was inconsolable. Dakota was gone. Although we stopped at the same rest stop on the way back, there were no signs of Dakota. After our fruitless search, we got back in the minivan and continued the journey home to Michigan. I felt surprisingly sad considering it was a stuffed animal we were looking for. Still, it wasn't just any stuffed animal. It was Dakota.

As the car pulled back on the highway, and over Katie's tears, Denni said a nice prayer for Dakota. She ended by saying, "And I pray Dakota ended up in a nice and happy home."

"I do too," I added, with a heavy heart.

PART IV
Lightning Strikes Twice

CHAPTER 56

If Walls Could Talk 2007

§

In the spring of 2007, the entire Proctor family and the Pritchard House were showcased on HGTV's show *If Walls Could Talk*. The curator of the local museum in Allegan contacted the TV show and informed them of the Pritchard House and our story in moving there. Figuring it might be fun, we agreed to participate.

The show highlighted the General's capture of Jefferson Davis and featured several historical items in the Pritchard House. As the segment ended, the narrator spoke of the six generations that had occupied the house, and concluded with a line that turned out to be quite ironic.

"The Pritchard House and its furnishings have been in the family for the last one hundred and forty years. And if the current owners have anything to say about it, they'll be in the family for another hundred and forty years."

Or not.

After more than a dozen years of living in the Pritchard House, I had a change of heart. It wasn't an overnight process, but I'd come to a conclusion. As much as I loved the Pritchard House, living in the house, and Allegan, forever was no longer the dream I once thought it was. I'd planted the seed with Denni in a number of conversations, and it didn't come as a surprise to Denni.

The Five-Year Plan we started in 1994 had turned into the Five-Years-to-Life Plan. With one renovation after another, the house was becoming a lifelong project. It was financially draining, but it wasn't just the money that was taking its toll. It took an incredible amount of energy to live in the house. There was work to be done almost every weekend, and the size and scale of all it was sometimes overwhelming. With almost fifty windows, changing out storm windows and screens for the Michigan seasons was a monumental task. I had to buy a commercial leaf vacuum for the incredible amount of leaves that fell every year. From removing asbestos to replacing knob-and-tube wiring, everything we touched needed expertise, knowledge, and money to renovate or repair.

More than twelve years into the process, I had concluded that no matter what, it would never end. When opportunity knocked, I answered the door.

"I've been offered a chance to interview for a job in Bloomington," I said one night.

"You know what that means," Denni responded.

"Leaving this house," I said. Just the sound of those words made me sad. "This house has been in our family for over one hundred and forty years. When we came here I really thought it was for good. I knew it might be hard, but I really thought it was possible. But things have changed. We've changed."

"Yes, we certainly have," said Denni.

"As much as I love the house I just can't envision living in it forever," I continued. "Dealing with Katie's situation has made us all realize there are a lot more important things in life. I love it here and I know you do too, but it's a house. When you get down to it, its boards and bricks and plaster and furniture. We've seen just how time consuming and expensive it is to do what we want to do with this house. And the reality is that we know it's never going to stop. We'll renovate rooms and have ongoing house projects forever if we stay here. I'm just not sure that is how I want to spend either our time or our money from here on out. And the other piece is my job."

"There it is," Denni said.

"There's what?" I asked, as if I didn't understand.

"Oh, come on," Denni said. "It's State Farm. She's your mistress. In some ways, I'm surprised you lasted this long. We talked about this when we moved up here. I asked you lots of times, 'Are you sure? Are you sure you can limit yourself being in Allegan?' You've seen other people promoted and opportunities go by, and I could tell it was eating at you."

"Fair enough," I said. "But it's more than State Farm. As much as I love Allegan and this house, I just feel like there's more for us. And a change would do us good. Leaving is going to be hard, I know that. But I think it'll also be good for all of us. Let's at least think about it."

Over the coming weeks, there were more conversations along the theme of leaving the Pritchard House. The move to Allegan in 1994 involved just the two of us and that was emotional enough. This time there were two children involved.

"If we move, it's going to crush the kids," Denni said.

"Yeah, I know," I answered. "But kids are resilient and the timing is about as good as it gets. Both kids have to change schools next year, anyway. Katie will be going to middle school, and Brian will be heading to elementary school. And she's had a few speed bumps with friends this year."

Near the end of the school year, the small clique of girls she had hung with throughout elementary school went through some internal turmoil. In the end, Katie was left on the outside looking in. It was a normal part of childhood that impacts all little girls, not just ones with brain tumors. But this was the first time anything significant had come up in the relationship area, and having Katie sad about her friends added to everyone's stress.

"We both know the middle school and high years are likely going to be rough for her, whether we're in Allegan or somewhere else," I said.

"I know, and that breaks my heart," Denni agreed. "And yes, it will be different buildings, but the kids will be the same kids. Most of her classmates know her story, and I just think that it might help."

"Well, it might help a little," I replied. "But kids are kids. This year didn't end all that hot for her. I'm sure they'll mend the fence, but that's not going to be the end of it. In fact, for that kind of stuff, the big issues are just starting. It might not be a bad thing for her to get a clean slate with a group of new kids."

"Brian loves it here," Denni added, changing the direction away from the conversation about Katie. "He loves Allegan and this house, he loves his buddies, and he loves his school. He loves everything about being here."

"That's exactly it," I said. "That kid loves everything. He'll be upset for a while, but he could live on Mars and be happy as long as he could find a Martian kid to play with. Look at him at the beach or a playground. He goes up to kids all the time and starts to play like they've been pals forever. That's one of the coolest things about his personality. I'm less worried about Brian than I am about Katie."

"Me, too," Denni said.

Family roots run deep, and I had been very happy living in Allegan. I absolutely loved my job at State Farm and teaching at Western Michigan University. I also knew Denni had come to love Allegan as much as I did, but I'd convinced myself that the lure of the Pritchard House had run its course. For me, it was time to consider broader horizons.

In the summer of 2007, I was offered a position at State Farm's home office in Bloomington, Illinois. After some serious consideration, prayer, and lots of discussion with Denni, I decided to take the job. Telling my mom would be difficult. Telling the kids would be heart-breaking.

My mom was very understanding. She'd seen the amount of work that had gone into the house and may have had an idea as to the cost. She visited frequently, and on most of her trips there was some sort of house renovation project proposed, underway, or recently completed. It had been a never-ending construction project. She told me she was grateful that we had made the commitment to restore the house, and was glad that the house had stayed in the family longer than it would have if we had sold it back in 1994. Naturally she was sad, but fully supported the decision to leave.

Shortly after I received the offer, Denni had another high school reunion in New Jersey. Since we had enjoyed her 20th reunion so much, we were excited about returning. We decided to make a vacation trip out of it by extending the trip to include Cooperstown, New York, and Niagara Falls. Denni and I had been to Cooperstown previously, and Katie and Brian had been properly brainwashed by their mother into being die-hard Cincinnati Reds fans. Denni wanted to show them the Reds exhibit at the Baseball Hall of Fame, and we found Cooperstown to be an incredibly quaint town. I also thought it would be a good opportunity to get on some neutral ground to inform the kids of the new chapter in our lives.

"When do you plan on making the announcement?" Denni asked me as we loaded the car for the return trip home to Michigan.

"When I find the right time," I replied.

"Hmmm," Denni said. Shortly into the trip, Denni said, "So, what's on your mind?" as the necessary prompt. I didn't bite.

Outside of Buffalo, we stopped at an Applebee's for lunch.

"You'd better do this now," said Denni, out of patience. "It's not fair to wait until the last minute."

I knew she was right. Again.

As we got back into the car, I started the engine, and Denni sensed that I was going to get back on the road, so she paused the movie that I had just started in the DVD player.

"Now," Denni said, and I knew I had no more time to borrow. I've been involved in a number of difficult conversations in my life, and I rarely shied away from them. For some reason, this was tough for me. But it was time to face the music.

"Guess what? I've got some big news." The kids looked away from the now frozen DVD screen and I had everyone's attention.

"You know how we've lived in Allegan a long time? And how we've been working on the house a lot, and I've had to go back and forth between Kalamazoo and Grand Rapids with my job at State Farm?" The only response was blank stares from both children.

"I've decided to take a new job with State Farm and it's in Illinois. So we're going to be moving there. What do you think about that?"

It took a few seconds for what I had just said to sink in. Katie was the first to respond.

"So we have to move away from Allegan?" she asked in that sweet tone only a child can muster.

"Yes, honey, we're going to be moving to Bloomington, Illinois," I responded with confidence. "You went there last summer with Mom when I had a business trip. Remember? They had a neat putt-putt course at State Farm Park," I said, trying to find any connection that might interest my children. It didn't work.

"But I like Allegan. I don't want to move." Katie said, her voice starting to register the shock.

"Do we have to move out of our house?" Brian asked as the logistics of the situation were moving his near seven-year old thought processes along.

"Yes, honey, it does," I said. "That makes me and Mommy sad, too. But we can go back and visit it and in lots of ways, it will always be our house."

"But I like Allegan. I like our house. I don't want to move," Katie said, restating her case with a voice that sounded so sad I could feel it.

"I know it seems that way now, but I have a feeling we're all going to love it there," I said, again hoping that my upbeat answer would help.

With those words of assurance, both kids began to cry.

"I'm not moving! And I'm not talking to you!" Katie exclaimed, as she put her headphones back on and continued to cry.

Brian was in a full-blown meltdown.

"I'm going to miss my friends. I don't want to go." His sobs were enough to get Denni crying and I felt I was losing control of the whole situation.

"I know you don't," I said, trying to show some understanding. "But you'll make some new friends in Bloomington, you'll see. You know…"

Denni interrupted me.

"Why don't you let this sink in and stop trying to sell everyone on it," she suggested. As usual, it was good advice.

For the next few hours the Proctor children sat in silence, watching movies. When the car pulled in the garage both kids jumped out and ran into the house.

"Give it a few days and they'll be in a better position to talk about it," I said optimistically.

I was wrong. For several weeks Katie and Brian lived in the land of anger and denial about leaving Allegan, and for a while it was best to avoid the topic entirely as far as the kids were concerned.

Some weeks passed, and as the moving date neared, the kids had come to terms with the impending move. Although they were very sad to leave Allegan, they seemed somewhat excited about their new adventure. They'd gone to Bloomington with us on a house-hunting trip and looked at a few houses. Denni took them to State Farm Park again, a large complex for the employees and their families who live in Bloomington. It had a huge pool with a lazy river and several water attractions, and the park had softball fields, volleyball courts, and a putt-putt course. All in all, the kids seemed to be dealing with everything as well as could be expected.

If anyone was having an emotional meltdown, it was me. The logical reasons for leaving were all still there, but still I felt an overwhelming sense of sorrow. It had a finality that I hadn't expected. The one hundred forty year run of the Pritchard House in our family was coming to an end. From the time the first brick was laid, the house had been in our family, and now, over six generations later, another family would call it home. The home had been in our family since the end of the Civil War, before cars, planes, and anything else that we'd refer to in the modern world. That hit me hard.

"I feel like I'm letting my family down, the living and the dead," I said as we sat on the covered porch one evening. It was one of our favorite parts of the house and had been the location for lots of fun and memorable events over the years. I'd taken my first steps over forty years earlier, just a few feet away, on the very same porch.

"We're your family, too, you know," Denni said. I didn't mean to, but at times, when it came to the Pritchard House, my conversation about "the family" seemed limited to only my brother, mother and grandparents, the inner circle related by blood to General Pritchard.

"You know what I mean," I said. "This house is leaving the family on my watch. It's exactly why we moved up here thirteen years ago. I thought I'd gotten my head around the fact that we were going to be here forever, like Mimi and Grandpa. I remember the reasons, and I'm glad we've done what we've done to the house. I'm proud of that piece. But the thought of leaving here is harder than I thought it would be."

"It's hard for me, too," Denni added. "This is my home, too."

"I know it is," I agreed. "In lots of ways, you've been connected to Allegan more than I have. Since we moved here, I've worked in Grand Rapids and Kalamazoo, and you've spent more time here in Allegan than I have. Plus, you've been more involved in the community."

"I don't know about that," Denni said. "But I hope you've really thought through what all this means. Once we're gone, we're gone. And the house and many of the things in it are gone. There will be no going back."

"I know," I said. "I know." The thought of it gave me goose bumps.

The Congregational church threw us a going away party, and there were several get-togethers with friends that we'd come to know and love over the previous thirteen years. Judi McCall came over frequently and doted on Katie and Brian. Judi had become part of the family, and saying goodbye was so much harder than I thought it would be. I wrestled with the thought of contacting my new boss in Bloomington and telling him that I'd changed my mind. One hundred and forty years of family history was a lot to give up. I struggled with a number of emotions, and at times I couldn't convince myself with certainty that we were making the right decision.

I argued with myself about the move. Dealing with Katie's brain tumor had reset the playing field when it came to priorities. While I knew there was more to life than a job and promotions and money, I was also certain there was more to life than a house. We'd devoted almost all of our time, energy, and money to restoring the Pritchard House. I was glad for that, and Denni was too. But with the "life is short" philosophy that I had adopted so strongly in the wake of Katie's illness, it seemed like there was more for our family to see and experience outside the walls of Allegan and the house.

And it seemed like something bigger than us. Was it a God thing? I just couldn't tell. But in the end, I decided we were past the point of no return, and it really was going to happen.

The week of the move, an estate auction was held on the grounds of our house. Denni and I, along with my mom and brother, had quickly decided what family heirlooms would remain in the family. Everything else was up for sale. For one, our new house in Bloomington didn't have the space to house the fifteen rooms of antique Victorian-era furniture. Secondly, I was convinced that these items belonged in Allegan, and to the extent possible, I naively hoped as many items as possible would go to local homes where they'd be appreciated. Antique dealers and curious bargain hunters came from Chicago and Detroit, and there were phone bidders from as far away as New Jersey and California. The General Pritchard House was a historic landmark and many people had waited for years for this sale to take place. So much for the items staying local.

Neither Denni nor my mom could bear to be present at the auction. On several occasions, I felt like I was close to losing control of my emotions as bidders postured and attempted to get the antiques for the lowest possible price. I didn't blame them; it was just hard to watch.

At the end of the day, all that was left of the Pritchard House contents could be loaded in the back of a passenger van. Furniture, art, oriental rugs, and knick-knacks that had sat untouched, some sitting in the same place for as long as my seventy-two-year-old mother could remember, were now gone. I walked through the empty house, and the wooden floors echoed the sound of my footsteps. Our family took one last walk around the grounds and through the house. I was numb with sadness. I sat on the steps of the porch one last time as the caretaker of the Pritchard House.

I felt a prayer coming over me. "Thank you God. Thank you for allowing me and my family to have this unbelievable journey in Allegan and living in this house. It's been a big part of our family's lives for over one hundred and forty years. That may not be a lot of time to you, but to us, it's more than a lifetime – more than several lifetimes. I know it's just a house, but it means an awful lot to us. I pray you take care of it as only you can. Amen."

The move to Allegan thirteen years earlier was one that no one saw coming. The move away from Allegan and the Pritchard House was even more shocking. We said our final goodbyes around town and began the trip to Bloomington to begin yet another chapter.

CHAPTER 57

Fragile Moments
2007

THE BLOOMINGTON MOVE TRAUMATIZED US. We knew leaving the Pritchard House would be difficult, but it was painful in many ways. The HGTV show filmed at our house a year before focused on several items in the house, including a turn of the century Handel reverse painted lamp. The intrinsic value of the lamp was around $10,000, but the lamp was one of the most special pieces in our family, and was, to us, priceless.

We were moving a number of antiques, and the moving company promised us their "A team" of movers would be particularly careful with the items. Marble top tables, leaded glass art, and a few other valuable artifacts were crated for extra protection.

In Bloomington, the movers began the process of unloading the boxes and crates as quickly as they could. They were marked "Family Room," "Office," "Kitchen," etc. for easy delivery. I was busy with a number of items when I came into my office and noticed a large number of boxes of books on top of the crate containing the Handel lamp.

The stack of heavy boxes of books sitting on the crate stood over five feet tall. The weight of it had crushed the crate, and when I threw the books off the crate and opened it, I looked inside to find the Handel lamp broken in a dozen pieces. I was literally fighting tears. I understood it was just a lamp, but that lamp represented so many things to me and my family. Outside of some Civil War letters from the General to his wife Mary, the lamp was the quintessential heirloom artifact that everyone in our family treasured.

Throughout the process of the move, I'd made the comment that the Pritchard House and its contents were just "things" and that we'd all come to learn that life was so much bigger than things. Perhaps I was being tested to see if I really meant it.

Brian met several boys in the neighborhood, and before the moving truck had pulled away, he and a boy named Logan were playing as if they'd been lifelong friends. Within weeks, he had established himself with a number of boys in the neighborhood and at his elementary school.

Katie, on the other hand, began middle school and was slower to make friends. She'd always been an observer, watching silently and patiently from the sidelines. Slowly, she developed a small group of friends, and she, too, began to get into the new routine.

As the months passed, parts of Bloomington were becoming more like home, although both children frequently mentioned Allegan. Brian asked on several occasions when we were moving back.

"I don't think we are moving back. Don't you like it here?" I asked.

"I like it OK. But it's not like Allegan. I miss our real house and my friends," he said.

"Me, too. I miss my friends, too," Katie added. "I love our old house. And our old yard."

Katie had a point about the house and yard. The Pritchard House had character, and the two and a half acres of trees and gardens were undeniably beautiful. The small lot in Bloomington had a nice enough house, but the comparison wasn't even close. Or fair, I concluded. There was simply no way to put any house up against the family home, let alone the first house we moved into after the one and only Pritchard House. But we were in Bloomington now, and we needed to make the best of it, which is what we tried to do.

For the next year, I traveled in my role as Claim Consultant. I went to California and Canada frequently. Denni and the kids got used to their new environment, and things seemed to stabilize. Although Katie seemed to enjoy her new friends, we noticed that she seemed stressed and depressed. Denni found a Christian-based counselor, and while the counselor was unable to share some of the particulars, we were able to glean that Katie had some deep-rooted anger. As the counselor came to know more of Katie's story, she became more amazed at all Katie had endured.

"It's not uncommon for children with significant health issues to have stress. A good portion of their lives isn't in their control. And most of all, kids don't want to feel different. Having health challenges, especially ones that make someone look different, makes it all the more difficult."

"So what do we do?" Denni asked.

"There's no magic answer. Some of her feelings are going to be completely natural. And teenage drama is part of growing up, especially with girls. The hard part will be determining when something is above and beyond the norm. Until then I'll give you the same advice I give all parents. Do the best you can," she offered at the end of one of Katie's sessions.

"You need a Master's Degree in counseling to give that advice?" I asked Denni sarcastically on the way home from the appointment.

A few months later, I received an urgent call from Denni.

"Come home – now!" she said in a panicked voice.

"What's wrong?" I asked, thinking something significant had happened to Katie or Brian.

"It's Tillie. I think she's dead," Denni said.

We lived only a few miles from State Farm's headquarters and I made it home in a matter of minutes. I found Tillie in the garage, and there was no doubt about it. Tillie was dead.

Denni had left our very healthy seven-year-old dog Tillie less than an hour earlier to run an errand. In the months since we'd moved, Tillie never understood what happened to the two-and-a-half-acre playground she had become accustomed to in Michigan. Our lot in Bloomington was less than a third of an acre, and the closest thing to a tree was something we would have called a sapling in Allegan. But she had figured out her new boundaries and seemed to be adapting. We nicknamed her Silly Tillie, and the moniker seemed very fitting. She was a total basket case, but a lovable one. As far as her health was concerned, we hadn't observed anything unusual.

It was early afternoon, and as soon as Katie and Brian got off the bus, Denni and I told them the news. They were heartbroken, and in a few minutes, word had spread around the block. I'd placed Tillie's body in the back of the minivan to take her to the vet, and we used that setting for an impromptu funeral service with a dozen or so neighborhood kids in attendance. Tillie was only seven years old, and the vet said she likely died instantly of a heart attack. The fact that she didn't suffer was some consolation.

Time marched on and the school year flew by. It was unbelievable to us how fast Katie was closing in on her teenage years. Denni and I were excited for Katie but we were also nervous. The doctors had told us about the potential for additional issues as Katie went through adolescence. And the counselor's comments made us think about just what a difficult path Katie had already experienced in her short life. Teenage years for most children are an incredible and fascinating time. They can be some of the best years of one's life, and for some, the worst years. How would it play out for Katie? Only time would tell.

CHAPTER 58

Pick a Number 2008

IN EARLY WINTER, KATIE BEGAN to complain of significantly increased headaches. The pediatrician couldn't find anything specifically wrong with Katie, and suggested reaching out to the doctors at Children's. Denni was very happy with one of the pediatricians she'd found in Bloomington, Dr. Brian Emm. His wife, Lisa, was an OB-GYN, and both of them had done their residency work in Cincinnati, he at Children's and she at University Hospital. Both were friendly, and Brian had a great grasp on Katie's condition. They also possessed a quality that we found endearing and sometimes rare in the medical field: a humble ego.

I have great respect for anyone who has completed the rigors of medical school and passed the examinations required to obtain the title of Medical Doctor. And in the years since Katie was diagnosed, we have seen *a lot* of doctors. Most of our treatment has been with the fantastic neurology and oncology doctors at Children's, but there have been a number of times we've seen other doctors, such as when Katie was referred to a specialist, or when we've been traveling and needed to seek medical attention. We've seen a number of pediatricians, orthopedics, ear, nose and throat specialists, eye doctors, etc. Most of them are great people and great doctors. Some are great doctors and not such great people, and a few we've even had to put into the category of "bad doctor-bad person."

A handful of the doctors we've dealt with seemed to think they were singularly equipped to handle any medical condition and took great offense at the notion of second opinions or going elsewhere for advice or treatment.

"I can handle this," was their retort. That type of doctor usually dismissed our questions, or talked circles in medical terms they figured we couldn't understand. We generally saw those doctors one time. I even walked out during an appointment when a doctor was being rude to Katie and me to the point it was a deal-breaker.

Dr. Emm was very clear that he would be happy to treat Katie for the routine medical issues, and we felt every confidence that he was more than qualified to do so. But Dr. Emm felt that for the conditions arising from Katie's brain tumor, which he determined to be out of his scope, that we needed to go to Cincinnati or a similar hospital since they were best-suited to handle those needs. He could accept the fact that hospitals like Children's specialized in higher levels of care for good reasons, and he was secure enough in himself that he wasn't threatened by it. And in the end, we respected him more for it.

Katie's headaches surfaced on and off for years, but as soon as she hit her menstrual cycle at the age of ten, the headaches occurred every day.

Although Katie had them for years, the recent headaches were much more severe. We needed to figure out if these were just a short-term issue related to puberty, or possibly something else.

Katie's MRI scans had revealed a stable tumor for a number of years now, with only a few hiccups. Dr. Crone felt she was stable enough that he transferred Katie's care to the neurology team of Dr. Sutton and Dr. Fouladi several years earlier. Dr. Sutton was a neurologist and Dr. Fouladi a neuro-oncologist, and between the two of them they'd provided Katie with excellent care and were very aware of her headaches.

From the start of treatment with Dr. Sutton, we were instructed to keep a medical chart that captured Katie's vomiting cycles and headaches. Katie was asked to rank her daily headaches from zero to ten, with zero being no headache and ten being the worst imaginable headache. On many days, Katie would report a headache in the one to two range, but occasionally they'd flare up, and for headaches over the five to six range, Katie had several heavy-duty medications to take. We kept her chart on the refrigerator. Some parents have their kids' artwork on the refrigerator; we had a headache chart. Welcome to our world.

Over the Christmas holiday and into winter, Katie's headaches continued to worsen, until on any given day, her headaches would be as high as an eight and no lower than a six on the scale. With me traveling, Denni made several trips to Cincinnati, and Dr. Sutton prescribed new medications in an attempt to get the headaches under control. Katie got to the point where she couldn't tolerate school, so Denni arranged for a home tutor to keep Katie current in her class work. As the days passed, the medicines were not working, and a new development occurred that changed the situation altogether.

Katie started complaining of tingling pain and numbness in her right arm, and on more than one occasion as she walked down the hallway, she veered into the wall. On two instances, she fell to the ground, and the second time her headaches were so bad she lay crying on the floor after she fell.

Denni called Dr. Sutton, and due to the urgent nature of the situation, she recommended an immediate trip to the hospital in Bloomington. A neurologist was contacted and met us at the conclusion of the MRI scan. We felt strange as we sat in the doctor's office. This was the first time since her diagnosis that we'd dealt with a neurologist outside of Children's.

"I don't want to alarm you, but we're concerned the tumor has grown," the neurologist began. "The radiologist had the measurements from the prior scan, and in his opinion, the tumor is larger and so is the cyst next to it." The doctor started to talk about a treatment plan when Denni stopped her.

"We need to get to Cincinnati," Denni said. Within an hour, Denni had made arrangements for Brian to stay with a neighbor and we were on our way. Both Denni and I were trying our best to not go into all-out panic mode. But who were we kidding?

In Cincinnati, another set of scans was completed. While the tumor measurements were the same, it appeared the cyst next to it was "pulsing."

"When kids hit puberty and their teenage years, this stuff can flare up," said Dr. Sutton. Dr. Fouladi added, "It's concerning, but we can treat the cyst and the headaches, and it's not a sign that the tumor has grown or changed." They both did their best to reassure us, and we felt grateful that we were in the care of such incredible doctors.

"I know it's not their fault, but they had us so worried." Denni said of the doctors in Bloomington. "I'm not doing that anymore. We've been coming here for eight years, and unless it's a regular check up with Doctor Emm, I'm coming here." I agreed and saw no point in arguing anyway. Determined mothers are a force to be reckoned with.

Over the next seventy-two hours, Katie received a new headache medicine through an I-V drip, and although the drug made her horribly nauseous, at the end of the treatment, her headaches were in the two to three range on the pain scale. Crisis averted.

Katie's headaches diminished, we headed home to Illinois, and everyone thought Katie was on the track to her normal state. Suddenly, she came down with a significant fever and complained of a severe stomach ache. Dr. Emm looked her over and said, "I'm not sure what's going on, but if it's OK with you, I'd like for Lisa to take a look." His wife's OB-GYN office was a short distance away, and with a call from her husband, she saw Katie immediately. By the time we got to the other Dr. Emm's office, Katie was doubled over in pain. An ultrasound revealed a large tumor on her ovary, which had severely contorted and was in danger of rupturing. Katie had emergency surgery that night.

All in all, Katie's past few months could be described in one word - miserable.

The "one thing at a time" philosophy that we'd embraced when Katie was in the hospital back in 2000 was coming into play. Sometimes it was hard to keep that attitude, but both Denni and I tried to anchor ourselves around that mindset. Over the years, Denni and I made quite a team in this area. When one of us was struggling, we'd help each other get through it. Sometime it wasn't always a fifty-fifty deal, as there were times I'd need more support, and other times Denni needed the boost.

It was a good thing we'd rehearsed this philosophy. We were going to need it.

CHAPTER 59

Lightning Strikes Twice, Part I 2008

§

In late February, holly and David were making final preparations for their annual trip to Hawaii. While they both loved their hometown of Cincinnati, winter was a beautiful time to be in the islands. Holly was giving some last-minute instructions to the dog sitter when she suddenly felt dizzy. David sat with her on the couch and looked over what she'd written. He noticed her normally neat handwriting was hardly legible. Then she became physically ill.

Their next-door neighbor was a physician, and after a short examination, he instructed David to get Holly to the hospital immediately. She had a complete work-up of neurological tests and an MRI scan. The news was stunning; Holly had a brain tumor.

Within a few days, Holly had surgery with the Riverside Neurological Group in Cincinnati, a renowned surgical outfit in its own right. As bad as the initial news was, the lab results were worse. Holly had a Glioblastoma Multiforme, a GBM - the Grade IV tumor that had one of the lowest survival rates of any of the one hundred and twenty types of brain tumors. The tumor was deep in her brain, and removing it caused a large scar over the left side of her head. There were other residual effects as well.

Holly had difficulty speaking, and for several months she stuttered and missed words as she spoke. Holly attacked all of her therapies with a vengeance. She had aggressive chemotherapy and radiation treatments and by early summer had made a remarkable recovery. The T-shirt she wore to her radiation treatments summed up her feelings on the matter: "Cancer Sucks." For her radiation treatments, she had to wear a helmet. As an interior designer, Holly wouldn't settle for any old helmet. Her design school classmates fashioned her one fit for a queen, complete with bedazzled jewels. As long as any of us had known Holly, absolutely nothing she did was "off the rack."

Denni, the kids, and I managed a number of trips to Cincinnati to visit with Holly over the spring and summer. We had all grown to love Holly very much and were deeply concerned. For Denni and me, our relationship with Holly was one that had grown considerably over the years.

When Denni and I first started dating in 1986, David and Darlene were in the process of getting divorced. Coincidentally, so were my parents. Our parents had each been married over twenty-five years, and the divorces affected us in different ways.

I had sided early on with my mother, and the relationship with my father wasn't a great concern to me. Denni had been close to both her parents and wanted to have a great relationship with each. She really wanted everyone to get along and for her parents to be happy. When Holly entered the picture, Denni wasn't sure how to handle it. There were some awkward moments initially, but the relationship grew into an incredibly strong and loving one. Holly was caring and happy and fun, and she loved David dearly and made him happy. To Denni, that was the most important piece.

When Denni and I first moved to Allegan to undertake restoring the Pritchard House, David and Holly made frequent trips to help us. Although he had progressed to a senior executive-level position, David had originally started his career with the phone company climbing telephone poles, and was also an electrician. David and Darlene had built their house in Blanchester, and when I say built, I mean physically. They dug the basement, and from foundation to the roof, they built their house. David helped us tear out wiring, rip up floors, and other things we could do to help keep the costs down and the projects on schedule. While David was helping with the structural piece, Holly was our go-to resource for the aesthetic part of the renovation work.

Holly had a flair for interior design and had returned to school to get her degree in that area. When it came to restoring the Pritchard House, she provided us with a number of ideas, some of which we considered and some of which we ignored, much to her frustration. But over the course of time our relationship evolved to one of affection, respect, trust, and enjoyment. Holly turned out to be an incredibly nice person.

When Katie and then Brian came along, the relationship deepened for all of us. Holly never had children of her own, and she took a shining to both our kids. The feeling was mutual; Katie and Brian adored Holly. As Katie grew, their relationship was fun to watch. Holly nurtured her inner teenage spirit, and she and Katie would talk endlessly about "girl stuff." When Holly was diagnosed with her brain tumor, Katie was old enough to understand the magnitude of the situation.

As the months passed and treatment continued, we all did our best to keep a positive spirit. In September, Holly and David came to Bloomington for a visit. We went to Brian's soccer games and out to dinner, and Holly seemed to be holding her own. Holly had been adamant about getting pictures taken with everyone during the visit, and in the back of my mind I wondered about her motive. One evening, as the others played a game of Uno, Holly and I sat on the couch and talked quietly.

"So, how am I doing?" Holly asked me.

"I think you're doing great, but the important question is how do *you* think you're doing?" I responded.

"I don't know," Holly answered. "Some days I feel like I might have a chance with this thing, and other times, not so much."

Over the years, Holly and I had a number of conversations on the topic of brain tumors. I had made several comments that although Katie had a lot of issues, at least she was fortunate that she wasn't diagnosed with a Glioblastoma, one of the worst of all the brain tumors. It was pointless to wish I'd never said those words to her, but still, I wished it.

"I know the odds," Holly said. "David won't talk about it and I know why, but I know them."

"All you can do is fight this disease as hard as you can and take things one at a time," I offered as small consolation.

"Ain't it the truth," Holly said. Then she looked at me, and with a hint of sadness in her voice, she touched my arm and said, "Take care of David, OK?"

"Well, I'm hoping you'll be around for a long time so you two can take care of each other," I said, feeling like I had glossed over the issue. But I knew what she was saying and figured she deserved a better response than that. I looked her squarely in the eyes. "Trust me, Nana, we'll take care of him. I promise you."

With that the conversation ended.

Katie & Nana – two peas in a pod

CHAPTER 60

Lightning Strikes Twice, Part II 2009

LATER IN THE FALL, HOLLY had a scary episode driving home from Christmas shopping. She felt dizzy, and although she didn't black out, as a result she forfeited the keys to her blue Volkswagen Beetle convertible with the license plates that read NANA-BUG. She was self-aware enough to know that she might not be in total control of herself, and said she didn't want to hurt anybody else.

In December, I had a business meeting in Las Vegas. Since I had begun travelling in my consultant role, Denni asked on several occasions to go with me. She especially wanted to accompany me on one of my many trips to California, after I made the mistake of calling one February afternoon from Napa where it was a beautiful sunny day. Back in Bloomington, it was another bone-chilling day of frigid temperatures, and I didn't endear myself to anyone when I informed Denni that I needed to cut the conversation short so I could go on a winery tour.

Denni wasn't a gambler, but she was interested in seeing Las Vegas just the same, so she joined me on the trip. We were walking down the strip one morning, and I was taking Denni's picture in a variety of gaudy tourist spots. As we stood in front of the Eiffel Tower at the Paris hotel, Denni's cell phone rang. I looked for additional photo opportunities, and Denni wandered over to some steps and sat down to talk. I could see Denni put her head in her hands, and in a short while the conversation ended.

"Well?" I said, as I walked up to Denni, figuring whoever it was didn't have good news.

"It was Holly. The tumor's back. It's in a much deeper part of her brain and they're not even sure they can operate on it. Dad was so upset he couldn't even make the call."

Holly was in the hospital over Christmas and the New Year, and we all went to Cincinnati to try our best to cheer David up. In the hospital, Katie and Brian enjoyed a few short visits with their Nana. Her speech had started to waver and she slept a lot. The doctor was still trying to determine if surgery was feasible. The tumor appeared to grow by the day, and the surgeon said he couldn't guarantee anything, but that if Holly wanted to have the procedure, he'd perform it. Ultimately, David and Holly decided that it was worth a try.

The surgery took place in mid-January, and although the surgeon did what he could, he couldn't remove much of it because it was embedded in her inner brain. For the next week, Holly went in and out of consciousness. She said few words and seemed incoherent.

I went back to Bloomington, and as I sat working at my desk a few days later, the phone rang.

"Holly's gone. She just died," Denni said, through choked tears. "It was awful. Dad had been with her almost non-stop, and the nurse said if he wanted to take a break, she'd stay with Holly. He wasn't gone thirty minutes, but in the time he was away, she died."

I hung up the phone and took a walk around the building. My head flooded with emotions.

Two brain tumors in our family. How could this happen? Katie and Holly had been as close as any family members could ever be. But the reality was that Denni was adopted and Katie and Holly had no blood relationship. The odds of one person being diagnosed with a brain tumor are incredibly remote. The fact that we had two in our family was like being struck by lightning – twice.

I had another conversation with God.

"God, I don't understand. I just don't get this," I said through my tears. "Holly was one of the most kind-hearted people I've ever known. And Katie is my daughter. I've looked for answers, and I've asked you for guidance. But this I just don't get. We've tried to be positive as much as we can. I often say how grateful and thankful I am. But right now, saying thank you is hard. And I don't feel terribly grateful. You're a forgiving God, and you're just going to have to forgive me. Because at this moment I'm hurt and sad and confused. And I'm really angry at cancer. And at you."

Holly Cook was fifty-three years old when she died. Her funeral was as emotional as one might expect. Her father attended, and I could scarcely imagine what might be going through his mind. Although Denni and I had our fair share of horrible moments with our own daughter's experience, Katie was alive. I thought back to the situation with our young friend in Allegan, Courtney Grauman. I don't think it matters how old a child is if they die before their parents. It's certainly a tragedy when a young child or teenage life is cut short through illness or accident, but I'm not certain there is much less pain to the parent if that child is an adult. Having to bury a child is something no parent can be emotionally prepared for. My heart broke as I watched Holly's father, who just sat in his chair and wept. I'm sure he'd never looked older in his life, and I don't think he was ever the same. I'd concluded after reading a number of entries on the Squirreltales website that some wounds are so horrific that one never recovers. Losing a child seems to fit in that category.

David was equally unprepared. After all, he was a number of years older than Holly and he had figured that he'd go long before her. But life – and death for that matter, doesn't come on our terms or our timing. And as hard as Holly fought, she lost her brain tumor battle less than a year after being diagnosed.

I couldn't help but think about Holly's gift of interior design. Heaven, beautiful as it must be, certainly must look even better now. At the funeral, a picture slideshow of Holly throughout her life played along with Kenny Chesney's "Don't Blink." As the words to the song poured out, I sobbed, and could feel Katie and Brian looking at me. It was one of the few times they'd seen me cry, and I was actually glad they got to see me like this. They needed to know it was OK for Dad to cry.

The sting of Holly's death lingered throughout the spring and summer, and David didn't attend the Ride for Kids event in Ann Arbor. For years, he and Holly had made the trip to be a part of the festivities. We determined it was a good thing he chose to pass it up. While it was nice to see the families and Stars, there were clearly some issues going on with a few of the kids. Kevin had been to the ride for the previous two years, but this year he was confined to a wheelchair, and he looked tired and gaunt. And Matthew, although still the life of the party, had seemed to be a bit under the weather.

Kevin died several months after the Ride, and Matthew just a few weeks after Kevin. Throughout the years, several of the Stars had lost their battles, and even with all the medical advancements being made, no matter who was in the PBTF gang, over one in five would not survive to adulthood. It made us all the more motivated to keep our fundraising efforts going.

For the majority of my life cancer had been some vague and mysterious disease that impacted other people. Then it came crashing into my world and the worlds of people I loved. By now I'd lost count of the number of kids and adults I'd known who were battling or had lost a battle to this disease.

Nana's T-shirt was 100% on the money. Cancer sucks.

CHAPTER 61

Cinderella 2009

IT WAS ONE OF THOSE moments when I realized just how much my life had changed. I couldn't help but smile as I looked at the concert tickets I had purchased. They were for Katie and I to see Christian music artists Steven Curtis Chapman and Michael W. Smith in Peoria, Illinois. It was a far cry from the concerts of my past life.

The first concert I ever attended was the Doobie Brothers in 1978. Over the years, I'd seen REO Speedwagon, Styx, Kansas, Paul McCartney, Def Leppard, and Journey among many others. In the 1980s and 90s, I saw Jimmy Buffett at least ten times. The experience of a Jimmy Buffet concert at Riverbend amphitheater in Cincinnati was legendary. I joked after my last Buffet show, which was well into my thirties, that I was too young to be witnessing all that was going on.

Denni had enjoyed some of those shows, too, and over the past several years she and I had attended a couple of Christian-based concerts at the Allegan County Fair. I knew the upcoming concert would be vastly different from a number of my other concert experiences, but I was very excited to be going with Katie.

Steven Curtis Chapman had been in the news over the prior year. In addition to his public campaign for international adoption, his family suffered a tragedy that was almost unthinkable. In May of 2008, Maria, Steven's five-year-old adopted daughter, ran undetected into the path of an SUV coming down their driveway and was struck and killed. The SUV was driven by Steven's eighteen-year-old son Will. Just as the tragedy occurred, Steven had a hit on the radio, entitled "Cinderella." It was a song about a little girl growing up before her father's eyes, and the heartbreaking story of Maria's death elevated the emotional impact of the song. The last chorus of the lyrics aligned with Cinderella's ball. As the girl's father, he didn't want to miss a single dance because when the clock strikes midnight, "she'll be gone."

At the concert, as Steven and his band played, everyone in the auditorium wondered if he'd play the song. Then, near the end of his set, he walked up to the microphone and took a few seconds to collect his thoughts.

"Tonight is a special night. This is my son Will's first night back on tour with us. You all know what happened, and our family is touched by the outpouring of support you've shown us. We have an incredibly loving God, and I'm confident right now Maria is being held in His loving care. And with the strength that only the Lord can provide, we're going to try to play a very special song. It's the first time we've played this song since the accident and we're going do our best to get through it. It's called 'Cinderella' and my friend Michael W. Smith is going to help us."

Michael joined him on stage and began the piano introduction to the song. As the lyrics poured out, I looked at Katie standing next to me. It was all I could do to stop myself from sobbing, but as I looked around, tears were flowing from the eyes of everyone in the audience.

I put my arm around Katie, and closed my eyes. "Lord, I don't understand so many things. I don't understand why little girls die in accidents, or get cancer. I don't understand why some kids get sick and live, and other kids get sick and die. But thank you for sparing Katie. She is a gift from you, and I know Denni and I are charged with keeping her in our care until you're ready to keep her in your care. I hope it's after she enjoys a long and happy and healthy life here on earth. But that's not up to me. It's up to you. And I have to trust completely that you'll do what's best."

As I finished, Steven was beginning the last chorus. His emotions piled up on him, and as he came to the last line, he had to take a moment. Then he sang the last line, about the ball coming to an end as the clock struck midnight, and as I clutched my own Cinderella tightly, my heart melted.

Music is powerful. It has the ability to take an individual to a place in time or to an emotional level that no other medium can. I've always connected music to special events and moments in my life, and that night will go down as one of my favorite musical memories. Like Cinderella's glass slipper, it was magical.

CHAPTER 62

Locks of Love
2010

§

DENNI AND I STOOD IN the dance studio and looked through the window as Katie practiced her dance moves. A reporter with the local paper peppered us with questions, and we did our best to answer. A week later, the following story ran in the local Bloomington newspaper, *The Pantagraph*:

§

BLOOMINGTON -- Katie Proctor is a fourteen-year-old survivor who deals every day with symptoms of having a portion of a tumor remaining in her brain stem. Monday after school, she will celebrate the tenth anniversary of her brain surgery by donating her hair to Locks of Love. It will mark Katie's fourth donation to the charity that provides wigs and hairpieces to children' who've lost their hair due to life-threatening illnesses such as cancer.

"I think it's nice for other kids to have hair after it's fallen out because of chemo (therapy)," Katie said last week. "I know some kids who have lost all their hair."

Neither Katie's parents -- Denni and Rob Proctor of Bloomington -- nor her teachers at Chiddix Junior High School, Normal, are surprised that Katie is celebrating her anniversary with a donation.

"That's Katie," said Nancy Brown, a seventh-grade language arts teacher who taught Katie last year. "She's one of the most unselfish persons I've ever met. Katie has to be one of the strongest and most determined young people I've dealt with in twenty-six years of teaching," Brown continued. "She missed a couple months of school when a cyst on the tumor caused her to have severe headaches, dizziness and loss of balance," Brown recalled.

"But she never lost that smile from her face and didn't want people to feel sorry for her or think she's different," she said.

At age four, Katie began having vomiting spells and her mom noticed that Katie would always move the telephone receiver to her left ear. A hearing test prompted a CT (computed tomography) scan, then a phone call that no parent wants to get.

A doctor told Denni Proctor -- who was pregnant with the Proctors' second child, Brian -- that the scan revealed a mass about the size of a small egg at the base of Katie's brain. The diagnosis was a brain stem glioma.

The Proctors lived in Michigan then and took Katie to Cincinnati Children's Hospital, where a pediatric neurosurgeon would do the procedure. Denni and Rob Proctor kept it together until Katie turned to them while she was being prepared for surgery and said "Don't worry, Mommy. I'll be fine."

"I just lost it," Denni Proctor recalled. The surgery took almost eight hours because of complications. During the surgery, Katie stopped breathing several times and her heart stopped as doctors discovered that part of the tumor was embedded in the brain stem. The surgeon had to leave fifteen percent of the tumor -- about the size of a thumbnail -- to reduce the risk of brain damage.

Less than two weeks later Katie developed bacterial meningitis -- an infection of the spinal fluid -- and spent almost six weeks in the hospital. That was followed by speech, physical and occupational therapy.

In October 2008 Katie began to experience severe headaches, dizziness, loss of balance and cyclical vomiting because of a cyst beside the tumor.

"They were just horrible," she said of the headaches. "I couldn't do anything because it hurt so badly."

Katie was excused from school and returned to the Cincinnati hospital, where medicines got her headaches under control. While her most recent test in December revealed that her tumor and cyst were stable, she continues to get daily headaches. Other symptoms of the tumor are that the right side of her throat is paralyzed, meaning it's hard for her to swallow and she chokes easily; she is deaf in her right ear; vision is her right eye is blurred; and the right side of her face and right vocal cords are paralyzed.

She has balance and coordination problems with her right side but still takes tap and hip-hop dance classes at Dance Factory in Bloomington.

Being ten years out from surgery increases Katie's odds of long-term survival. But she knows nothing is guaranteed and tries to appreciate each day.

"This is your life," she said. "You don't get a second one."

§

"Wow, she gets it," I said as I read the article with Denni. "As unfortunate as it is that she's had to go through all of this, you do have to love the fact that she's got a perspective on life that few people will ever get. That is definitely a God thing."

"I know," Denni said. "But I wish she had an easier path to get that perspective."

CHAPTER 63

Wishful Thinking 2010

As we waited for our appointment with Dr. Sutton and Dr. Fouladi, a social worker asked us if we were interested in participating in the Make-a-Wish program. Denni and I were startled. We knew Katie had hit a rough patch over the past year or so, but wasn't Make-a-Wish for kids who were dying?

The social worker quickly clarified. "I know that a lot of people think only kids who are terminally ill get to participate, but Make-a-Wish grants wishes to kids with life-threatening illnesses. Many of the Make-a-Wish kids make full recoveries and lead healthy lives now."

Later, Denni and I discussed the possibilities. "I don't know if I'd feel guilty if Katie took a Make-a-Wish trip. We're not rich, but we can afford to take Katie to some of those places the social worker mentioned, like Hawaii and Disney."

"Why do you do this?" Denni asked.

"Do what?" I asked, not sure what she meant.

"Why do you somehow feel like our family isn't entitled to things that are offered to us? Like somehow we'd be greedy if we took advantage of a trip like that. You heard what she said. She said income plays absolutely no part in the Make-a-Wish program. You don't even know what Katie would wish for, so how do you know we could afford to make it happen?"

"Good point," I said. Denni wasn't done.

"And frankly, after all Katie's been through, and you being a first-hand witness to all of the pain and suffering she's had to endure, you're shortchanging her. For you to somehow conclude that maybe Katie isn't as deserving as other kids, like she hasn't earned it. Well, I think that stinks."

The truth of Denni's comments settled in my head. I had absolutely no legitimate rebuttal.

"You're right." I added meekly, "You're right."

Katie was very excited about the prospect of a Make-a-Wish trip, which merely reinforced Denni's multiple points on the matter. But for Katie, figuring out what to wish for was difficult. Back in Bloomington, two Make-a-Wish volunteers from the chapter in Chicago sat on the couch and facilitated the family discussion.

"So what do you like to do?" one of them asked. "Do you like to shop? Some kids take a shopping spree to New York City, or the Magnificent Mile in Chicago, or even the Mall of America."

Katie was unresponsive.

"She's not much of a shopper," her mom chimed in.

The other volunteer weighed in. "When we say think of anything, we mean it. If you'd like a swimming pool, a big TV, your room made over, really, anything."

"Ooh, a pool!" Denni said.

"The wish is for Katie, not you," I added with a bit of sarcasm.

"I don't think so," Katie responded.

"Well, there are celebrities you could meet," the volunteer said, trying to get the conversation back on track.

"She's a huge Jonas Brothers fan," I said. "Would you like to meet them?"

"I dunno," Katie said, less than enthusiastically.

"Well, you don't have to make up your mind today," the volunteer said. "In fact, you have until you're eighteen years old. There are also lots of trips. Almost half of the wishes are for Disney and Hawaii."

"Katie, tell her how many times you've been to Hawaii," I said.

"Three," Katie said matter-of-factly.

"Wow," said both of the volunteers almost simultaneously. "You might have a pretty hard time coming up with a wish to beat that! Well, we'll check back in a few months, and until then, be thinking of what you'd like to do."

"OK," Katie said and the volunteers left.

Several weeks later, Katie and I were sitting on the couch watching a Minnesota Vikings game. We'd had several conversations about potential wishes. She had seemed to rule out a celebrity encounter or a shopping spree and focused her attention on places she'd like to go. It looked like possibly a trip to Greece was the front-runner. Katie was a huge *Mamma Mia* fan, and the scenery in the movie had her spellbound. I had been to Greece during a summer semester in college, and the thought of a trip there was very appealing to me, as well.

As we sat and watched the game, an advertisement came on and in an instant, everything changed. "NBC Sports is proud to bring you the twenty-first Winter Olympic Games from Vancouver, Canada." The Olympic theme played in the background as the film clip showed a variety of the Olympic events that would soon take place. Katie jumped to her feet.

"That's it, Daddy. That's it! That's what I want to do for my wish! I want to go to the Winter Olympics!"

"Well, alrighty then!" I said in my best Jim Carrey/Ace Ventura impression.

I relayed Katie's wish to the volunteers who had visited us from Chicago. In less than two weeks we received a response in the mail.

"You open it, Katie. After all, it's your wish," Denni said as she handed Katie the envelope. Katie opened the envelope and in a few seconds, she was beaming.

"They granted my wish, and they said you guys can come, too!"

Several weeks later, Katie received a packet requesting more specific information on her wish. There were a number of details to consider, including what Olympic events she wanted to attend as well as a detailed medical questionnaire to be completed by the doctors at Children's in Cincinnati. The list of Olympic events in the seven-day itinerary was impressive, and included the Opening or Closing ceremonies, men's and women's skiing, hockey, speed skating, a medal ceremony with a Barenaked Ladies concert, and several figure skating competitions, including the pair's finals.

Brian and I were subtly lobbying for a hockey game, but I realized Katie wasn't a hockey fan and this was not our wish. Katie quickly settled on her choices: the Opening Ceremonies, moguls skiing, the gold medal celebration with a Barenaked Ladies concert, and her piece de la resistance, the pair's finals figure skating competition.

The holiday season passed quickly, and with the Olympics starting in less than six weeks, it was hard to be excited about anything else.

On the morning before the Olympic Games were to begin, a limousine showed up in our driveway. The Make-a-Wish packet indicated there would be transportation to and from O'Hare airport in Chicago, two hours away, but they had not mentioned that the transportation would be a stretch limousine, complete with a Tuxedo-wearing chauffeur.

After landing in Vancouver, we were met by Make-a-Wish staff who gave us a guided tour of the city and checked us into the hotel. When we got to our room, which turned out to be a full two-bedroom suite, there were four large boxes, one for each family member. The boxes included Make-a-Wish shirts, hats, and gloves, Olympic souvenirs, and complete sets of Olympic tickets for all of the events Katie had chosen.

I looked at the Opening Ceremony tickets and noticed two of them were in the eleventh row on the floor of the coliseum and the other two tickets were in the middle section. The face value of the floor tickets was printed in the upper corner - $1,100 each.

"Wow," was all I could say. "This is unbelievable!"

The Opening Ceremonies were just the beginning of our adventures. Katie and our family were treated like royalty, gaining access to places many other Olympic fans couldn't go near. We were given a tour of the Olympic Village and attended a party in the VIP tent. The first sporting event we attended was the mogul's competition, where Canadian Alexandre Biledeau won the first ever gold medal on Canadian soil, causing a celebration in the streets of Vancouver unlike anything we'd ever seen. Later in the week, we were special guests at the Canada House, the facility where the Canadian Olympic Team and their family members gathered. We watched the Canada-Finland hockey game with a number of the athletes, and for one afternoon, Katie and Brian were as Canadian as a bottle of Labatt's beer.

While it was all spectacular, the highlight of the week for Katie was attending the pair's finals figure skating competition at Pacific Coliseum. Our seats were directly behind the broadcaster's booth, and we immediately recognized one commentator, former Olympic gold medalist Scott Hamilton. Denni and I remembered Mr. Hamilton from his days in the 1980s when he stunned the world by completing the first back-flip in competition. The 1984 Sarajevo Olympics were his shining moment, and in the years since, he'd become an international superstar in the skating world. Katie had been a figure skating fan for years, and had seen replays of his skating glory, so she was an ardent Scott Hamilton fan to say the least.

Denni took the opportunity to ask the Make-a-Wish staff and the assistant behind the broadcast booth if it would be possible for the Make-a-Wish kids to meet the famous skater. The assistant said she'd check and came back a few minutes later with positive news.

"Scott said he'd love to meet the kids, but it'll have to be after the broadcast and follow-up interviews, so it'll be about forty-five minutes after the skating program ends and the medals are awarded."

"That's fine with us," Denni said.

When Scott came out of the booth, the first thing we noticed was his feet. He had on a full suit and tie, complemented by a pair of bright red tennis shoes. As he approached, he could tell Denni was looking at his shoes.

"Hey, I have to sit there a long time and nobody sees my shoes," he said with a smile. "Hi, I'm Scott."

"Hi, Scott. I'm Denni Proctor, and this is my daughter, Katie, my husband, Rob, and my son, Brian. Katie and I both have things in common with you."

"What's that?" he asked.

"Well, I went to Bowling Green," Denni said. "That's where I got my teaching degree."

"Go Falcons!" Scott said, a proud Bowling Green State University alumnus. The college was in Bowling Green, Ohio, in the northwest corner of the state, where Scott grew up and began his skating career.

"And Katie's connection is even more special," Denni said. "She's a brain tumor survivor."

"Hi, Katie. It's a pleasure to meet you," Scott said. With that, he began a conversation with Katie that lasted several minutes. In that time, several others had come up to see Scott and were waiting for his attention. We were thoroughly impressed with this Olympic legend. As the crowd around him grew, he never once broke eye contact with Katie, and when they finished their conversation, he looked up.

"Well, what do you know?" he said. "Proctors, I'd like you to meet a couple of my skating buddies." He promptly introduced us to Olympic bronze medalist Debi Thomas and Canadian Olympic silver medalist Elvis Stojko.

Scott posed for pictures with us, signed autographs for Katie and Brian, and signed my Vancouver Olympics ball cap. When he was done, he proceeded to turn his attention to his other guests. His expression of hospitality and kindness was the epitome of Katie's Make-a-Wish trip. The fact that Scott Hamilton had turned out to be such a class act was our gold medal moment.

As we rode home from Chicago in the limousine, it was difficult to capture the emotions we were all feeling. We were tired to be sure, but it truly had been the trip of a lifetime. Within a week after Katie returned from her Olympic trip, she was interviewed on the local television news and she wrote a blog that was posted on the Make-a-Wish web page. As for Denni and me, we couldn't have enough good to say about the charity or our experience.

A few months later, we were asked to participate in a fundraiser for the Make-a-Wish Foundation at Illinois State University, located in Bloomington, Illinois. Chi Omega sorority supported Make-A-Wish as their national philanthropy, and we were to speak during the Greek Week fashion show event. We felt honored to do what we could as a small repayment for the kindness shown to us by the Make-A-Wish organization.

The Braden Auditorium at ISU brimmed with over 2,000 students on the night of the fashion show. Two Chi Omegas were assigned to be escorts for Katie. They were outgoing and bubbly, and both Denni and I flashed back to our own Greek-filled days in college. The girls showed Katie around and helped her with her make-up, and the director of the event gave everyone some last-minute instructions.

The lights went down and a huge movie theater screen projected an image of Katie and the rest of our family. The next slides took the Chi Omega escorts by surprise and their eyes began to water as the slideshow chronicled Katie's journey over the years, including pictures of her in the hospital, while the narrator told of Katie's battle with her brain tumor.

As much as the girls had good intentions, it was like many other situations we had seen. People saw a smiling and friendly Katie, but they really had no idea what she'd been through. I could see the girls looking at Katie and wiping their eyes as the slide show continued. After a few minutes, it ended with more pictures of our family at the Winter Olympics, courtesy of Make-a-Wish. Then it was Katie's turn to take the stage. When she was introduced, the crowd cheered loudly.

Katie thanked the audience and talked about what a fantastic organization the Make-a-Wish group was, and that, in her opinion, it was a great cause to support. She only spoke for a few minutes, but Denni and I were amazed at just how well she articulated not only her appreciation for the Make-A-Wish foundation, but her sincere gratitude for the outpouring of caring people had shown her over the years. And she made an impassioned plea to continue to help fund organizations like Make-A-Wish as well as groups that do research to help cure cancer, so that kids in the future won't have to go what she's gone through.

As she finished, Denni was a mess, and my eyes filled with tears as the crowd erupted into a full-blown standing ovation. It was incredibly loud and probably lasted over thirty seconds. Katie didn't know what to do, and she looked at us and slowly moved away from the podium. It was my turn.

"There aren't a lot of perks when it comes to having a brain tumor," I began. "Katie has been at or in the hospital every holiday but Easter since her diagnosis. She's had five surgeries and has at least two more to go. She's endured more painful procedures in the first fifteen years of her life than most of us could ever imagine. And she lives with the effect of her brain tumor every day, from headaches and facial paralysis to limited vision and deafness. After seeing what she's gone through, I won't use the word lucky. But in the world of brain tumors she's pretty fortunate, or better yet, blessed. She's alive. A number of the kids we've met along the way since Katie was diagnosed with her brain tumor have lost their battles.

"That's why groups like the Make-a-Wish organization are so special. These kids have so many things they have to face in life. And although most of us never see that part of their lives up close and personal, I can tell you many of the things they have to deal with are truly awful. You wouldn't wish them on your worst enemies. But the Make-a-Wish program gives kids and their families a chance to escape from hospitals and doctors and painful tests to focus on having the experience of a lifetime. That is what they did for us. We'd like to thank the Make-a-Wish foundation for all they've done, for us, and the thousands of other wishes they've granted."

It was time for me to close. But I wanted to use the opportunity to do more than say thanks.

"And thanks to you for helping this great cause. It takes money to support the incredible work that they do. I'm very thankful that you've chosen to help in the Make-A-Wish cause. But I hope you'll do one thing for Katie and all the other kids suffering from some pretty awful diseases. Next year, and the year after, when it's not part of Greek Week, won't you please make that same commitment to help? Thanks again, and God bless you."

The Proctors with Olympic Gold Medalist Scott Hamilton at the Vancouver Winter Olympics.

CHAPTER 64

Gentle Giant
2010

AFTER TILLIE PASSED AWAY A few years earlier, we had considered whether or not we should get another dog. The more we thought about it, the more we felt something was missing. Like before, the questions centered on which type of boxer to get.

I found a breeder about forty-five miles from Bloomington and we went to take a look. The litter included six puppies, and one in particular caught my attention, the runt. Katie and Brian were enamored with all of the pups, and while they were playing in the pen with the dogs, I ventured over to where the father of the litter was to talk to the breeder.

"I've been breeding boxers for twenty years, and his line is the most docile bunch of boxers I've ever seen," the breeder said, pointing to the dad, who was lying quietly in the yard. I walked over to the dog and he sat up and sniffed my hand. It's what he didn't do that surprised me. He didn't jump all over me.

Our previous boxers had ranged from hyper to downright crazy. Most of the other boxer owners I'd known over the years had the same descriptions. Boxers are loving, loyal dogs to be sure, but they are emotional basket cases and, considering their size, they can create havoc.

I remembered our boxer jumping on practically every guest who arrived at our house when I was a child. He even tore the sleeves off several of my friend's shirts, as his way of playing. Rocky III, before Tillie, had been great with our family, but he had been so strong and aggressive that we couldn't take him anywhere. I wasn't interested in another dog with that temperament.

After a second visit to see the litter, we landed on the runt and on the name. From my perspective, it was simple - he was my fourth male boxer so he should be called Rocky IV. I didn't get much resistance and everyone in the family was thrilled with our new addition.

It became clear that Rocky IV would be the best-behaved boxer we'd ever have. From the puppy stage to adulthood, he had a demeanor that simply amazed us. He was friendly and playful, but never in the out-of-control way like our previous boxers. He stayed in the yard, came when he was called, and after a brief sniff on the hand of arriving guests, he'd go lay down and ignore whatever was going on around him.

Since Rocky was the runt of the litter, Denni and I were ill-prepared for what was to come. By the time he was a year old it was obvious that he was going to be huge. And when he reached full-grown status, he towered about three inches taller than the average male boxer, and his ninety-four-pound frame, rippled muscles, and twenty-inch neck created an imposing initial impression. In reality, he was a gentle giant.

Rocky IV quickly lost the numerical surname and Katie embraced him as her best friend. Brian enjoyed him too, as did the rest of us, but Katie forged a bond with Rocky that was impenetrable. She spent hours with him, and it was clear that he was as fond of her as she was of him. That relationship would prove to be invaluable as Katie entered high school.

CHAPTER 65

School Daze 2011

THROUGHOUT HER CHILDHOOD KATIE HAD a small but close group of friends. Many of them were aware of her condition and its side effects and treated her pretty normally. There had been a few friendship speed bumps along the way, as would be expected in any setting involving children. We knew it was all a part of growing up that Katie needed to deal with. Still, after everything Katie had been through, it was hard to watch.

Since moving to Bloomington from Michigan in 2007, Katie was slow to build friendships. Unlike the kids in Michigan, none of her classmates in Illinois knew what she'd been through. But the girls she hung around with were very nice. They weren't the most popular crowd and didn't seem to care, which I found especially refreshing. They got along very well and seemed to respect one another. One girl, Madison Dixon, seemed to embrace Katie, and Katie in turn embraced Madison. Denni and I were glad to see her gravitate to a best friend like Madi. Most of the other students at Katie's middle school treated her decently, either by ignoring her or accepting her. Except for a few kids, and one in particular.

Ahmad (not his real name) was a different story. He seemed to be angry at everyone, and for some reason he directed much of that anger toward Katie. For a while, Katie didn't tell anyone about what was going on, but Denni noticed Katie's behavior had changed. Katie seemed tense and even a bit depressed. Apparently, Ahmad had been intimidating and bullying Katie. When we discovered the situation, both Denni and I were furious.

Ahmad told Katie how much he hated the United States, and that he was glad for what happened on September 11. Although somewhat shy, Katie is pretty outspoken as far as her patriotic views are concerned. When she pushed back, Ahmad said something to the effect of, "You better watch your mouth or the same thing could happen to you."

Over a number of weeks, he'd made comments that were intended to upset or harass Katie. As we probed Katie to explain the conversations in more detail, several seemed to be veiled threats of one kind or another.

Denni contacted the school authorities, and she was stunned at the guidance counselor's initial recommendation that we should look at changing Katie's schedule of classes to keep her away from Ahmad.

"Absolutely not!" Denni said as her voice rose. "Why should Katie have to move? This kid is the one who's been picking on her, and *she* has to move? I don't think so."

Denni had several conversations with the school administrators, and the situation was eventually resolved, or at least brushed under the rug, to their satisfaction. The administration said they visited with Ahmad and his parents and surmised that he really didn't mean anything by his comments. They decided not to move either student out of the class, but said they would move Ahmad's seat away from Katie and have the teacher "keep an eye on it."

"Wonderful. What a stellar way to deal with the situation," Denni said sarcastically to the counselor. Fortunately, Ahmad ignored or avoided Katie, and things seemed resolved. Katie's stress was reduced and her overall spirits improved. By the time Katie started high school the next year, we thought Ahmad and the bullying was a small and distant memory.

When the first surgical attempt to correct Katie's smile failed in 2001, the doctor told us there was a second procedure available. It was a complex procedure, performed in two stages up to a year apart. The procedure was much more invasive and painful, and the doctor had said it was such an extensive procedure that it was not recommended for young children. As Katie grew, we told her more about the procedure and said the decision was entirely hers, but that if and when she decided to do it, we'd fully support her. Katie opted to have the surgery at the end of the first semester of her sophomore year in high school. She said she didn't want to miss school so she planned to use the holiday break for some of her recovery.

The first stage of surgery took a several-inches-long section of nerve from her ankle and implanted it in the functioning side of her face, where it would spend the next six months regenerating and growing in its new location. Katie also had a gold weight inserted in her right eyelid to help it close. Her right eye hadn't blinked since the original tumor surgery, and her vision had deteriorated to 20/200. The gold weight procedure is over ninety percent effective, but, unfortunately, Katie's procedure was unsuccessful. The doctor said she had too much scar tissue built up inside her eyelid and felt there was not much more that could be done to make the eye close.

Katie recuperated over the Christmas break following her surgery, and was able to return with the start of the winter classes. The doctors tutored us on the importance of protecting the nerve as any trauma or damage could kill the nerve before it took root. The doctor explained to us prior to the surgery that a tradeoff would be involved. Because the nerve graft would be needed from her ankle area, the removal of the nerve would cause her to lose sensation in part of her right foot. Cutting nerves was not something to be taken lightly, and any chance of failure was cause for concern. We instructed Brian that he had to suspend his usual habit of jumping out of nowhere to shock and scare his sister, and I think if Denni could have, she would have made Katie wear a football helmet to school.

Shortly after Katie returned to classes in January, Denni knew something was up. We could sense that Katie's mood was off, and Denni knew she needed to press further.

"You seem so stressed out. Katie, honey, what's going on?" Denni asked.

Even with direct questioning and our increased attention for a period of a few weeks, Katie's reply was a less than convincing "nothing." But on one afternoon, she'd endured too much and when Denni pressed her, she crumpled to the floor and sobbed uncontrollably. When Katie calmed down enough to speak, Denni was able to ascertain the series of events leading up to the current state.

At the start of the school year, a few new girls joined the group that Katie sat with at lunch. One girl in particular seemed to be very concerned with controlling the group, including who sat in a particular seat. In addition, the girl was rude, demeaning, and seemed intent on dividing the group. Katie said she had tried to ignore the situation, but it had continued to escalate and very recently had gotten even worse.

According to Katie, she would put her books on the table and go through the lunch line. When she returned she often found that the girl had knocked Katie's books on the floor and had placed someone else in her seat. Though upset about the situation, Katie sat in her newly assigned seat. Apparently, this happened for several days in a row. And on the most recent day, not only were Katie's books on the floor, but another girl's as well. Katie had put up with enough, and when both girls saw the situation, Katie confronted the bully and the conversation included raised voices that got the attention of the cafeteria monitors.

Katie admitted raising her voice and saying something to the effect of, "You can't treat people like this!" The cafeteria monitor told the girls to break it up. According to Katie, the girl leaned in and said, "This isn't over," and walked away.

After the lunch period, Katie went into the bathroom and as she turned to leave, the girl and one of her friends blocked her exit.

"Nobody disrespects me like that," said the bully. "Nobody." Katie attempted to walk around the girl, and the girl leaned into her and forced her up against the wall.

"I'll punch your face so hard it will fall off," the bully said.

Denni was in full-blown Momma Bear mode.

"*Nobody* threatens my daughter like this," she said with clenched teeth. "This is absolute insanity."

In an instant, I could gauge Denni's level of anger. Denni was an emotional mom, but this time she was in a rage, and for good reason.

The initial conversation with the counselor was less than satisfying. As with Ahmad, it seemed to Denni as if the school counselor was afraid to confront the bully and her parents. One of the other counselors mentioned to Denni that the girl's name was familiar in the administration office, and not because of any academic achievements or community service.

After several frustrating phone calls, Denni pushed for a face-to-face meeting with the administration and a few of the guidance counselors. At the beginning of the meeting, the first counselor laid out the events from their perspective. Denni was flabbergasted at how twisted the scenario had become and felt it was obvious the counselor was more concerned over the reaction of the bully's parents to the accusations.

"That is absolutely ridiculous!" Denni said, stunned. One of the other counselors spoke up and said several girls in the group seemed to support Katie's version of the incidents. Even so, the first counselor suggested that no one came forth regarding the bathroom scene, and that the girl's parents were complaining that everyone was ganging up on her daughter.

"So this bully threatens to punch my daughter in the face, and you're worried about this girl and her parent's getting upset?" Denni asked with a full dose of sarcasm.

"Katie had a nerve transplant in her face a month ago and it's an incredibly delicate time. If there is any impact to the nerve, it could die and ruin the whole procedure. But that's not important here, is it? I forgot, we're worried this poor bully and her parents might be upset."

"It's not as simple as that," the first counselor said. I felt the same sense of rage that Denni did.

"Yes, it is," I added. "One party is the bully and the other party isn't. Based on several witnesses, we know which is which, don't we? It sounds like this kid has a history of this behavior, and if we pressed, I'm sure we'd find some other things, wouldn't we?"

"We weren't there," said the first counselor, and Denni and I were both convinced was siding with the bully. "There are two sides to every story."

"Yeah, because Katie has a lot of reasons to make this up," Denni said, quite disgusted by the conversation. "And you can't face it, but we can, the bully has every reason to lie. Sure, pick on the kid with the brain tumor and if there's fallout, play the victim."

"Even by cowardly bully standards this sucks," I added.

"I understand your concerns," the counselor began. Denni would have none of it.

"No, you don't! How dare you!" Denni responded. "Don't sit here and tell me you understand our concerns! Katie's had to deal with so many difficult situations her whole life. She's had six surgeries because of her brain tumor, and she's had to overcome things you can't imagine in your worst nightmare. She's had to put up with incredible physical pain and it goes far beyond that. She's been bullied before, too. It's tough enough being a kid, but she's had to put up with so much more than almost any kid you can think of. And you insult her and us with some lame 'there's two sides to every story' response? My husband said it nicely, this sucks. And if you think for a minute we're going to give up and give in on this, you haven't seen *anything* yet. I can promise you that!" Her eyes could have drilled through steel at that moment.

One of the other counselors seemed to be much more understanding and realistic about the situation. He was very helpful, and after several more conversations, Denni convinced the counselors to put the accused bully in another lunch period rather than moving Katie, as was originally suggested.

That was the only period in which the girls had a common setting, and the other counselor assured Denni he'd pay special attention to the situation.

Fortunately, the scenario played out as the counselor suggested. The lack of proximity appeared to be enough that the girl did not approach Katie. Or, equally possible, I thought, was that she found another target.

I continued to be amazed that in spite of the considerable issues confronting Katie her schoolwork continued to excel. Katie was almost a straight A student. When teachers commented about Katie to us, they raved about what an incredible kid and student she was. She was by no means perfect, but many teachers told us they were genuinely moved by her effort and attitude.

Katie had been provided with a Section 504 plan by the doctors at Children's Hospital. These are accommodations aimed at giving kids assistance in the educational setting where it is deemed necessary. Being deaf in her right ear and having limited vision, she was to be provided a seat near the front of the class. She was allowed to have a water bottle with her due to her choking episodes, and she had a number of medications stored at the nurse's office. In addition, she was allowed a break from some of the physical activities in gym, had an additional set of textbooks at home, and could take additional time for testing if she needed it.

Aside from the water bottle and the extra books, Katie almost never used any of the accommodations. Teachers told us Katie did everything in her power to be like all the other kids. The teachers said although they could tell Katie had some medical issues, unless they saw her Make-A-Wish trip story or were in her small circle of friends, most the kids never even knew she had a brain tumor because she never mentioned it. Katie didn't seem to want anyone to know she needed any extra help.

Denni and I had several conversations with Katie over the years on the topic of disclosure. While we did our best to try and make Katie feel as normal as possible, we felt it was important that when it was necessary, she should explain her situation to others. For example, we had to stress to Katie that she really did need to tell some of her friends and classmates about her right ear deafness.

Especially in areas where there was a lot of noise, like school hallways, Katie had a hard time locating sounds. Often she didn't hear anything specific, so she wouldn't react. We told Katie kids might misinterpret her lack of response as being rude or unfriendly. Katie made a point to walk on the right side of people so she could hear them, and after a while, she and her friends would automatically fall in sync. Overall, Katie did a pretty good job of interacting with her peers, friends, and teachers. And none of the issues Katie dealt with seemed to have an impact on her studies or her grades.

As I thought about it, I concluded that the private counselor she'd seen before had been correct. Schoolwork was one of the few areas in Katie's life that she had much control over. She wasn't dependent on other people, athletic abilities, or doctors. She was in control, and she wasn't going to let herself down by getting less than excellent grades. There were so many things about Katie that I had come to admire. She had her moments and her issues, like we all do, but considering everything she'd had to deal in her young life, I was amazed and impressed. She was turning into quite a young woman.

CHAPTER 66

Georgia on my Mind 2012

As Katie ended her sophomore year of high school and Brian ended his last year of elementary school, I was presented an opportunity at State Farm that was, to us, a more attractive location than Bloomington.

In the fall of 2011, I had been offered the position as Director of the call center operation in Bloomington. After spending the first twenty-five years of my career in the Claims department, I decided it would be a great chance to try out something new and took advantage of the opportunity.

Within six months of taking the job, things began to change quickly. In order to meet increasing customer needs, State Farm announced plans to build massive operation centers in Atlanta, Dallas, and Phoenix. I had done some initial work on the strategy behind the structural reorganization, but was still surprised with the offer to relocate to set up and launch one of the new call center operations.

"I've been offered the job and can pick either Atlanta, Dallas or Phoenix," I said, as I talked to Denni on the evening of the job offer. Although the conversation felt similar to the one we'd had in Michigan almost five years earlier, there were also a number of differences. To begin with, we weren't leaving a six-generation house that had been in the family for one hundred and forty years. And for Denni, as much as she loved Allegan, she didn't feel the same way about Bloomington. She liked many of the people she'd met and especially the good friends we'd made, but Bloomington wasn't home and felt very different than Allegan.

For valid reasons, Denni had mixed feelings about my employer. She understood and even forgave some of my workaholic behaviors, and she appreciated that it was a great company to work for. She knew it had been a big part of my life even as a kid when my dad was a State Farm agent.

But in many ways, she frequently had to compete with State Farm. While that was hard enough living in Cincinnati and Allegan, where only a few of our friends were associated with State Farm, Bloomington had a population of about 70,000 people, and at least 15,000 of them worked for the insurance giant. As we looked at the other houses on our street, at least one in three was occupied by someone employed at State Farm. In some cases, both spouses worked there.

In the fall of 2011, Denni had obtained a teaching position as her first return to the full-time working world since she quit her job at Perrigo Drug Company in 2003. The school was thirty-five miles from Bloomington, and as much as she liked teaching, it didn't entirely overcome her dissatisfaction with living in central Illinois. When it came time for the conversation about leaving Bloomington, especially for a place like Atlanta, Denni was very enthused.

The conversation with the Vice-President who'd offered me the position was a short one. I'd ruled out Dallas. I mean, seriously, home of the Dallas Cowboys? That wasn't going to happen. To me, there was only one logical choice.

"I'm from Ohio and Michigan," I started. "Frankly, even though the winters in Illinois are bad, the desert doesn't interest me or my family. More importantly, Katie treats at Children's Hospital in Cincinnati. Atlanta to Cincinnati is a very doable commute when necessary; Dallas or Phoenix to Cincinnati, not so much. I'll take Atlanta."

"Atlanta it is," said the Vice President. "Considering that's my hometown, I think you made a wise choice."

"I haven't even moved there yet, and I'd have to agree with you," I said.

CHAPTER 67

Boo Boo Bunny XXL 2012

AS EXCITED AS WE WERE about the move to Atlanta, something much more pressing occupied our minds. Katie had the first stage of her nerve transplant the prior December, and the final stage was set for June. This was the most complex part of the procedure, and the idea was to give Katie the entire summer to recuperate so she could return to school. At least that was the plan.

When May arrived, Denni received a call from Children's explaining that Katie's surgery would need to be moved to late July due to some medical issues going on with the plastic surgeon. Having resolved the bullying episode in school, we were all were anxious to get the surgery completed, and this was a development that we neither expected nor wanted.

Denni and Katie headed to Cincinnati two days before the scheduled surgery in July. I planned on joining them the following day in order to wrap up what I could in preparation for the move to Atlanta the next month. On the day before the scheduled surgery, Denni got another phone call from Children's. The surgery was going to have to be delayed again due to the medical issues with the doctor, this time until mid-August.

I thought back to the time twelve years earlier when all the events piled up on Katie: the meningitis, the faulty lumbar drain, among others. History was repeating itself. Mid-August finally arrived, and in between the chaos of packing the house in Bloomington and readying for the move to Atlanta, we headed off to Cincinnati for Katie's surgery.

When Katie was little and had an ouchy, we would use "Boo Boo Bunny" to help her get through whatever pain she was in. It was a wash cloth folded to resemble a bunny that held a couple of ice cubes.

Throughout her journey, we learned that dealing with pain would become part of the program. Occasionally no amount of Boo Boo Bunny would be sufficient to handle what she was going through.

The first stage of the surgery had taken a nerve from her ankle and implanted it in the functioning side of the face where it spent six months regenerating in its new location. The procedure wasn't pleasant, but in reality, it didn't hold a candle to what was to come. The second and final phase of the nerve graft surgery involved removing the atrophied muscle on the right side of her face, and replacing it with a muscle about the size of a deck of cards that was taken from Katie's inner thigh. The now-functioning transplanted nerve from the ankle was then connected to the new muscle.

It all sounded complicated, and it was. And not only complicated, but extremely painful. In fact, none of us, including Katie, were prepared for the intensity and length of the pain, not only in the thigh where they removed the muscle, but in her face, as well. When we first saw her in recovery after the six-hour procedure, we were shocked. Katie had her right eye sewn halfway shut with sutures coming through her top and bottom eyelids. The scar on her thigh was much larger than we'd expected, and she had a wire sticking out of her neck connected to a Doppler radar machine, the kind the weather anchors refer to on TV, to monitor the blood flow in the new muscle.

"I wasn't prepared for this," Denni said to the plastic surgeon. "It just seems like it's so much more than what we bargained for."

In the doctor's defense, she had told us the procedure was a big deal. In fact, she'd said it several times. She'd said that removing a leg muscle of that size was a significant procedure and that nerve surgery was particularly painful. We knew it was a major procedure. Even so, none of us counted on this.

Denni had learned over the years that on occasion she needed to be a patient advocate for Katie in ways that didn't endear her to the nursing or medical staff. Speaking of endearment, there is a scene in the movie *Terms of Endearment* in which Shirley MacLaine is trying to get the nursing staff to give her terminally ill daughter, Debra Winger, pain medication. And when the medical staff doesn't respond quickly enough with the medication, Shirley goes off – and I mean really goes off, on the staff.

Over the years I've witnessed several episodes like that. Katie has received incredible medical care, but in the few instances when things haven't been going right, I have casually mentioned to the nursing staff that if things don't improve, Denni might "go all Shirley MacLaine" on them. And when she has done it, it has been every bit as dramatic as in the movie.

In this instance, I could sense it coming. Katie's pain was intense, and relief was short term. Not only that, but a few of the doctors and nurses didn't seem to put as much emphasis on Katie's pain as either Denni or I expected. Katie had endured several very painful procedures over the years and she had at least an average, if not above average, tolerance for pain. Throughout her treatment we'd never seen her exaggerate her symptoms. In fact, if anything, she downplayed them. To see her in this state of agony was difficult. Denni complained and then complained some more, and finally went off on a nurse to get a doctor to come take a look at the situation. As in, "RIGHT NOW!"

The doctor who arrived wasn't in the normal rotation and hadn't seen Katie much over the past few days. When he arrived to see the situation, he was stunned.

"How long has she been like this?" he asked the nurse.

Denni jumped in before she could answer.

"On and off for a long time. Too long. The pain meds don't seem to last and we can't seem to convince anyone that she needs something different, stronger, just something to make this better. She shouldn't have to be in this much pain!" Denni said, her voice filled with emotion and frustration.

"I agree," said the doctor bluntly. He didn't raise his voice, but he made it clear to the nurses present that this situation should have never gotten as far as it had and he wanted an immediate prescription filled and to be notified if this didn't do the trick. In addition, he wanted the meds administered in specific intervals to keep Katie ahead of the pain cycle.

"I didn't see that coming." Denni said. "The only time I remembered seeing that doctor, I really didn't think much of his bedside manner. But the way he jumped on things and got things under control was impressive."

It took a while to get her pain under control and fortunately, many of the heavy-duty pain medications Katie received had the side-effect of causing temporary amnesia, so she recalled only bits and pieces of her week from Hell.

Her mother and I weren't so fortunate.

CHAPTER 68

It's All About That Grace 2013

After spending over a week in the hospital for the second stage of her nerve graft surgery, Katie was discharged. We came back to Bloomington to start her recovery, but stayed only a few days. We said goodbye to our friends and left Bloomington for our new home in Alpharetta, Georgia, twenty-five miles northeast of downtown Atlanta. Yet another new journey was beginning for Katie and our family.

Katie's recovery was slow and painful, and it became clear she wouldn't be returning to school for the first semester of her junior year. Denni arranged for Katie to participate in the online high school program. It was difficult, and Katie had to take a full load of classes, including Physics, without the benefit of a live teacher. She managed to get through it and continued to earn exceptional grades, but both Denni and I could tell that the events of the prior year had taken their toll on Katie.

As the months passed, Denni and I again became concerned about Katie's mood. In the prior year, she'd gone through two significant and painful surgical procedures and moved 700 miles away from the few friends she had. She seemed tense and depressed and nothing we did seemed to help. We invited her best friend from Bloomington, Madison Dixon, to spend part of the Christmas break with Katie. Madi and Katie had forged an incredible friendship over the years, and we were happy they were keeping in touch.

Shortly after the Christmas holiday, Madi arrived, and Katie's spirits were lifted. But one evening, Madi got to experience an explosive side of Katie that she'd likely not seen before. I asked Katie to pick up something from a place Katie had never actually driven to before. Although it seemed like a trivial task, Katie resisted, and finally I flat out told her to go. In an instant, the explosion occurred.

"You don't get it! I don't know where it is!" Katie said, her voice rising, and clearly distressed.

"Katie, honey, it's right down the road from where you go to the doctor. It's literally two more turns and you're there," I said, hoping to move on.

"You're not listening!" she yelled, now in tears. Madi was sitting in the family room and could hear everything, but pretended to watch TV as the scene played out.

"Katie, you need to do this." I said, having lost my patience. "You're seventeen years old and we're not asking you to drive an hour into parts of town you don't know. This is no more than twenty minutes from here and you know the roads. You need to go."

"You're not listening! You're not listening! You never listen! I'm not going!" Katie was screaming and crying uncontrollably at the same time. She stormed past Madi and went upstairs to her room where she slammed the door and went into a fetal position on her bed.

I just looked at Madi and shrugged my shoulders.

"I'm sorry, Madi." I said. "Katie has been stressed out for a while now. Between surgery and moving, this whole thing has been pretty tough on her."

"I know it has," Madi replied. "I just wish I could do something to help."

"We all do," I said.

In bed that night, Denni offered her assessment of the situation.

"You know sometimes Katie just isn't comfortable going places she hasn't been to. Once she's gone somewhere with us, then she's OK with it. She just needs to get familiar and comfortable with the situation first."

"Yes, but that's not always possible. Like tonight, it was no big deal, it was just down the road from where she's already been," I protested.

"Honey, Katie's right. You're not listening. It's no big deal *to you.* Clearly it is to her. She's been through a lot."

"Yes, I know she has," I said.

"Please let me finish," Denni said. "We've been with her through all of it, and you and I still can't believe all that she's had to go through. She's coped with so many big things for so long, and now it seems like the little stuff is what puts her over the edge. Isn't it better that she copes with all that big bad stuff and if she has to blow a gasket over the little stuff, might we just grant her some additional grace there?"

"Grace," I said. "Yeah, that girl is definitely entitled to some grace. With a capital *G*."

I decided to have another conversation with God. As I often started my conversations with God by talking about Katie and her struggles, I was confused. I didn't understand the need for perpetual challenges and setbacks.

"OK, I get it, God," I said. "If you're trying to make Katie and us stronger, we're stronger now."

CHAPTER 69

The Beast 2013

I SCANNED THE ROOM AND tried to put the finishing touches on my presentation in my head. I'd made presentations like this before, and have always been comfortable speaking in front of a group. Even so, I tend to work myself up a bit to get the right amount of adrenaline going. This was a service club, and I reflected on the days when my father was President of the Noon Optimist Club in Lima. Back then it was the exclusive domain of men, businessmen, specifically. Those days were long gone, and more than half the room was comprised of women. Secretly, I was glad, since I felt my message landed even better with women, many of whom were moms.

As I was introduced, I hit "play" on the remote in my pocket and the overhead screen came on, displaying the picture of a doctor on the phone. Then the audio began.

"Hello, Denni Proctor? This is Doctor Profit. We got the results of Katie's scan... Are you sitting down?"

That was my cue.

"Just like in the movies," I began, "nothing good can ever follow those words, 'Are you sitting down?' My wife got that call, and the conversation changed our lives forever. Because in the very next sentence the doctor would tell my wife that our daughter Katie had a brain tumor.

"Hi, I'm Rob Proctor, better known as Katie's dad. I'd like to take the next few minutes to tell you a bit of Katie's journey and the journey of our family. Plus, I'd like to give you some information on brain tumors. And I'll tell you the real reason I'm here. I hope to motivate you to give money to the Pediatric Brain Tumor Foundation so researchers can find better ways to fight, and maybe even cure, the brain tumors that are maiming and killing our kids."

I hoped I had their full attention by then.

"Katie was four and a half years old when she was diagnosed. She's gone through an incredible journey, including multiple surgeries, hospitalizations, doctors' appointments, painful tests, and tons of other things you and I would never want to go through. I'm happy to tell you that, today, she is alive and, for the most part, well. This is a classic case of 'I wish I'd known then what I know now.' But that's not how these journeys work. You have to find your way one day at a time. And that's exactly what Katie and our family have done."

I recounted the details of the original diagnosis and the surgery, along with the consequences she's had to live with. I did my best to move quickly through those parts to get at the heart of my message. In my presentations, I used a number of metaphors to help make my points. In this instance, I used one of my favorites. The screen projected an image of a roller coaster. I let the slide linger for a few seconds and I noticed the confused look on some of the members of the audience.

"This is a roller coaster at Kings Island amusement park in Cincinnati, Ohio, called The Beast. It's pretty famous as roller coasters go. It's the longest wooden coaster in the world, and if any of you have ridden it, you know it creates a sensation unlike anything else you've ever experienced. From the clink-clink sound you hear as the car climbs the steep incline, to the shuddering sounds the wooden frame makes as it hurls you towards that first tunnel entrance, it's an awesome ride!"

"Katie has battled a beast of her own in her brain tumor journey. When you think of a beast, you think of some monster who is out to do you harm. Using that description, calling a brain tumor a beast is very accurate. But I prefer to put a different spin on this beast. I equate Katie's brain tumor journey with the roller-coaster ride, not the monster."

"Obviously, I'm not comparing Katie's brain tumor battle with a day at an amusement park, but I hope you see the metaphor. As I said, The Beast is the longest wooden roller coaster in the world. The ups and downs and unexpected twists and turns make for one exciting ride. Although parts of it look and feel like you might jump off the track at any moment in a disastrous crash, the car somehow manages to stay on track, giving you the opportunity for another ride."

"Katie has experienced the terrible lows in her journey. They include physical pain that range from the sharp sting of a needle or the cut of a scalpel, to the dull ache of chronic headaches and the heart-wrenching sorrow she felt when some of her brain tumor pals and her grandma died from brain tumors."

"She has felt the anxiety of the climb, not knowing exactly what's over the next hill. Is it a smooth descent with a great view, or is it a plunge into the abyss? We'll know soon enough... clink-clink."

"Katie has experienced the incredible highs of being on top of the peak and looking at the wonderful views. You want that feeling to last forever. Katie's felt the inner glow of being first in line in that front car as the special passenger. Between the VIP treatment of her Make-A-Wish trip and a number of other occasions where she's been the guest of honor, she knows what it feels like to be special."

"And she has been at the back of the line on that spot that says the wait from where you're standing is two hours for a four-minute ride. At that point you're not sure if the wait is really worth it. From dealing with people who've treated her badly, to having a legitimate complaint that this brain tumor journey is inherently unfair, Katie knows the feelings of frustration that come with it."

"Katie loved The Beast. For a while we made Kings Island a mandatory stop on our trips to Cincinnati when she had appointments at Children's. As Katie grew and her headaches changed, she had to stop riding it. After the ride, she'd be a bit disoriented and onlookers wondered if she had just come from the Beer Garden. At least Katie got to ride The Beast, experiencing all of its exhilarating ups and downs and twists and turns. And when she did, she didn't even scream like a little girl. Her father, on the other hand…."

There was laughter in the crowd and I looked back at the screen that projected a picture of Katie and me riding a caterpillar-themed kiddie roller coaster the year before her diagnosis.

"Not exactly The Beast, huh?" I said. Softened by a little laughter, they were ready for my pitch.

"I told you the real reason I'm here. It's to have you open your hearts and wallets and give money to the Pediatric Brain Tumor Foundation. I'm not bashful about asking for money for this great organization. But let me tell you the 'why' part before I get to the 'how' part."

I rattled off some background information and gee-whiz numbers concerning brain tumors. I talked of the dozen or so kids diagnosed every day with a brain tumor and of the one hundred and twenty types of brain tumors, from the brain stem glioma like Katie's, to the Glioblastoma Multiforme that killed her grandmother. I felt I needed to shift the focus away from numbers to make a better connection.

"I've learned over the years with our involvement in the PBTF that these kids are so much more than statistics. Let me tell you a little about them." I clicked the remote again to show pictures of the Ann Arbor PBTF Ride for Kids Stars.

"First, here's Ruth. She's the senior member and anchor of what I call the PBTF Gang. She was diagnosed as a teenager. After battling her brain tumor, she found out a few years ago that she has melanoma, a type of skin cancer, as well. She received a PBTF academic scholarship to study at the University of Michigan, and I'm happy to report that the last time I saw Ruth, she was doing well."

I changed the slide to show a picture of Katie with another girl. "LeeAnn is Katie's age, and we met her at our first ride in 2000. Katie and LeeAnn are like twins, each with eye and facial paralysis that mirror each other. Matthew, Kevin, Cara, TJ, Andrew, Zach, Cara, Guy and several others round out the group. Every year when they see each other, they pick up right where they left off."

"As helpful as it's been to be a part of the PBTF family, it's been painful when several of the Stars lost their battles."

I clicked my remote and the slide changed to a picture of Denni and me standing with a group of the PBTF kids.

"See the tall bald kid with his arm around my shoulder in this picture? That's Guy. Guy was in high school when he was diagnosed. He came to the Ride for several years, and he and I really hit it off. Guy went to Stanford on a

PBTF scholarship, until he died at the end of his freshman year. He was only 19 years old."

My own voice caught on the last sentence and my eyes watered, aware of the raw pain still present. I quickly changed slides again.

"Matthew was ten years old and had the energy of the Tasmanian Devil. He was the entertainer at the ride, taking on the biggest, toughest bikers in an all-out effort to make them laugh. And he laughed harder than anyone. He died about two months after this picture was taken. Two weeks later, we lost Kevin," I said, as I clicked the remote and the picture showed Katie and LeeAnn standing next to Kevin, who had been reduced to a wheelchair in his last ride.

"TJ died as well, and as The Gang lost members, the tragic cycle continued when they added three-year-old Clare, Jacob, and others since. Statistically, no matter who is in the Gang, too many of them won't make it to adulthood."

I could tell that the pictures resonated with the audience. I shifted gears again. The screen was now divided into four equal parts with Katie's picture in one corner and blurred out images of three other children filling out the remaining squares.

"About one in ten thousand kids get a brain tumor, and of those, one in four of them will die. Imagine four kids you know, your neighbor's kids, your brother's kids, your grandkids, or your own children. How do the one-in-four odds sound now?" I tried to make direct eye contact around the audience.

"The reality is that over ninety percent of all cancer research dollars are allocated to adult cancers. Pediatric brain tumor researchers have to fight for every dollar they get. For reasons I think you can understand, our family made a vow to help them in the fight for those research dollars, and we'll continue as long as we have to."

It was time for me to close.

"Our aim is to motivate as many of you as we can into making a donation to the Pediatric Brain Tumor Foundation. Our goal this year is to raise as much money as we can for brain tumor research. Cumulatively, the PBTF hopes to raise several million dollars this year. The doctors and scientists need money for research to find better drugs to kill the tumors, instead of the tumors killing our children."

"On the positive side, in addition to funding medical research, the PBTF has established an academic scholarship fund for patients and their siblings. That may not sound like much, but not too long ago they didn't *need* such a program." I was confident most of the audience understood the implications of that statement.

"I'm asking that you prayerfully, or not prayerfully, if that's not your thing, consider a donation of any size to the PBTF. We don't want to guilt anyone into giving money. You shouldn't give to a charity out of guilt. You should give to a charity because you're moved to do so or because you want to truly help that cause. I can promise you this organization is worthy of your donation. Thank you so much for time. I thank you, and these brave and wonderful kids thank you, too."

The Ann Arbor PBTF Ride for Kids Gang

CHAPTER 70

Senioritis
2014

KATIE WAS ABLE TO JOIN her classmates for the beginning of the second semester during her junior year. She made a few friends, and Denni encouraged her to get more active in the senior high youth group at church. Katie had been involved in youth groups since she was a little girl and had always enjoyed them. We had begun to attend Andy Stanley's North Point Church in Alpharetta, and loved it. The high school youth group was huge, and although the leaders tried to reach out to her to get her more involved, she didn't make the connection like she had with her groups in Michigan or Illinois.

Katie's spirits fluctuated over the months, and we did our best to be supportive. Katie communicated with Madi frequently and seemed to be holding her own in the positive attitude department. Just prior to the start of Katie's senior year, we took a trip to Kauai and Oahu, Katie and Brian's fourth visit to Hawaii, and it lifted the spirits of the entire family.

Katie entered her senior year as excited to get out of high school and on to college as anything else. Denni and I had mixed feelings about it.

"High school was one of the best times of my life and I hate for her to rush out of it," I said. "But I totally get it."

"What's that?" Denni asked.

"You and I had a ball in high school. We still keep in touch with a lot of our high school friends. We've gone on vacation with them, and they come to visit. Outside of Madi, Katie's had a couple friends here and there, but her high school experience hasn't been all that great, especially since we moved here," I said.

"I can relate that moving during high school is tough," Denni added, which made me feel even worse about the situation. "I knew it would be hard, we both did."

"Yes, I know, and I feel bad about it," I agreed.

"I do, too. But she really wasn't happy in Bloomington, either," Denni admitted. "I just think those last two surgeries knocked her down."

"That kid has been knocked down so many times," I said. "I'm amazed and impressed. For so many years she not only got back up, she bounced back up with a smile on her face. But this last batch of stuff over the past year just knocked her down so hard. In all honesty, I've been concerned," I said.

"Concerned about what?" Denni asked.

"That one morning we'll walk in to Katie's bedroom and find that she's checked out."

"I've been concerned for her, too, but I think Katie's stronger than that," Denni responded. "In fact, I think she is the most resilient kid you and I will ever meet. God made her that way for a reason."

"I know you're right," I said. "I just wish He'd have made *me* that resilient."

Katie's high school GPA was over 3.6, and, combined with a high ACT score, allowed her to choose between a number of schools to attend. Denni was only half-joking when she encouraged Katie to consider the University of Hawaii, as Denni had big plans to be Katie's onsite college chaperone. Katie said the University of Cincinnati, the University of Georgia, and Kennesaw State University were her main considerations, so we visited those campuses and a few others.

The University of Cincinnati was an interesting choice to us. Katie had spent considerable time in Cincinnati throughout her life, whether visiting her grandparents or during the countless trips to Children's Hospital, which sat on the very edge of the UC campus in Clifton. As the college visits progressed, it appeared that UC had fallen out of the running. It was quite a distance from Atlanta, and we were secretly happy when Katie announced she was no longer considering that option.

The University of Georgia was a beautiful campus, but at over 700 acres and 35,000 students, the campus seemed daunting. Katie mentioned several times during the orientation how very large everything seemed. On the other hand, as we walked the 300 acres of the campus of Kennesaw State University, where 24,000 students attended, Katie seemed very impressed with the campus and the friendliness of the students and staff. She applied to all three schools and was accepted to each of them. In the end, Katie elected to be in the Honors Program at Kennesaw State University, which was located north of Atlanta and a little over an hour away, so Mom and Dad were both pleased with her selection.

As Katie's senior year ended, and she walked across the stage to pick up her high school diploma, I couldn't help but think about the journey Katie had taken to get to this point. In my mind, I began to think about all the things that had happened, and a number of images flooded my head. My mental PowerPoint included images of Katie tugging at my leg as I dropped her off at preschool at The Looking Glass, images of Katie playing with her brother at Lake Michigan, and playing with her friends in the Pritchard House. I saw Katie with all of our family, and with Holly. There were vivid images of Katie in Hawaii and enjoying the Olympics. Those were the images I chose to allow into focus that evening.

There were other images too. Images of hospitals and doctors and things related to her fourteen-year battle with her brain tumor. They were a big part of Katie's life to be sure, but on this graduation night, they didn't make the grade. Her journey had its share of pain and struggles, more than most people could ever imagine, in fact. But her journey was also one of incredible triumph and bravery and courage and optimism. That was the part I chose to focus on. Yes, it had been an incredible ride so far. Both Denni and I were excited about the possibilities that lay ahead for Katie. After all, a whole new chapter of her life was beginning.

It was just what the doctor ordered.

Katie Proctor senior portrait.

PART V
Silver Linings

CHAPTER 71

Role Model

Over the years, Denni and I have lost count of the number of times people have told us that Katie is a role model, a hero. Time and time again we've heard that the manner in which Katie has handled all of the issues and challenges in battling her brain tumor has inspired them.

Every so often, I've thought about Katie's journey and how she evolved into a role model. I've thought about how hard it is just being a kid, much less a kid with serious medical issues that have left visible differences. And I've thought about how little of Katie's journey most people got to see. Close friends who came to visit at our house, or at the hospital, often saw Katie in a pretty normal state. Even from those glimpses, she has inspired others. I can state with confidence that what they didn't see would have shocked them.

In truth, there are parts of Katie that are an absolutely normal part of any person going through adolescence into adulthood. Or, as I put it, Katie can be a real stinkpot. When her mother and I have reminded her about doing chores, cleaning her room, or asking her questions when she's deeply engaged in a television program, we've had the pleasure of meeting Stinkpot Katie. It has been pretty predictable stuff - drama tantrums, complete with eye-rolling, and emphatic use of the word "whatever." But I conclude that there haven't been too many of these episodes, and I can easily say Katie is one of the most positive, optimistic people anyone could ever meet.

She has always been connected to a small but wonderfully loving group of friends, she's traveled to spectacular places, and she's experienced so many incredible things. Katie's been the recipient of love and support from her family, friends, and even strangers from all over the country. She has returned that love to countless others. In many ways, she's had a fantastic life.

As often as not, when people ask Katie how she's doing, her response is a simple, "I'm fine." It's the same response Denni and I give most of the time. Denni and I have said that outside of that pesky brain tumor, Katie has been one happy kid. Aside from a few pockets here and there, it's been true.

That said, I can't help but think that sometimes when we say, "she's fine," it feels like we're shortchanging Katie's journey. Yes, she is *fine* in the sense she is alive and mostly healthy, and for that we are eternally grateful to God. But in addition to all the wonderful things she's experienced, she's endured dozens and dozens of things that no one would even remotely consider as "fine."

Katie's journey has touched so many people over the years and she's been a role model, but it's been by default, not choice. I can say without hesitation that I couldn't have handled what Katie has been through with half the courage, optimism, dignity and humor that she's shown. The way she's handled all of this is truly awe-inspiring, to me and many others. Some of the other kids with brain tumors I've met have been role models as well for the same reasons.

The more I think about it, the more I imagine being a role model is tiring. Overcoming tremendous obstacles and dealing with painful challenges time and time again may be inspiring to others, but for the one who has to live through it, it's kind of a raw deal.

Sometimes, I figure, maybe they just want to be a stinkpot.

CHAPTER 72

Silver Linings

DENNI AND I HAVE SAID we wouldn't wish a brain tumor on anyone. In her journey, Katie has had to deal with more than most of us could imagine. Even considering all that she and our family have been through, there have been upsides – silver linings, if you will.

To begin with, it's helped us gain a much clearer perspective on what is truly important. I still whine about some petty stuff, but I have a better gauge of what's significant on the worry meter, and what shouldn't even register. It sounds cliché, but it's true - life is way too short to worry about things that in the end don't amount to a hill of beans. While everyone agrees with the concept, I think our family has an exceptional appreciation for that philosophy.

Especially in the first few years after Katie's brain surgeries, when Denni and I would hear individuals complaining about trivial matters, we'd just look at each other and roll our eyes. We're still guilty of the occasional whining, although both Denni and I are pretty good about helping each other get off the pity train to remind ourselves of the truly important things in our lives. Sometimes we don't even need each other to do that; it just hits you like a two-by-four.

I was driving to work recently and had a lousy morning. We were in the midst of remodeling our master bathroom, and the contractor had run into some extensive and expensive snags. I was in full gripe mode, talking to myself and lamenting all the things wrong with the bathroom. I made eye contact with myself in the rear-view mirror, and it hit me. Here I was, griping about the issues taking place with a bathroom, which happened to be one of multipl*e* bathrooms in our house.

I thought about my attitude. *Oh, poor me! One of my bathrooms has issues.* I thought about the people who were lucky to have one bathroom, and the millions who didn't have any. Things like that have caught my attention, and although I'm not entirely cured, my whine disease is less severe than it probably would be were it not for our brain tumor odyssey.

This philosophy has also given me less patience with others over the years. I've tried hard to internalize my feelings; otherwise, I know I'd come across as some holier-than-thou hypocrite, and I'd like to keep that character flaw to a minimum. But sometimes it's difficult to do. After seeing firsthand what Katie and a lot of other kids have gone through, listening to people gripe about absolutely unimportant things can be challenging.

I think we've fostered several generations of whiners who've lost the ability to distinguish between what's important and what's not. I have nothing against the Starbucks crowd, but I have an example that captures this approach to life. A co-worker came into my office one day with a horrible dilemma.

"My latte just doesn't have enough whip. I can't face my day without a perfect latte."

Really? Your attitude for today centers around a cup of coffee? Wow, I feel sorry for you...

Unfortunately, that outlook is seemingly embraced by thousands more people with each passing month. Or, maybe they're just finding their way onto social media.

As frustrating as it is for Denni and me, it's been far more difficult for Katie. In the first few years after her diagnosis, she was heavily involved in treatment. In elementary and middle school, Katie took a lot of things in stride. Going to the doctor all the time, spending holidays going to medical appointments at Children's, carrying a water bottle for when she choked - it was just her life. I love the quote she gave to the newspaper when they interviewed her about her Locks of Love donations: "This is your life; you don't get another one." I think that statement encapsulates an incredible philosophy of living life here on earth. Yet, as positive as Katie has tried to be, it hasn't been without its challenges.

As she went through high school, Katie had a few instances where the frustration mounted to a near boil. Katie had some of the most significant and painful procedures of her life during high school, and frankly, that period of time probably won't go down as one of her favorites. As she faced serious health issues and suffered considerable pain, she got to hear of the insignificant issues facing some of her peers. Bad hair days, fights with boyfriends, clothes that didn't fit perfectly all rose to the level of near catastrophe. That had to be extra hard for her to deal with, but overall, Katie handled it remarkably well.

Denni and I attempted to explain to Katie that her peers weren't trying to be difficult. It's just part of the growing up process. That has come as small consolation to Katie at times, and we can't say we blame her. Seeing their reactions, or more accurately their over-reactions, has been a double-edged sword. On the one hand, it had to be frustrating to listen to people who made a bad hair day sound like the end of the world. There were several times that as she relayed their issues it was obvious that she was upset. They really had no sense of how self-centered they sounded, but Katie had a great sense of it.

On the other hand, it did help Katie understand how petty those thoughts and actions were. Countless times teachers and counselors have relayed to Denni and me how mature Katie is. Considering everything she's had to deal with, it makes sense. Katie has had no choice but to confront some pretty harsh realities. Most of the time she handles it incredibly well.

And I'm optimistic that this mindset will serve her well throughout her life.

Overall, I'm very happy to say our family gets that things in life don't always go our way. We get that life's not fair, and occasionally, that it's horribly unfair. Don't mistake a positive outlook for foolish naiveté. The fact that unfair things happen is sometimes hard to accept. I still struggle to understand how a kind and loving God allows such horrible things to happen, not just to sick kids, but horrible things all over the planet. In spite of those realities, focusing on the positives – finding the silver linings – has been the key to our family's ability to "survive and thrive" as we like to say.

Every person and family has issues to deal with. Some may not be as challenging as what we've faced, but everybody has something they have to deal with. We're not special in that regard. It's how you approach each day that matters. And while we have our moments, individually and as a family we've chosen to face things as positively as we can. It doesn't always work, but in my book, it sure beats the alternative.

This journey has shown us the true meaning of friendship. Katie, Denni, Brian, and I have felt the incredible support of family and friends. I could fill pages and pages describing the kindness our family and friends have shown us over the years. People have done things for us that I could never repay in a million years. They're not looking for repayment anyway.

A number of friends prepared meals for our family when we first got back in Allegan after being in the hospital for six weeks. Our neighbors have taken care of our house, our pets, lawns, and errands while we've been at the hospital or dealing with some significant medical situation. And the list goes on. As much as we've appreciated the physical assistance, the emotional support has been just as important. Sometimes, it's been the only thing keeping us afloat.

We have had people surprise us in many ways. Mostly in good ways, but to be candid, not always. We have encountered a few people who seemed to think Katie's brain tumor might be contagious, and they shielded their children from her. And we've met a few people who can only be described as heartless or thoughtless. But we've only encountered very few folks who fall into that category. The overwhelming majority of people we've run across along the way have strengthened our faith in humanity.

We see bad things and bad people every day on the news. What's really tragic is that we begin to think that's the way most people are, when in fact, most people are good, very good. Our family has been blessed to experience some of the most heartwarming gestures you could ever imagine. Seeing so many positive gestures from family, friends, and strangers alike makes the glass more than half full. In fact, oftentimes, it's overflowing.

In spite of the struggles and challenges, I remind myself that so many other parts of life are great – in fact, really great. If we focus on the truly great stuff, keep today front and center, and not waste energy on stuff that doesn't deserve it, it certainly does help set your mind at ease. Even if your latte isn't just perfect.

Our pilgrimage has changed our understanding of the word perseverance. Getting knocked around is part of life. Seeing what Katie has gone through, it takes perseverance to a whole other level. It's not only the physical challenges that she has had to deal with, it's the emotional component as well. Not feeling well takes its toll on anyone, but imagine not feeling well for weeks and even months on end. That can break your spirit. Sometimes we've seen Katie at the edge of the abyss physically and mentally. Having daily headaches and needing to take medications to control them is something she takes for granted. But it doesn't mean it's easy.

Watching someone you love suffer is hard, and watching your own child suffer is even more difficult. Especially in the beginning stages, Denni and I received of lots of comments of support, and many of them were to the effect of "I can't imagine going through this. It must be so hard." Looking back, it was very hard. Seeing Katie in pain, having issues that we couldn't fix, or being subjected to poor treatment – all of that has been hard to deal with. And it had an impact on our entire family. But Denni and I persevered, just as Katie did. We went into a survival mode of our own to get Katie and us through what we needed to in the moment. Because we had to – we had no other choice. And sometimes, it's as simple as that. We've built an attitude regarding perseverance that has helped us in a number of situations over the years.

Sometimes it's hard to find the silver linings. They can be hidden in some pretty dark clouds. But the silvers linings are there, and if you look long and hard enough, you'll find them.

CHAPTER 73
Crime & Punishment

I've struggled a lot with the concept of punishment. Over the years, between Katie, Holly, and the countless others I've become acquainted with in our brain tumor journey, I've seen a lot of suffering. At times, for me, it can be difficult to separate suffering from punishment.

I have offered up a lot of prayers for the families on the Squirreltales site and in other places where I saw widespread suffering. Through it all, I have never understood why kids and their families have to endure these struggles. Even with a strengthened sense of faith, I still can't understand, nor do I want to accept, that this is part of some holy or divine plan. I've gone through several thought processes on the matter, but none of them have brought clarity.

If God wanted to punish people, why would He punish kids who really hadn't done anything? Why make them and their families suffer? I've begged God numerous times that if He was going to punish me for things I admittedly deserved to be punished for, that He should punish me and not Katie. I've thought about whether God uses things like sickness and suffering to bring others to Him. Even if bringing others to Him is ultimately a good thing, in my mind I believe there must be better ways to accomplish the goal.

One time, when I was questioning the concept of suffering, I ventured into a new territory of thinking. I hated to see Katie, or any person, suffer, especially when there appeared to be no reason for it. I thought of some of the passages I'd read in the Bible, particularly the ones about the crucifixion of Jesus. It intrigued me enough that I went to the Internet and found some horribly graphic descriptions of the Roman practice of crucifixion.

According to the Biblical account of the death of Jesus, which I believe is true, it started with his public flogging. After a night of being beaten by the guards and having a crown of thorns jammed on and into his head, Jesus was taken to a public place and tied to a post. At that point a whip with shards of glass and lead embedded in the tips was used in a series of lashings that removed a good portion of all layers of the skin from his back. He would have likely blacked out on several occasions from the intense pain, and would have been repeatedly revived to endure the process.

After that, he was forced to carry the wooden cross a distance until they reached the site of the crucifixion. There, he was thrown on the ground, and the soldiers drove six-inch spikes through his wrists and his ankles. There is some dispute, but a good portion of academic research around the topic suggests the nails weren't driven through the palm of the hand or the top of the feet, as most churches portray. According to many of the scholars, those locations weren't strong enough to support the weight of the body, and placing the nails in the wrist and ankle joints intensified the pain.

His body would have been unable to support itself in the upright position, and over a period of hours, the weight would sink down onto his feet where the nails would cause excruciating pain, and he would have attempted to push himself up, causing even more agony. Jesus' back, whipped clean of its skin, would rub up and down on the beam, causing even more pain. Over the hours, his body would have gone back and forth in the slow death ritual, until finally, he would be unable to lift himself up enough to gather air, and he would have slowly suffocated. Or, possibly because of the hours of unimaginable pain, his heart may have given out.

It is an almost incomprehensible way to die. As I've reflected on this topic, I've thought of some things in ways I'd not considered before. Jesus was God's son – His chosen child, whom He loved. And God watched His son endure that kind of agonizing death, knowing Jesus had done absolutely nothing to deserve it, and knowing He could have prevented it. Yet it happened to serve a greater purpose. A much, much greater purpose.

As much as I have thought how hard it is to see Katie or others suffer, God knows better than anyone what suffering is. There is simply no comparison for anyone on earth who can come close to understanding God's perspective. It doesn't lessen my sadness about the suffering going on in the world. But it certainly gives me a different viewpoint to consider it.

I've also thought about some of the descriptions of Heaven I've read about. No pain, sadness, or suffering. And no cancer. What if God, who really does have a perfect plan, knows that these kids' lives on earth aren't going to be happy and healthy? If that is true, then bringing them to Heaven for all of eternity, as hard as it is for us to accept, could perhaps ultimately be a more humane outcome.

As much as I've thought about all the angles of the suffering equation, I never have been able to close the loop on my understanding of it. Like many things associated with God, I've struggled to get my mind around the "why" details. That's probably because, well, He's God and I'm not.

CHAPTER 74

Questions and Answers

AT TIMES IN OUR JOURNEY there have been as many questions as there have been answers. And some of the questions remain unanswered.

One of the nagging questions Denni and I have had is whether or not the Pritchard House contributed to either Katie's or Holly's brain tumors. We wonder if the elevated lead levels Katie had when she was a toddler could have been the source of her brain tumor. We discussed it with Dr. Crone and several others in the medical profession, and the truth is, we'll never know. There are over one hundred twenty types of brain tumors. Even with the research taking place, the causes of brain tumors remain one of the least understood components of the disease.

We wonder whether Katie's brain tumor was present when she was hospitalized for vomiting when she was about two-and-a-half years old. If that had been the case, and they could have detected it... Well, again, we won't know. We've learned thoughts like those aren't terribly productive. We can beat ourselves up about it, but none of it changes the course we've been on.

When we were in the early stages of the house renovations, Holly and David helped us enormously with some pretty non-glamorous projects. We ripped out floors and wiring and got into the guts of the house. Along the way, we removed asbestos and some other things that are pretty nasty. None of the adults got checked out for medical issues, but could exposure to some substance in the Pritchard House have caused tumors for Katie or Holly? With all my heart, I can say I hope not, but I just don't know the answer.

As far as the Pritchard House is concerned, a lot of folks ask us whatever became of it. After living in the house for thirteen years, we sold it when we moved to Bloomington in 2007. I don't think about it often, but to this day, a big part of me still struggles whether it was the right move for us and especially Katie.

The house was purchased by a family with Allegan connections and they remain there today. We've been back to Allegan only a few times in the nine years since we moved away, and the house looks a lot it did when we left it, which is a good thing to us. The Pritchard House will always be home, no matter where we live.

When Holly was diagnosed with a brain tumor in 2008, it rocked our world. I've racked my brain countless hours trying to figure this one out. And even applying my brother's Ph.D.-level math to this, I can't calculate the odds. How could two individuals, although in the same family, unrelated by blood, be stricken with such a rare medical condition?

One lingering question that remains is whether Katie's cyclical vomiting will be a lifelong residual effect. In the eighteen months since I started writing this book, Katie has been hospitalized twice for the condition, and it doesn't seem to be loosening its grip on her. Being in an Honors program in college is difficult enough, even when one can get to class regularly. Missing large blocks of time for illness makes it even more challenging for her. We hope and pray that it can be eliminated from her list of medical issues. But so far, that hasn't proven to be the case.

A lot of people have asked me over the years, "How do you cope?" That is an interesting question, and the answer is complex.

First of all, you've seen that I made some pretty lousy choices. Throughout this book, I've tried to be honest in telling what I felt and how I responded to the situations facing me. My way of coping and reacting to things is what I chose to do, not necessarily the best or right thing to do.

Coping is, by definition, dealing effectively with something difficult. The problem is that it's a useless definition, as it is incredibly person-specific. If my way of dealing with something is to ignore it, is that dealing with it, and if so, could that be considered coping? And what is considered difficult for me might not be difficult for you, and vice versa. With that limitation in mind, here are some of the mechanisms our family has used to cope.

Take one day at a time. We fell into that mode pretty quickly when Katie was in the hospital. Watching Dr. Crone and the medical staff handle situation after situation showed us the value of dealing with what's in front of you. Not to get too religious on you, but if you think about it, it's a biblically-based philosophy. Jesus said several times to live for today. Don't worry about yesterday and although we can *plan* for tomorrow, don't *worry* about tomorrow. It's a pretty simple philosophy, yet probably one of the most difficult to implement.

What we've gleaned from our journey is that everything has to play out. We've learned to be cautious about running too far down the path in front of the events. And that's helped us all manage expectations and deal with issues as they appear.

Laughter really is the best medicine. Some things in life are tough to deal with, but I'm a firm believer in finding the lighter side of anything we can. Along the way, our family has found fun and humor in some otherwise unfunny situations. And I'm glad that Katie, with all that she's had to deal with, has discovered the importance of humor. I'll give you an example.

Needles have been a big part of Katie's life. And I'm not aware of any kid who likes needles. One time, when Katie was younger, and was about to get a contrast injection for her MRI scan, the nurse asked her which arm she wanted the needle put in. Katie took a moment, looked at both her arms, and then said with great emphasis – "Daddy's!"

A quote came in my head one day and I've often used it regarding Katie's ability to find humor wherever possible:

"The tumor has impacted a number of Katie's senses; her sense of hearing, and sense of sight among others. We're just grateful that it didn't impact her sense of humor."

Life's too short to go through it with a scowl. Laugh. Find the funny things you can laugh about, including yourself, and the journey will be a lot more pleasant. Our family has embraced humor wherever we could.

And throughout this journey, we've laughed more than we've cried. It's not even close.

Don't worry and don't overthink. Worry is a dangerous emotion. There are parts of our brain that are hard-wired for the right kind of worry, like the kind that tells you not to walk down a dark alley in a dangerous part of town. But worry depletes you of energy, and rarely gets you closer to a solution in the end. It forces the mind to play devil's advocate, and although the ten-foot ledge isn't any higher off the ground, the mere act of worrying makes it seem a hundred feet off the ground, or a thousand. Avoiding worry has helped us avoid playing the "what if" game, a dangerous and unproductive use of time and energy.

My advice on worrying? Stop it. There, I saved you hundreds of dollars in counseling fees. You're welcome.

Find your happy place. I'm not talking about naively ignoring reality, but there is something to be said about mentally finding a place where you can find comfort. Sometimes it's the only safe haven in a world full of storms. I have a picture on my desk taken from a hammock in Hawaii looking through a palm tree to a perfect blue ocean. I can't tell you the number of times I've retreated to thoughts of me lying in that hammock, and it has made my stress lessen if not completely disappear. We all need to find places that give us comfort, and for me, there isn't a happier place than that hammock in Hawaii.

Let it out. This is one I've really struggled with, and my wife Denni has been an incredible help in this area. As I began this journey with Katie, I felt I needed to keep my emotions in check. I'm not an overly macho guy, but part of me thought I was failing in my role if I showed that what was happening was getting the best of me. Sometimes, you have to let it out – whether it's crying, yelling, venting, or just talking. Bottled up stress is like shaking a can of pop – eventually it's going to come out and when it does, you're a mess!

Put one foot in front of the other. It's a continuation of the One Day at a Time theory, but it's more than that, too. Sometimes you simply need to focus on putting one foot in front of the other and keep moving. At times, it's easy to feel like you're standing still, in a rut, in a pit, in a living Hell. It brings feelings of frustration and despair, and as hard as the path can be, keep moving! Eventually you'll find your footing.

Friends & Family Plan. Every year, when Jerry Lewis sang the song "You'll Never Walk Alone" at the end of the Muscular Dystrophy Association telethon, I'd get choked up. The song is absolutely on point. No matter what you're dealing with, whether it be a brain tumor (or multiple brain tumors), or some other struggle, you are never alone. Aside from the obvious relationship with God, which I highly recommend, there are a number of mere mortals who can provide unbelievable support. Lots of people want to help in situations like the ones our family has faced. The advice here is simple. Don't be silly - take it.

Alan Jackson was right. Shortly after the attacks on September 11, Alan Jackson released a song entitled, "Where Were You When the World Stopped Turning?" and it includes a lyric that suggested that the greatest gift God gave us was love. He is absolutely right on the money. I would further suggest the greatest gift is unconditional love. I've seen enough examples, including some shown to me from God, but also from Katie, Brian, and Denni, among others, and at times when I truly didn't deserve it. It just doesn't get any better than that.

What we have discovered in our journey is that there is no answer guide. Although not having all the answers is unnerving at times, it's also nice to know we don't need to. We continue to have faith that the One who ultimately has the answers is the One who created us all in the first place.

CHAPTER 75

Me, God, and Wally World

THERE HAVE BEEN A NUMBER of "a-ha" moments in my spiritual journey. The most significant moment was when I first felt the manifestation of God in Katie's hospital room on that unforgettable night. I'm embarrassed to admit it took an event like that to make me realize the presence of God, but it hit me like a freight train. It changed my life in an instant, and I can say I haven't been the same since.

Spiritually, I'm still a work in progress; honestly, in the last fifteen years, I've wandered back and forth feeling close to God and feeling distant. Denni has said it a number of times and she's right - God doesn't move, I do. Sometimes knowing that isn't enough to keep me from moving. It's just that now I recognize when He is feeling distant, and so far, I've taken steps to come back closer to Him. I pray I always make that choice.

As far as my encounters with God over the years are concerned, and especially the instance where I felt His immediate presence in the hospital room, I imagine there are skeptics. I understand that. All I can tell you is what I heard and felt. Be skeptical if you want to, but I'm betting my life on what I heard and felt that night.

Even with a 100% belief in the existence of God I still struggle with the concept of "religion." I especially struggle with those who are self-proclaimed speakers on behalf of God. They frequently end up in disgrace, begging for forgiveness of their shortcomings. To me, it seems like they are mostly sorry because they got caught. I'm not out to judge them, as I'll be having my own set of explanation issues when I face God, but I have a feeling some of those self-righteous religious figures are going to have a conversation with their maker that is entirely different than what they thought. And I doubt they'll be hearing, "Well done, my good and faithful servant." Instead, I suspect it'll be more like God handing them a Snickers and saying, "Grab a seat. We're going to be here a while."

One thing I don't struggle with. I have a personal relationship with a loving God who really does have a master plan for each of us. But, here's the rub. At first blush, we're in control, as far as making choices go. I have the free will to do or not do something, but the choice drives actions and consequences I'm ultimately responsible for. I'm fully confident that one day I'll be in front of God with absolutely no good explanation for some of the choices I've made. What I'm equally confident of, though, is that He is a loving God who shows mercy and grace and forgiveness. And thank God for that!

I can't explain why some pretty bad things have happened to Katie or our family. But I've seen God's love first-hand and have no doubt that Katie and our family has been in His loving care the entire time. And each member of our family has a very special relationship with God that warms my heart. I've been given three incredible gifts from God. Their names are Denni, Katie, and Brian.

To say I'm proud of my family is an understatement. I'm proud of our family, and not just because of the way we've handled ourselves in this journey. But much more so, I'm proud because of the things we've learned and the people we've become. Let me start with the star of our show, Katie Proctor.

It wouldn't be out of bounds to say that Katie has been dealt a very unfair hand in life. Having a brain tumor that has required seven surgeries by the time she was out of high school has had a significant impact on her life. Being partially deaf and losing some of her vision has been hard on her. Having to work through chronic headaches and choking spells is not something most of us can imagine having to endure. The plastic surgery has improved some of the facial paralysis, but it's clearly visible and always will be.

Katie has handled all of these things with a level of courage, dignity, humor, and class that is hard to describe. And the emotional aspects have been every bit as challenging as the physical ones. She's endured countless instances of being subjected to insensitive comments by thoughtless or cruel people. She's been left out of things and has been treated as an outsider in some ways. She's developed some wonderful friendships, but that, too, has been a challenge at times.

With all of those things piled up on her, it would be easy for Katie to take the road of despair and bitterness. But those are two words I'd bet wouldn't come up once if you polled a hundred people and asked them to describe Katie Proctor. Instead, you would hear words like loving, brave, compassionate, funny, caring, spirited, smart, and role model. And two words I bet would be most common – courage and perseverance.

Katie has been knocked down a number of times in her life. In fact, she's been knocked down so hard with things that would take most of us out of the game. But not her. Katie is living proof that it's not how many times you get knocked down, it's how many times you get back up that counts. I'm proud of her beyond words.

My wife Denni has been simply amazing throughout this journey. She's sacrificed and done things with total disregard for her own self. She's been an incredible mom to both Katie and Brian, nurturing and loving them in a way that only a mother can. She has poured every ounce of herself into our family, as a mother and as a wife. Denni has shown me time and time again unconditional love and support, and at times when I didn't deserve it.

As long as I've known Denni, she has been a woman of faith. But over the years, she has lived out that faith in ways that have helped me and others in so many ways. Those same words I used to describe Katie – kind, caring, compassionate – all of them apply to Denni as well. She too is a role model.

Denni and I have built a tremendous partnership over the years. First and foremost, I think it's because we respect each other. There are times I take the lead, and other times she takes the lead. We play off each other's strengths, and we've learned from each other. I readily admit I've learned from more Denni than she has from me. I've seen studies that reveal a higher divorce rate among couples with children who have life-threatening illnesses, and I can see why. The added stress is incredible, from the financial burden of the non-stop medical bills, to the hectic schedules for treatment, to the greater impact on the entire family. It's easy to see how it can take its toll on a marriage. I'd offer that Denni and I, just like Katie, have not only survived, but thrived. A great portion of the credit goes to Denni. She's the most incredible person I've ever met, and I can't imagine going through this with anybody else but her.

Our son Brian has known nothing else but having a sister with a brain tumor. For a kid who has barely had a fever, he's been inside the walls of more medical centers than any other healthy kid I can think of. Brian is very self-confident, which has been an incredibly important trait. There have been periods of time where almost all the attention and focus of our family and others has been on Katie. It's happened a number of times over the years, and rather than be bitter about it, he has handled it all exceptionally well.

There have been times that Katie had challenges and leaned on Brian. Throughout the years, Brian has shown an unbelievably positive attitude, as well as love and support. From the time he was a toddler, he'd listen to Katie and try to the best of his ability to make it all better for her. It's the kind of love that melts your heart.

Although he and his sister squabble like any siblings, he has one of the kindest, gentlest hearts I've ever known. To give you an insight into his character, Brian has often sat at the allergy table at lunch in school, not because he has allergies, but because he doesn't want the allergy kids to feel different. He loves his sister, and for every piece of grief he's given her, he's given her ten times that in love. OK, five times that in love. After all, he *is* her brother. I tease him a lot, but when it comes to my son I'm so proud of him I could burst.

It's hard to be proud of an animal, but we've had three dogs that have been a big part of Katie's life and a main component of her support structure. All three have meant the world to her, and they've helped her more than any medicine at times. From Rocky III, who protected Katie as a baby, to Tillie, who was the craziest dog we've ever had, to our current Rocky IV, they have always been there for her. Katie has had some rough patches throughout her life, particularly in the last few years. Since moving to Georgia, Rocky has been her closest friend at times. It's hard to describe, but he seems to sense her emotions, and when Rocky cuddles up to Katie and buries himself against her side, the impact is visible and heart-warming. It's been more than therapeutic; it's been a God-send.

I'm not a perfect father or husband by any means, but I think this journey has helped me be a better father and person than I would have been. I'm a workaholic and can be a stubborn and self-centered person. I can't say I'm thrilled to acknowledge that, but it's the truth. I like to think I'm also friendly, funny, and caring. I have a positive outlook, and I've been told that I have a positive influence on those around me. I'm a long way from perfect, but I'm better than I was, and that is no small something.

Over the years I've found ways to make work the most important thing in my life. While I still struggle at times, I can also point to a number of times when I've intentionally backed away from work, especially in the last few years. That is something I likely wouldn't have done had it not been for this journey. I've been blessed with a great job. We're not rich, but I know people who work a lot harder than I do and for a lot less money. I've gained an appreciation and a perspective that although I love my job and my career, it doesn't even make the Top Three in terms of priorities. My faith, my family, and my fitness (my health) occupy those spots.

Throughout my life, I've tried to find humor wherever I can, and I'm confident it has helped me immensely in dealing with a lot of the not-so-pleasant portions of this journey. There have been a few times along the way that I feel my ability to find humor was the only thing that rescued me from despair. I like to think my humor has helped others as well. At the end of my life I want my tombstone to read;

Here lies Rob – at least he made us laugh.

That, or,

Please move to the left – you're standing on my head!

Geez, I crack myself up.

Growing up, my family wasn't rich, but we always had plenty. Denni and I started our life together in the "acquiring stage" like many young couples, and in our culture, it's easy to get carried away with the material things in life. In this odyssey we've been on, we've learned the truly important things in life don't come in a box, and we've changed our outlook on "stuff." We've decided we'd rather be a family that *does* things rather than *has* things. Except for the 70" HD TV for watching Minnesota Vikings games. God totally understands that one.

Even with the expenses connected to restoring the Pritchard House and all of the medical bills, we've been able to have and to do things beyond what a lot of people would ever dream of. God has blessed our family in so many ways. He's provided me with a job and an income that allowed Denni to quit her job and focus on the kids. That in and of itself is more than I ever deserved. Denni was already an incredible mom, but allowing her to devote herself to that role without having to work outside of our home was a blessing.

With the passage of time, we've become less and less worried about the things that we have. We have a nice house, but none of us are too caught up with the stuff that goes into it. As we came to realize in Allegan, at some point, it's just stuff. It's bricks and furniture and gadgets, and not a single possession is worthy of too much attention. Once you've held your daughter's hand when it seemed like she was dying, no inanimate thing can ever feel that important. Not a house, not a car, not a job. It's that simple.

As an offshoot of our perspective on stuff, we have been able to do more as a family. We've traveled and gone to more places, and have done more than we ever would have if our journey had taken us down a normal path. The whole idea of "we'll get around to it" changes when brain tumors invade your family. We've embraced the concept of doing everything we can, seeing everything we can, and doing it while we can. Denni finds a way to fit it in the budget and we make it happen. Too many people are holding out for that dream trip that will never come for one reason or another. Not us. We'll find a way.

We're the Griswold's - Clark, Ellen, Rusty and Audrey, on that family vacation quest to Wally World. We're all about taking that detour to see the world's second largest ball of twine. Because Clark Griswold was right; getting there is half the fun.

The Cast of Characters: Alice (Gigi) Proctor, David (Bald-Bald) Cook, Rob Proctor, Denni Proctor, Katie Proctor & Brian Proctor

EPILOGUE

The Final Katie Update Spring 2016

To: Friends of Katie
From: Rob Proctor
Re: The Final Katie Update

I figure it's time for one last Katie Update, so here's what Katie and the other cast of characters in this book have been up to.

With assistance from Pediatric Brain Tumor Foundation and Georgia Hope scholarships, along with some money from my mom, Alice, Katie is attending Kennesaw State University, where she's in her second year. She is in the Honors Program and is majoring in History. After earning a 4.0 last spring, Katie spent the summer in an exchange program in Montepulciano in the heart of Tuscany, Italy, and ventured to Rome, Venice, Florence, Pompeii, and Sicily. It was her second trip abroad in as many years, as her grandpa, the one and only Bald-Bald, took her on a Viking river cruise as a high school graduation gift in 2014. Katie and Bald-Bald saw the sights of Switzerland, Germany, France, and the Netherlands. Adding Katie's four trips to Hawaii and her Olympic experience, you could say she has become quite the traveler.

As far as her health is concerned, Katie still has cyclical vomiting bouts as a residual effect of her brain tumor. One came during Finals Week her first college semester and she ended up in the hospital over the Christmas break. Then, in the fall of 2015, she had a lingering episode that began shortly after Labor Day and affected her for four months. She had a procedure at Children's in Cincinnati, and, fortunately, the procedure worked, and Katie has felt almost total improvement in her symptoms since then. There has been some movement in her facial paralysis, as the plastic surgeries were partially successful in restoring some of the function to her facial muscles. She may consider an additional surgery down the road if she so chooses. She remains the bravest person I've ever known.

In order to make certain Katie was having the time of her life in Italy, Denni felt compelled to join her, so she, too, spent some time in Tuscany this past summer. Denni is teaching Advanced Placement Government and Economics classes at a high school near our house in Atlanta. Her passion for teaching is obvious and the amount of time and attention she devotes to her students – like many teachers, is largely unrecognized. Sadly, Denni lost her brother David in December of 2015, and, in an eerie similarity to Holly, he too was fifty-three years old when he died. He had skin cancer that metastasized to his brain. His death shook Denni, but she continues to find her footing in her faith. She remains my rock, and I love her dearly. When it comes to Denni, I consider myself the luckiest man on the face of the earth.

Brian is a freshman in high school and recently received his driving permit. The "Chunk-A-Load-A-Buddha-Boy" is now six feet tall, muscular, and towers several inches over his dad. He enjoys playing football, baseball, swims on the neighborhood swim team, and plays video games far more than his parents would like. He threatens the sanctity of our house by occasionally rooting for the Dallas Cowboys, but I'm hoping it's a phase he'll grow out of. Brian is active in the North Point Church high school youth group. He is proud to acknowledge and even share his faith, and I admit he seems much less concerned about peer pressure and going along with the crowd than I did at his age.

His grades are exceptional, and he has not only his father's gnat-like attention span, but also a quick wit and biting sarcasm. Suffice it to say, between the two of us, Brian and I drive Denni nuts most days. He still has one of the kindest hearts I've ever seen, and plain and simple, he's turning into an exceptional young man.

As for me, in addition to my day job, I've spent the past year-and-a-half writing this book. It's been quite a journey in its own right. It's been therapeutic on some levels, but it's also been emotionally challenging and outright gut-wrenching at times. Some of the memories I had to relive had been put out of my mind for good reason.

In the end, like Katie's journey, I feel this book is part of something bigger. My aim wasn't to make you feel sad, nor was it to make you feel sorry for Katie or the rest of us. My intent was to give you a glimpse inside our world as we coped with the life-threatening illnesses within our family. Along the way, I'm sure I didn't handle everything as well as I could have. But I did the best I could under the circumstances. And to my defense, that's about all any of us can do.

I've tried to show you the roller-coaster world cancer patients and their families go through. Cancer is a horrible and cruel disease. It attacks with no concern for age, gender, or ethnicity. It tricks people into believing it's gone, only to attack again with a vengeance. Cancer is a cowardly disease, and writing this book made my hatred for it grow exponentially.

If you get anything out of this book, I hope it's the message that throughout any of life's trials and tribulations, hope, faith, and love are the most important things one can have to cope and to overcome. A positive spirit and a will to persevere can succeed against almost any obstacle. God doesn't build us to go through these things alone. And, as I've discovered, it's nice to know we don't have to.

Let me leave you with one of my favorite musical quotes. If nothing else, you'll be singing it in your head for the rest of the day.

I get knocked down, but I get up again,
You are never going to keep me down
I get knocked down, but I get up again…

"Tubthumping," Chumbawumba

God bless you,
Rob W. Proctor

PS: If you'd really like to make a difference, go to one of these fine organizations and make a donation. I promise you'll feel better for doing so.

www.curethekids.org (Pediatric Brain Tumor Foundation)
http://wish.org (Make-A-Wish)

To purchase this book, visit www.robwproctor.com

Rob W. Proctor